Photoshop® CS3 Channels and Masks Bible

Photoshop® CS3 Channels and Masks Bible

Stephen Romaniello

Wiley Publishing, Inc.

Photoshop® CS3 Channels and Masks Bible

Published by
Wiley Publishing, Inc.
10475 Crosspoint Boulevard
Indianapolis, IN 46256
www.wiley.com

Copyright © 2007 by Wiley Publishing, Inc., Indianapolis, Indiana

Published by Wiley Publishing, Inc., Indianapolis, Indiana

Published simultaneously in Canada

ISBN: 978-0-470-10264-0

Manufactured in the United States of America

10 9 8 7 6 5 4 3 2 1

For general information on our other products and services or to obtain technical support, please contact our Customer Care Department within the U.S. at (800) 762-2974, outside the U.S. at (317) 572-3993 or fax (317) 572-4002.

Library of Congress Control Number: 2006939503

About the Author

Stephen Romaniello is an artist, educator, and writer. He began his career in graphics in 1980 as a production artist and typesetter; soon he was promoted to designer and then art director. In 1982, he became a partner at Armory Park Design Group. Three years later he founded Congress Street Design, a full-service design firm. In 1987, at the beginning of the digital revolution in graphics technology, he purchased his first computer. Romaniello accepted a faculty position in 1990 at the Advertising Art program at Pima Community College in Tucson, Arizona, with the intention of developing a state-of-the-art digital graphics program. He served as department chair of the renamed Digital Arts Department for eight years.

Romaniello has developed curriculum and training materials for many of the mainstream graphics programs, and has offered seminars at the Maine Photographic Workshops, the League for Innovation, and National Business Media. A certified instructor in Adobe Photoshop he currently teaches digital art courses at Pima Community College. He is the coauthor of *Mastering Adobe GoLive 4* with Molly Holtschlag and the author of *Mastering Photoshop 6*, *Photoshop 7 Savvy*, *Photoshop CS Savvy*, and *Photoshop CS2 Savvy*, all published by Sybex. He is also the author of *The Perfect Digital Portfolio*, published by Sterling and *The Photoshop Visual Encyclopedia* published by Wiley. His column, "The Digital Eye," appears in *Digital Graphics* magazine. Romaniello is the founder of Gorilla Geeks, a company that offers onsite training and consulting throughout the country. His home and studio are in Tucson, Arizona.

*For my brother Chuck whose vision has inspired
me to attempt the highest peaks*

Credits

Acquisitions Editor
Tom Heine

Project Editor
Beth Taylor

Technical Editor
Rob Barnes

Copy Editor
Beth Taylor

Editorial Manager
Robyn Siesky

Production Manager
Tim Tate

**Vice President and Executive Group
Publisher**
Richard Swadley

Vice President and Executive Publisher
Barry Pruett

Project Coordinator
Adrienne Martinez

Graphics and Production Specialists
Denny Hager
Heather Pope
Amanda Spagnuolo

Quality Control Technician
John Greenough
Brian H. Walls

Book Designer
Elizabeth Brooks

Proofreading and Indexing
Aptara
Tricia Liebig
Sherry Massey

Contents

Contents

Part III: Color Channel Techniques   145

Chapter 6: Exploring the Channels Palette 147

Part VII: Working with Type Masks and Vector Masks   409

Chapter 19: Working with Type Masks 411

Chapter 20: Masking Paths and Shapes 423

Part VIII: Compositing with Channels and Layers 453

Chapter 21: Blending Layers 455

Preface

Just about anyone who works with digital images needs to know to how to use Photoshop. But its complexity can be confounding even for experienced users. In *Photoshop CS3 Channels and Masks* the image looks, how they behave, and above all how you can manage and control them. It delves into the depths of the many types of Photoshop masks showing you how to use them to your advantage. This book combines theory with practical techniques to get results that are inspirational and satisfying.

With full-color pictures on almost every page, this book shows fine examples of every concept and technique and reveals how all types of Photoshop masks and channels are created and controlled. You can read this book from beginning to end for a comprehensive overview or use it as a primary reference and focus on any channels or mask-related topics.

This book is divided into eight parts that include:

— **Part I, Image Basics:** This introductory chapter is an overview that includes the fundamentals of image dynamics — how information is gathered, constructed, and organized, and the components of Navigation.

— **Part II, The Zen of Color:** Reveals the secrets of color channels from the inside out. Topics include color modes, creating color, color spaces, and color adjustment.

— **Part III, Color Channel Techniques:** Looks at the Channels palette and shows techniques for mixing channels, creating monochromes, duotones, and spot color.

— **Part IV, Color Channel Pyrotechnics:** Describes full-tilt production in Lab mode, creating and enhancing detail, and working with light and shadows.

— **Part V, Mask-Making Basics:** Looks at the different types of masks that work with selection techniques such as alpha channels, Quick Mask, and ambiguous edges.

— **Part VI, Masking Layer Content:** This part presents layer masks, clipping masks, and Smart Objects.

— **Part VII, Working with Type Masks and Vector Masks:** Reveals the secrets of paths, vector masks, shaper layers, and type masks.

— **Part VIII, Compositing with Channels and Layers:** Demonstrates blending modes and layer and channel compositing techniques.

These parts together put forth a comprehensive overview of the mechanics of working with Photoshop CS3. Each chapter reveals the aspects of a general topic in theory and is then put into practical application with the step-by-step demonstrations.

You'll find this book a valuable reference whether you're an artist, photographer, Web designer, printer, or desktop publisher. Even if your goal is to understand masks and channels and other aspects of the world's premier image-editing software, *Photoshop CS3 Channels and Masks Bible* is for you.

Acknowledgments

Photoshop CS3 Channels and Masks Bible was the result of efforts by my many friends who contributed their time and expertise. First of all, thanks are in order to Carole McClendon, my agent at Waterside Productions Inc. Thanks and kudos to the production team at Wiley including acquisitions editors Tom Heine and Courtney Allen, whose vision helped get this book going; to project editor Beth Taylor who knows her stuff; and to Rob Barnes the tech editor, for his expertise and attention to detail.

My thanks to artist and photographer friends who provided inspiration including Andrew Rush, Steve Meckler, Tim Fuller, Imo Baird, and Demitri Ivanovitch Sarnukov. And especially to my daughter Leah for providing some wonderful images for this book.

I also want to thank my close friends Joeanne Stur, Charlotte Lowe Baily, Katherine Fergison, and Karen Brennan whose support helped me through some tough moments.

My gratitude is owed to my colleagues at Pima Community College including Briged Murphy, Dennis Landry, Dave Wing, Patty Gardiner, Margo Burwell, and Jack Mertes, and of course to my amazing students.

Many thanks to the Adobe Photoshop beta team, for keeping me apprised of the many changes to the program during its development. Also, thanks to Image Stock, Corel, PhotoDisk, ImageIdeas, and Eclectic Collections for providing images from their CD library. Thanks also to my brother Chuck and my mom, Violette, for their effusive enthusiasm.

Part I

Image Basics

Chapter 1

Building Images

A Photoshop image is like a building. The color channels are the foundation that ultimately determines the image's core structure, just as the pixels are the building blocks of its visual elements. It may contain layers that are its multiple floors and it can have masks that act as windows.

Just as there are many different ways to construct a building, in Photoshop, the choices you make can also dramatically affect how an image appears, how it is edited, and ultimately how it is output. This chapter analyzes the elements that constitute the structure of a Photoshop image. It addresses how the elements are assembled and accessed and defines important terminology. Furthermore, this chapter demonstrates how to utilize these key features in the creation and manipulation of an image.

Distinguishing Between Vector and Raster

Two fundamentally different methods are used to create still images. Vector graphics are objects composed of mathematically defined points, curves, and shapes called *objects*. Raster images use a grid of colored squares, called *pixels,* to render variations of color.

Vector graphics

Vector graphics are composed of paths and points that define their shapes. The vector tools, such as the Pen tools, the Shape tools, and the Type tool are used to draw these objects. In Photoshop the vector tools can be used to select areas of an image or to produce type or shapes that when printed, produce clean, sharp lines and edges.

Vector objects are created by dragging a shape onto the Image window with one of the shape tools or by the technique of depositing points and line segments with the Pen tool. Both methods are shown in Figure 1.1. These paths are called *Bezier curves*, after Pierre Bezier who developed them for the European Automobile industry in the 1960s. Bezier curves can take the form of any combination of straight, curved, or scalloped paths and can be open ended or closed to form a shape but what makes them different from the pixels used by raster images is that that they are composed of mathematically defined points and segments.

Vectors are *resolution-independent*, which means that they automatically conform to the highest resolution of the device on which they are printed, whether it's a desktop inkjet printer, a laser printer, or a high-resolution imagesetter.

FIGURE 1.1

A shape drawn with the Custom Shape tool (left) and a Bezier curve drawn with the Pen tool (right).

Raster images

Although the vector tools are indeed quite handy, most of Photoshop's operations are designed to change the color of pixels. Raster images, sometimes called *bitmaps*, are different from mathematically defined vector images because they consist of a mosaic of little colored units called picture elements or *pixels*.

These usually square-shaped areas of colored light are the smallest editable unit in a Photoshop image. Pixels are usually so small that, when seen on a monitor, the colors blend into what appears to be a continuous-tone image.

Each pixel is assigned a color based on the numerical constitution of binary information. The variation of colored pixels within the grid matrix of a digital image produces the variations of tone and color.

Understanding Bit Depth

The computer is a high-speed calculator that uses the binary number system to calculate and describe information. The binary number system uses zeros and ones to describe all numerical values. The smallest unit of binary information is called a *bit,* which is an acronym for binary digit. There are 8 bits in a byte, which is a row of eight zeros or ones. There are 256 possible combinations in a string of eight zeros and ones. There are 1,024 bytes in a kilobyte. There are 1,024 kilobytes in a megabyte, 1,024 megabytes in a gigabyte and so on. A pixel, however, is the smallest *editable* unit in a Photoshop image and each pixel contains a certain amount of color information depending on its bit depth.

Bitmaps

The simplest graphic images called *bitmaps,* are composed of pixels that are only one bit "deep." In these images, only one binary digit of information describes each pixel. Think of each one-bit pixel as an on-off switch. There are only two alternatives—the light can be turned on or off. The binary number *zero* represents off or black, and the binary number *one* represents on or white. Bitmap images are frequently used to create black and white line art, as shown in Figure 1.2.

Graphic software for early PCs and Macs had the limited capability of editing bitmap images by replacing white with black or black with white. The scanners, video cards, and monitors that created and displayed the images on these early computers were also limited and could only process one-bit images.

Grayscale

In a *grayscale* image, each pixel is allocated eight bits of binary information. Each bit can either be on (black) or off (white). Eight bits of information produces 256 possible combinations ($2^8 = 256$). A grayscale image, therefore, contains a potential of 256 shades of gray where black is assigned a numerical value of zero and white 255. Grayscale is a mode that is most often used for editing and displaying black and white photographs, such as the one shown in Figure 1.3.

FIGURE 1.2

A bitmap image composed of only black and white pixels.

RGB color

Full-color RGB images are composed of three 8-bit primary color channels — red, green, and blue — which are actually similar to grayscale images and contain 256 shades per channel. When working with 8 bits per channel, RGB images the Photoshop Mode menu displays a check mark next to 8 bits/channel but they are more commonly called 24-bit color images. These three channels, when combined, produce a potential 16,777, 216 colors (2^{24} = 16,777,216). Photographic images require 24-bit color to describe their smooth gradations and subtle tonal variations.

FIGURE 1.3

A grayscale image potentially composed of 256 gray tones.

Most scanners can produce images in 48-bit color. At this bit depth, the information is distributed into three 16-bit channels — red, green, and blue — each with a potential of 65,536 possible colors (2^{16} = 65,536). These channels, when combined, can produce trillions of possible colors. Some professional photographers and photo retouchers prefer these high-bit images because they offer an extended dynamic range and more subtle tonal variations. Photoshop can read images with 16 bits of information per channel, designated in the Mode menus as 16 bits/channel.

Calculating File Size

An image's file size can be calculated by multiplying its height and width in pixels by its bit depth, or the amount of memory each pixel consumes. For example, an RGB image that is 5 inches tall by 7 inches wide and has a resolution of 72 ppi (pixels per inch) is 504 pixels by 360 pixels.

Because the image is an 8-bit RGB, each pixel contains 24 bits of information. We must convert the bits to bytes to streamline the calculation. There are 8 bits in a byte; we divide 24 by 8 and get a factor of 3. We multiply the height by the width by the bit-depth factor (in bytes), or $504 \times 360 \times 3 =$ 544,320 bytes. Because there are 1,024 bytes in a kilobyte, we divide 544,320 by 1,024 to get 531.56, or 532 kilobytes when rounded off to the nearest whole number.

The value derived from this formula is the raw file size. The addition of layers, channels, paths, layer masks, Smart Objects, and annotations will increase the file size. The file size may be reduced when the image is saved to an image format with a compression scheme, such as JPEG or TIFF.

64-bit CMYK

A 64-bit CMYK color image actually has four channels of 16 bits per channels. The file sizes of these images are much larger. Many of the color combinations that 64-bit CMYK images can produce are a 4-color ink composite of black. It's debatable whether it's worth creating CMYK images with so much information when they are going to be output to four color process separations and printed with a system of inks with a significantly smaller color gamut than RGB.

Even though images with higher bit depths contain more color information, they are displayed on the monitor at the bit depth capability of your video card, which in most cases is 24 bits. To see an image in 24-bit color depth on a Macintosh, the monitor should be set to Millions Of Colors; in Windows, the setting should be True Color.

HDR images

Photoshop supports High Dynamic Range (HDR) images that represent the entire dynamic range of the visible world. The luminance values of an HDR image are stored in 32-bits-per-channel images. You can create an HDR image using multiple photographs, each captured at a different exposure, and merge them using the Merge To HDR command.

CROSS-REF See Chapter 12 for more details on HDR images. All the luminance values in a real-world scene are represented and stored in HDR images. Adjusting the exposure of an HDR image in the Merge to HDR command image gives you the same range of exposure as when photographing a scene whereas 8- and 16-bit color targets only a small part of the visible spectrum. This capability has the potential to make your images look more realistic.

Understanding File Formats

Different file formats serve different purposes. Some formats compress data to make the file size smaller on the disk, while others are used to make a file compatible with another software program or the Web. The format you choose depends on how the image will ultimately be used. It is important to know what saving an image to a specific format will do. At worst, saving a file to the wrong format can lose important data that enables you to retain the images eligibility. At the very least, it could inconvenience you by losing the ability to place the document into another program.

Photoshop CS3 can open 32 different file formats and save to 21 different file formats. With the addition of plug-ins that attach to the Import and Export submenus, Photoshop supports even more, which means that it is a great program for converting files to make them compatible with other software programs.

When considering in which format to save your document, think about what features you want to preserve. The native Photoshop format (PSD) preserves all saved features of the document including channels, paths, layers, profiles, and annotations. Because the native format contains all Photoshop's features, consider working in PSD format until it is time to publish it. Then choose Image ⇨ Duplicate to quickly make a copy. Choose Save As or Save for Web to save the duplicate document to the new file format.

Determining Resolution and Size

A screen image is composed of pixels whereas a printed image may be composed of dots or lines. An image's resolution is determined by the number of these visual units per linear inch in the display or print. Each one of these units is a building block. The more building blocks that the image has, the finer the detail that can be created and displayed and, therefore, the higher the quality of the image.

Resolution

There are several kinds of resolution. Each kind has specific characteristics that determine how an image is displayed or printed. When you create an on-screen image in Photoshop, the pixel information may be converted into a halftone screen or color separations when preparing files to print on a printing press or a stochastic screen when printing to an inkjet printer. It is important for you to understand the qualities of each type of resolution.

Image resolution

Image resolution is determined by the number of pixels that occupy a linear inch of a digital image, usually measured in pixels per inch, or ppi. You can clearly see the pixels in Figure 1.4. Image resolution is determined when you scan an image or shoot a digital photo at a given setting.

FIGURE 1.4

A close-up of a full-color image showing the building blocks or pixels that determine its resolution.

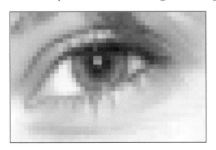

Monitor resolution

Monitor resolution is determined by the number of screen pixels that occupy a linear inch of a monitor screen (72 ppi for most Macintosh RGB monitors, 96 ppi for Windows VGA monitors). This resolution never changes, as it represents the physical matrix of screen pixels of the monitor. The actual size of what you see on-screen, however, is determined by the resolution settings of your monitor. You can choose specific display resolutions in which to view an image from your operating system's Control Panel ➪ Monitor (Windows) or from the System Preferences ➪ Displays (Mac). Depending on your monitor and video card, the smallest resolution available is 640 pixels wide x 480 pixels deep, which displays the image quite large on-screen. The largest setting depends on the size of the monitor and displays a much smaller on-screen image. When an image with the same resolution as the monitor's actual matrix is displayed in Photoshop at 100%, it appears at its physical size relative to the screen pixels and the monitor's display settings because at 100%, one image pixel equals one monitor pixel. If the image has a higher resolution, it will appear larger than its physical size. For example, a 3" x 4" image that is 288 ppi will appear four times larger at 100% than an image that is 3" x 4" at 72 ppi (4 × 72=288). If you copy and paste (or drag and drop) an image that is the same physical size but a lower resolution to a document of higher resolution, the pasted image will be proportionally reduced in physical size as in Figure 1.5).

If you want to see the image at the size it will be printed, choose Print Size from Photoshop's View menu. The image displays at the size at which it will print, no matter what its resolution.

Printer resolution

Printer resolution is measured by the number of dots that can be printed per linear inch (dpi). These dots compose larger halftone dots on a halftone screen or stochastic (frequency modulated) dots on an inkjet printer.

FIGURE 1.5

The tile on the left which is 72 ppi and 5″ wide by 5″ deep was dragged and dropped onto the image on the right which is the same physical size but has a resolution of 288 ppi.

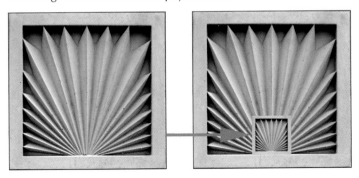

Halftone resolution

Printing an image on paper with a printing press presents a unique set of problems. How does a machine such as a printer portray variations in color and tone? It needs a method that will produce color and tonal range without blending ink. To accomplish this task, the ink is distributed to individual dots of variable size within a grid called a *halftone screen* (see Figure 1.6). The dot density of a printed image is measured in lines per inch (lpi) or, in some instances, lines per centimeter (lpc) which describe the vertical and horizontal lines of the grid. On a traditional halftone screen used to print black-and-white images, the size of the dots determine the darkness or lightness of an area. Larger dots portray areas that are darker than areas with smaller dots which allow more of the paper to show through. With full-color images, four different colored halftone screens — one each of cyan, magenta, yellow, and black — called *color separations*, are registered on each other (see Figure 1.6). These tiny colored dots combined in varying densities on the paper force the eye to mix colors when viewed and produce a full range of color. The resolution of the halftone screen determines the amount of detail that can be printed. The finer the halftone screen, the more detail can be displayed. The line frequency of the halftone screen is determined by the type of printing that is being performed. Table 1.1 is a list of common frequencies used in various types of printing.

When you print an image from Photoshop to color separations on a laser printer or imagesetter, the values of the pixels are calculated by a hardware device or software called a RIP (Raster Image Processor) that converts the pixel information into dot densities. The printer uses this information to produce a single halftoned image or a series of color separations.

TABLE 1.1

Common Halftone Screen Values

Frequency	Description and Commercial Uses
60 lpi	A coarse halftone screen, suggested for screen printing.
85 lpi	Less course. The dots are visible to the naked eye. Commonly used for newsprint and porous paper stock.
133 lpi	Finer detail. The dots can only be seen with a magnifying glass. Used on web presses for printing medium-quality weekly magazines, books, and stationary on uncoated paper.
150–175 lpi	Very fine dots. These frequencies are suitable for brochures, pamphlets, and commercial printing on coated stock.
200–300 lpi	These frequencies produce the finest images with lots of detail and color depth. You might use this option when creating annual reports or fine art prints.

Stochastic screen resolution

Rather than using variable sized dots to portray color, an inkjet printer uses a system frequency of modulated dots whose quantities determine tonality and color density. Figure 1.6 shows close-ups of the same photograph. Inkjet printers deposit tiny droplets of ink through a system of micro piszo jets. Higher-end printers sometimes use multiple shades of cyan, magenta, and black to produce a greater range of color and sublimate the dots so that they bleed into each other producing a continuous tone effect.

FIGURE 1.6

A close-up of a halftone screen of a black and white photograph (left); a close-up of the colored dots produced by color separations (middle); and a close-up of the colored dots printed by an inkjet printer (right).

Determining resolution

When you scan an image, it is crucial to acquire enough information to produce good-quality halftones from your laser printer, imagesetter, or direct to plate device. If the image is insufficient in resolution it may appear soft or pixilated. Scan your images at two times the screen frequency of the halftone screen. That means if your image is going to be printed in a newspaper or in a newsletter, on an 85 lpi halftone screen, scan it at 170 pixels per inch. If your image will be printed in a glossy magazine, at 150 lpi, scan your image at 300 ppi. If you will be increasing the size, factor in the percentage of scale. Here is the formula:

```
scan resolution =2 X line screen X % of scale.
```

If you plan to print to an inkjet or large format printer, scan your images at a minimum of one-third the desired print resolution. For example, for a print resolution of 720 dpi, scan the image at 240 ppi or higher. If you are going to increase the size of the printed image, then you should scan at a higher resolution. This equates to common scan resolutions of 120 ppi, 240 ppi, and 480 ppi — although anything more than 360 ppi is probably overkill. In fact, an image scanned at 300 ppi and printed at 100% is usually quite sufficient for any printer.

Line art or bitmap content is different. Ideally, scan at the same resolution as the printer's dpi resolution or in evenly divisible units of the printer's resolution. For example, you would scan at 360 ppi for a 1,440 dpi print.

Sizing images

Resolution and size are interchangeable factors. You can enlarge the physical size of an image with no loss of quality if you reduce its resolution. If you scan a picture at 600 ppi and print it at 300 dpi, for example, you can double its physical size without compromising its quality. And of course, scanning an image at 300 ppi at 200% using the scanner software's sizing feature collects the same amount of information as scanning the image at 600 ppi. Avoid exceeding the scanner's optical resolution as it may produce disappointing results.

Photoshop's Image Size command changes the size and/or resolution of the entire image. The features in this dialog box provide extensive control over how the image is reconfigured. You can size an image simply by redistributing its pixels. Essentially you can reduce its resolution and increase its physical size (or vise versa). To do so, follow these steps:

1. Choose Image ⇨ Image Size. The Image Size dialog box shown in Figure 1.7 appears. This particular image is 3" wide and 4" high, and has a resolution of 150 ppi.

2. Clear the Resample Image box, which also clears the Constrain Proportions box and grays out the option.

3. Type a new value into the Resolution field. In this example, change the resolution from 150 ppi to 300 ppi, doubling the resolution of the image but reducing its physical size to 1.5 x 2". Notice that the Pixel Dimensions remain the same because there is no addition or deletion of pixels.

4. Click OK to apply the changes.

When you clear Resample Image, as in the above example, you preserve the images pixels while changing its output size. When you check the Resample image box, you add or discard pixels. Use this feature to resize the image and retain or increase its resolution. Decreasing the size of the image or *resampling down*, usually doesn't affect the image's quality but be cautioned that enlarging the image by *resampling up* may produce a soft image with fuzzy edges and inferior contrast.

To resample an image, select the Resample Image box in the Image Size dialog box and pick from one of the five choices listed in the menu: Nearest Neighbor, Bilinear, Bicubic, Bicubic Smoother, and Bicubic Sharper. Each of the following algorithms programs how Photoshop adds or removes pixels from your image.

FIGURE 1.7

In the Image Size dialog box, you can redistribute pixels by deselecting the resample box or add and subtract pixels by checking it.

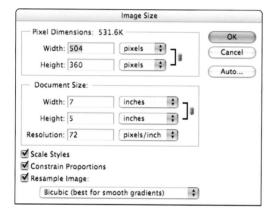

- **Nearest Neighbor:** Evaluates an adjacent pixel. Use this option for line art desktop icons, software interface screen captures, or any time that anti-aliasing creates artifacts.

- **Bilinear:** Averages the four pixels above, below, and on either side for smoother transitions.

- **Bicubic:** Averages the eight closest neighbors and adds a sharpening effect to increase the contrast.

  Although scanning an image at its ultimate output resolution and size is always a better option, sometimes it is simply not possible. If you must, use these two interpolation algorithms to help reduce the diminished quality of enlargements. Bicubic Smoother and Bicubic Sharper do not add detail to an image. They increase edge contrast to subvert the softening effect of resampling up. You should experiment and compare the effects of each algorithm for best results.

- **Bicubic Smoother:** Slightly blurs the edges of areas to produce the most contrast when it adds pixels for a more sublimated continuous-tone look. Bicubic smoother is often used to enlarge images to smooth out any artifacts that are created.

- **Bicubic Sharper:** Adds an additional sharpening algorithm to better enhance edge contrast. Bicubic smoother is recommended to reduce image size to maintain sharpness.

Constraining proportions

When you resample an image, you can constrain its proportions. When selected, the Constrain Proportions box ensures that image height and width will maintain their proportions — changing one dimension automatically updates the other. When this option is inactive, the link icon between height and width disappears and you can increase the height and width independently of each other.

Scale styles

When the Scale Styles option is selected, any Layer Style will be resized proportionally (see the section "Working with Layers" in this chapter). Clearing this box results in the layer styles retaining their original size.

Getting help with resizing images

If you're confused about resizing and image, choose the Resize Image Assistant (Macintosh) or Wizard (Windows) from the Help menu to guide you through the resizing process of choosing the best possible results for size and resolution. It automatically applies the resize command to duplicate the document so the original image is unaffected. To use it, choose Help ➪ Resize Image and wait for the Resize Image Assistant /Wizard window to appear. Follow the directions and make the appropriate choices.

Setting interpolation for the program

Choose General Preferences (Edit/Photoshop ➪ Preferences ➪ General) to display the default interpolation settings for the entire program. These defaults affect the sizing functions when using the transformation commands from the Edit menu or the Move tool and several of the distortion filters and the Crop tool when cropping to a specific size. Similar to the Image Size dialog box the Interpolation methods are Nearest Neighbor, Bilinear, Bicubic, Bicubic Sharper, and Bicubic Smoother.

Sizing channels and masks

If you resize an image with the Image Size command, all the channels and masks including color channels, layer and vector masks, alpha channels, active quick masks, and paths are sized proportionately with the image. If you add canvas to the image the outer edges of the channels and masks are enlarged to accommodate the new size. When you crop an image so too are the masks and channels cropped at their outer edges however, paths and vector masks retain their original size, shape, and position and extend outside the Image window.

Transforming images

Transformation commands affect selected areas or layer content. Transformation operations offer the ability to scale, rotate, skew, or distort the perspective and warp an image. They are accessed through either the Edit menu or can be applied with the Move tool with the Show Transform Controls selected in the Options bar.

When you choose one of the transformation options, a bounding box surrounds the selected area or layer content. You transform the image by dragging one of the corner or center or corner points of the bounding box, or placing the curser outside the box and dragging to rotate it. To complete any transformation you must click the check mark in the Options bar to commit it or the Cancel icon to abort it. Table 1.2 shows how to apply the transformation operations.

TABLE 1.2

Transformation Operations

Transformation	Menu	Operation	Move Tool: *Check Show Transform Controls in the Options bar*
Move	NA	Place the cursor anywhere inside the bounding box (except on the point of origin) click and drag.	Place the cursor anywhere inside the bounding box (except on the point of origin) click and drag.
Scale	Edit ⇨ Transform ⇨ Scale or Edit ⇨ Free Transform	Click and drag the handles of bounding box inward or outward. Press the Shift key to constrain the proportions. Press the Opt/Alt to scale from center.	Click and drag the handles of bounding box inward or outward. Shift-click to constrain the proportions. Opt/Alt click to scale from center.
Rotate	Edit ⇨ Transform ⇨ Rotate or Edit ⇨ Free Transform	Drag cursor outside of the bounding box. Click and drag clockwise or counter clockwise. Click and drag the point of origin to change the fulcrum of the rotation.	Drag cursor outside of the bounding box. Click and drag clockwise or counter clockwise. Click and drag the point of origin to change the fulcrum of the rotation.
Skew	Edit ⇨ Transform ⇨ Skew	Click and drag one of the corner points of the bounding box vertically or horizontally.	⌘/Ctrl+Opt/Alt click and drag a corner point vertically or horizontally
Distort	Edit ⇨ Transform ⇨ Distort	Drag one of the corner points of the bounding box in any direction	⌘/Ctrl click and drag a corner point in any direction

Transformation	Menu	Operation	Move Tool: *Check Show Transform Controls in the Options bar*
Perspective	Edit ⇨ Transform ⇨ Perspective	Drag one of the corner points of the bounding box in any direction	Press Shift+⌘/Ctrl and drag a corner point in any direction
Warp	Edit ⇨ Transform ⇨ Warp	Choose a Warp option from the menu in the Options bar and adjust the settings in the dialog box. or Choose Custom from the Warp Options menu, Click and drag a gridline or anchor point.	Click one of the points on the bounding box. Choose the Warp icon in the Options bar to display the grid. Click and drag a gridline or anchor point.

Other rotations and flipping

The Edit ⇨ Transform submenu offers five standardized transformations. The options listed in Table 1.3 work the same as their Image ⇨ Rotate Canvas counterparts, but they affect only the active selection or layer, and offer you one-click access to some of the most common image modifications:

TABLE 1.3

Rotations and Flips

Command	Action
Rotate 180°	Rotates a selection or layer content by 180 degrees so that appears upside down.
Rotate 90° CW	Rotates a selection or layer content clockwise by 90 degrees.
Rotate 90° CCW	Rotates a selection or layer content counterclockwise by 90 degrees.
Flip Horizontal	Mirrors a selection or layer content across the vertical axis, creating a horizontal reflection.
Flip Vertical	Mirrors a selection or layer content across the horizontal axis, creating a vertical reflection.

Transformations can also be made numerically in the Options Bar. Choose a Transformation from the Edit ⇨ Transform menu, or choose the Move tool and click the Show Transformation Controls box in the Options Bar. Click a segment or a corner point on the bounding box, and the Options bar will display numerical data, as shown in Figure 1.8. You can transform the bounding box by typing new values in the text boxes.

FIGURE 1.8

The Move Tool Options bar showing numerical values for transformations.

Using the Crop Tool

Sometimes it's necessary to discard part of an image. The Crop tool can precisely discard unwanted image areas. You can also crop to a specific height, width, and resolution and use the Crop tool's perspective feature to fit a portion of an image into a specific size. Follow these steps to perform a basic crop with the Crop tool:

1. Choose Image Duplicate to make a copy of the image.

2. Choose the Crop tool from the Tool palette.

3. Drag the mouse to define the bounding box. The area outside the crop will darken as shown in Figure 1.9.

4. Click and drag the handles of the bounding box to encompass more or less of the image. Drag bounding box by placing the cursor inside the boundaries and click and drag. Release the mouse when you are satisfied with the new position.

NOTE The Crop rotation option becomes active when the cursor is anywhere outside the crop selection; when the cursor is too close to the bounding box, a Crop Bounding Box Resize icon appears.

5. If you want to rotate the crop marquee, place the cursor outside the bounding box and click and drag clockwise or counterclockwise. Drag the mouse to rotate the bounding box. Make further adjustments by dragging any of the handles until you're satisfied with the new, rotated crop.

TIP After you've established the crop marquee, Shift-Click on a corner point drag and readjust the size of the crop while constraining the proportions. Opt/Alt click and drag to constrain the crop bounding box proportions as you radiate the marquee from its point of origin in the center of the marquee. Reposition the point of origin by clicking and dragging it.

6. To implement the crop, click Commit (the check mark in the Options bar) or press Return (Mac) or Enter (Win). You can also double-click inside the cropping area to commit your crop. If you decide to cancel the crop, press the Esc key or click the Cancel button.

FIGURE 1.9

FIGURE 1.9

The crop shield darkens to better define the area to be preserved.

Cropping to size

You can crop your image to a fixed size and new resolution by entering values for the height, width, and resolution in the Crop Tool Options bar, shown in Figure 1.10. When you drag the Crop bounding box it is automatically constrained. When you commit the crop, everything within the crop marquee will conform to the new specified size.

Most cropping is usually performed with the width, height, and resolution fields left blank. Click the Clear button on the Options bar to clear the number fields to restore manual operation. Click the Front Image button on the Options bar to automatically enter the current active document's width/height/resolution into the number fields.

FIGURE 1.10

Use the Crop Tool Options bar to crop to a specific height, width, and resolution.

Perspective cropping

You can distort an image to fit a particular area of the image content into a rectangular document of a specific size. After you've drawn a marquee, you can crop to perspective as in Figure 1.11. With the Perspective option selected in the Options bar you can adjust the corner anchor points of the bounding box independently. When you implement commit the crop, the image area distorts to conform to the new document's height and width.

FIGURE 1.11

Use the Perspective option to fit a region of an image into a rectangular shape.

Sizing the canvas

Choose Image ➪ Canvas Size to access the dialog box that allows you to expand or shrink your canvas. The Canvas Size dialog box, shown in Figure 1.12, creates more pixels around the image. When you perform this operation on an image that has background layer, by default, the new canvas is filled with the current background color. If there is no background layer, the new canvas extension will be transparent. You can choose a canvas extension color from within the Canvas Size dialog box. The Canvas Extension Color menu lets you choose the Foreground color, the Background color, White, Black, or Gray from the predefined color menu. Or click the swatch and choose a color from the Color Picker.

The Current Size field displays the current file size and the width and height of the image. Type a new overall width and height value in the New Size field to determine the new overall size or select the Relative box and enter the amounts you want to add to an existing canvas. You can choose from eight different units: percent, pixels, inches, centimeters, millimeters, points, picas, and columns in which to add canvas.

The anchor grid controls the position of the new canvas. Click the center cell, and the image will be framed on all sides by the new canvas. Click any of the cells to determine where the new canvas will be added.

The Canvas Size dialog box lets you specify color, size, and position of the new area added to the image.

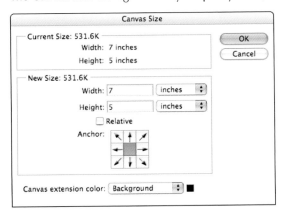

Rotating the canvas

The Rotate Canvas submenu found under Image ➪ Rotate Canvas, offers options that you can use to reorient your entire document. Experiment with the following options:

- **180°:** Rotates the image so that it appears upside-down. The image retains its left-to-right orientation.
- **90° CW:** Rotates the canvas by 90 degrees clockwise.
- **90° CCW:** Rotates the canvas by 90 degrees counterclockwise.
- **Arbitrary:** Displays the Rotate Canvas dialog box. Specify an angle of rotation by typing a number in the Angle field. Choose CW or CCW (clockwise or counterclockwise), and click OK.
- **Flip Canvas Horizontal:** Mirrors the image across the vertical axis.
- **Flip Canvas Vertical:** Mirrors your image across the horizontal axis with vertical mirroring.

Working with Layers

Layers enable you to work dynamically in Photoshop. This means that image content can be saved to individual layers and edited independently. Layer content can be moved vertically or horizontally.

The stacking order of layers can determine the depth and position of visual elements within the picture plane. Working with layers gives you tremendous power and control over your image and keeps the editing process flexible and dynamic.

The Layers palette

The Layers palette, shown in Figure 1.13, is the control center where you perform most of the layer functions. The Layers palette is clustered with the Channels and the Paths palettes. If the Layers palette is not visible, choose Window ➪ Layers or press the F7 key.

Layers are stacked and each is separated from the one directly below it or above it by a thin line. Each layer contains a thumbnail of the layer's contents, and the layer's name appears to the right of the thumbnail. Layer styles, masks, or locks are indicated by icons. In the far-left column is the visibility icon which controls layers visibility.

FIGURE 1.13

The Layers palette displaying a background, two content layers, and a type layer.

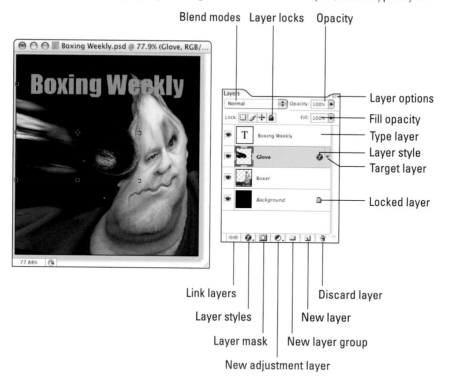

Above the layer stack you can select from the four check boxes, which lock transparency, image pixels, position, or all. At the top-left of the Layers palette is a list of blending modes that can alter the color relationships of layers in the stack. And to the right of the blending modes is the Opacity slider, which controls the level of transparency of a targeted layer's contents. Fill Opacity control is just below the master opacity control.

You can access many layer operations from the Palette Options menu, shown in Figure 1.14. Click the small triangular icon on the top-right to reveal the list of options.

FIGURE 1.14

The Layers Palette Options menu.

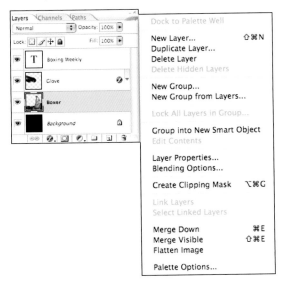

Working with the background

When you scan or import an image and open it in Photoshop, the Layers palette displays one thumbnail, labeled Background. A background is the Photoshop's default layer. If you delete the contents of a selection or erase a portion of the image with the Eraser tool, the area fills with the background color specified in the Tools palette.

All layers float above the background. Unlike a layer, the background does not support transparency. No matter how many layers are in the document, the background is always at the bottom of the stack and cannot be dragged to a higher position. When a layer is created, its content always appears in front of the Background. By default, the Background is locked. If you want to move its contents, adjust its opacity, or reposition it in the Layers stack, you need to convert it to a layer. As with many of Photoshop's operations, there is more than one way to perform this task.

To convert a background to a layer, double-click the background or choose Layer ⇨ New ⇨ Layer from Background. The New Layer dialog box, shown in Figure 1.15, appears. Name the layer and click OK.

FIGURE 1.15

The New Layer dialog box.

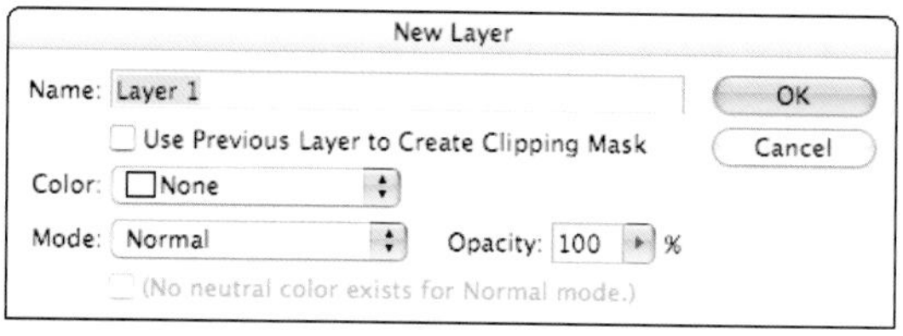

The New Layer dialog box presents options to color-code, specify opacity, and choose a blending mode. You can also group it with other layers if, for example, you're using it to make a clipping group.

A layer can be converted to a background, too. Click once on the layer to highlight it. Choose Layer ⇨ New ⇨ Background from Layer. The new Background is automatically placed at the bottom of the stack. Any transparent areas will be filled with the current background color.

Naming layers

Name your layers! The default numbers that Photoshop assigns to new layers become quite anonymous when their content is too small to be recognized on the thumbnail or when there are several dozen of them in the document. Type a name that readily identifies it. Naming each layer with a descriptive title is a fast way to organize the components of your image for easy identification and to increase the efficiency of your workflow.

To name a layer, double-click the current name next to the thumbnail in the Layers palette. A box appears around it. Type in the new name. Or you can choose Layer Properties from the Layer Options menu and type a name in the Layer Properties dialog box, shown in Figure 1.16.

FIGURE 1.16

The Layer Properties dialog box.

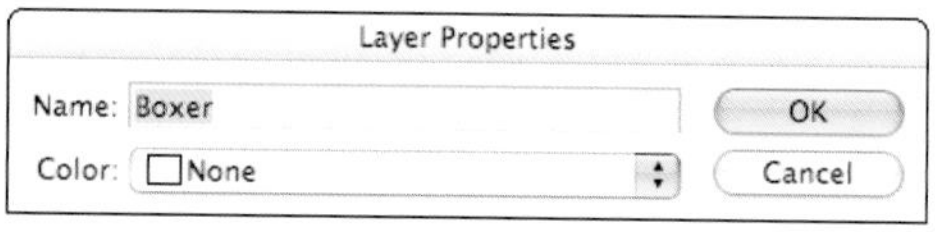

Viewing layer content

You can conceal the contents of a layer by clicking the visibility icon (the little eye) in the first column of the Layers palette. To see the contents, click it again. To reveal or conceal the contents of more than one layer at a time, click the eye next to each of the desired layers. To conceal all but one layer, Option/Alt click the visibility icon. With the same key held down, click the icon again to see all layers.

Choosing thumbnail size

A thumbnail is a miniature representation of a layer's content. Pick from three sizes of thumbnail, or no thumbnail at all. To specify a thumbnail's size, click the Layers Palette Options arrow. Choose Palette Options to display the dialog box shown in Figure 1.17. Click the desired thumbnail size and then click OK.

FIGURE 1.17

The Layer Palette Options menu determines the size of the thumbnails that are displayed.

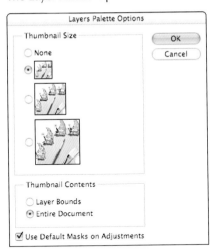

Highlighting layers

Before you can apply a command to affect the contents of a layer, you must highlight it first. A highlighted layer is targeted and ready to be edited. Click anywhere on the layer. A colored highlight appears on the layer. You can highlight more than one layer at a time by Shift-clicking on each layer to select contiguous layers or ⌘/Ctrl click to select noncontiguous layers. (See the section "Working with Layers" in this chapter.)

Understanding transparency

Transparency is indicated by a gray and white checkerboard. A transparent area can either be entirely void of pixels or the pixels are completely transparent. A layer is semitransparent when you can partially see the checkerboard or if you can see content from other layers through it. Figure 1.18 illustrates the difference between opaque and semitransparent images.

If the color of the image is predominantly gray and the checkerboard becomes difficult to see, the color and size of the checkerboard can be changed in Transparency & Gamut Preferences to better reveal the image.

Controlling opacity

Use the Opacity sliders to adjust the level of transparency of the pixels on a targeted layer. You can then see through layer content to the underlying layers in the stack. When you click the Opacity field on the Layers palette, a slider appears. Drag it to the right to increase, or left to decrease opacity, or enter a value from 0% to 100% directly into the box.

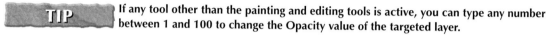 **TIP** If any tool other than the painting and editing tools is active, you can type any number between 1 and 100 to change the Opacity value of the targeted layer.

TIP Place the cursor to the right of the word Opacity in the Layers palette, click and drag to adjust the Opacity of the layer.

Understanding fill opacity

The Fill Opacity slider adds another opacity setting to a layer. Fill Opacity affects a layer's pixels without affecting the opacity of any Layer Styles that have been applied to the layer. (Layer styles are discussed later in this chapter.)

Changing stacking order

The stacking order in the Layers palette determines the plane of depth where the layer content appears. The content of the topmost layer in the Layers palette appears in the very front of the image. The further down in the stack a layer is, the farther back its content appears on the image, all the way back to the bottom-most layer, or the background.

You can change a layer's position in the stack and, consequently, its visual plane of depth in the image. In the Layers palette, click and drag the layer up or down to reposition it. As you placed the layer on a division line, it appears bold. The bold line indicates the new location where the layer will appear when the mouse is released.

FIGURE 1.18

The image on the top is opaque, surrounded by transparency. The image on the bottom is semi-transparent.

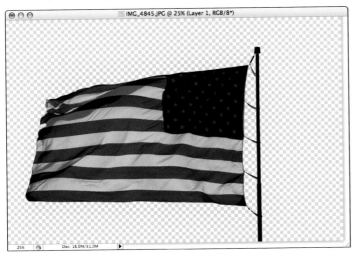

Another method of changing the position of the layer in the stack is to choose an option under Layer ➪ Arrange, or use the equivalent key command. The Arrange submenu presents you with four options, as shown in Table 1.4.

TABLE 1.4

Key Commands for Changing Stacking Order

Position	Macintosh Shortcut	Windows Shortcut	Result
Bring Forward	⌘+]	Ctrl+]	Positions the layer on top of the layer immediately above it
Bring To Front	Shift+⌘+]	Shift+Ctrl+]	Positions the layer at the top of the stack
Send Backward	⌘+[	Ctrl+[	Positions the layer under the layer immediately below it
Send To Back	Shift+⌘+[	Shift+Ctrl+[	Positions the layer at the bottom of the stack directly above the Background

Working with multiple layers

There are several ways to affect two or more layers simultaneously. To highlight multiple layers, Shift-click each layer to select contiguous layers, or ⌘/Ctrl click to select noncontiguous layers. When multiple layers are selected you can transform each layer's contents, you can do the following:

- Reposition layers in the stack
- Merge layers
- Align layer contents
- Lock layers
- Group layers into a Layer Group
- Create a Smart Object
- Create a clipping group
- Link layers

Linking layers

Linked layers are used primarily for the simultaneous transformations and repositioning of multiple layers. Linking layers is similar to selecting multiple layers but gives you the ability to reselect them quickly. After you've linked them, you need only to highlight and transform one of the layers and all the layers linked to it will also be affected. To link one or more layers, click one of the layers. From the Layers Palette Options menu, choose Link Layers. A chain icon appears to the right of the Layers name, as shown in Figure 1.19. Linked Layers can also be merged (see the section, "Consolidating Layers" later in this chapter).

You can apply other effects to multiple layers by using specific layer-based operations. (These effects are described in more detail in later sections of this chapter and in later chapters of this book.)

FIGURE 1.19

Linked layers are indicated by a chain icon.

These operations include the following:

- **Adjustment Layers:** Used for color and contrast adjustments and for color mapping.
- **Layer Masking:** Used to conceal and reveal portions of two contiguous layers.
- **Blending Modes:** Used to affect the relationship between the pixels on a layer and the layer immediately beneath it.
- **Layer Groups:** Used for organizing, controlling opacity, positioning two or more contiguous layers in the stack, and for transforming or moving layer content. (See the section on grouping layers in this chapter.)
- **Layer Comps:** Used for saving multiple versions of an image for efficient display.
- **Fill Layers:** Used to apply a solid color, gradient, or pattern to an independent layer.
- **Layer Content:** Used for changing the type of Adjustment or Fill layer.
- **Clipping Masks:** Used for the transparency of one layer to hide portions of a layer immediately below it in the stack.

Grouping layers

A Photoshop document can support an unlimited number of layers. You can consolidate layers into groups to better manage them. A Layer Group is indicated in the Layers palette by a folder icon as shown in Figure 1.20. Click the arrow to the left of the icon to expand the folder to see its contents.

By highlighting the folder, you can affect the layers as a group. The group can be revealed or concealed, repositioned in the stack, and similar to linked layers — moved and transformed.

You have several options for creating a new Layer Group:

- From the Layer menu choose Layer ⇨ New ⇨ Layer Group.
- From the Layers Palette Options menu, choose New Layer Group.

FIGURE 1.20

Layer Groups appear as a folder icon in the stack. When opened, the layers within the folder are indented.

- You can select multiple layers in the stack and then choose Layer ⇨ New ⇨ Group from Layers from the Layers menu or Group from Layers from the Layers Palette Options menu.

- Click the Layer Group icon in the Layers palette. By default, the layer set will be named Group 1, Group 2, and so on. With the first three commands, a dialog box shown in Figure 1.21 appears. You can name the layer set, color-code it, and specify the color channels that comprise the image.

- After you've created a new Layer Group, you can add layers to it by clicking and dragging individual or multiple highlighted layers to it, then, release the mouse.

FIGURE 1.21

The New Group dialog box.

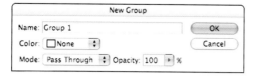

Layer Groups and color channels

To change the characteristics of a highlighted Layer Group, choose Group Properties from the Layers Palette Options menu or from the Layers menu. In the dialog box shown in Figure 1.22, click the Red, Green, or Blue color checkboxes to determine the color information will be visible. The boxes display the individual or combined color channel information of all the layers in the Group. This is can be useful if you want to limit the color information of a particular layer. You can produce some rather interesting effects especially if you are applying a blending mode to the Group as in Figure 1.23. From this dialog box you can also color code a Layer Group for easy recognition.

FIGURE 1.22

The Layer Group Properties dialog box.

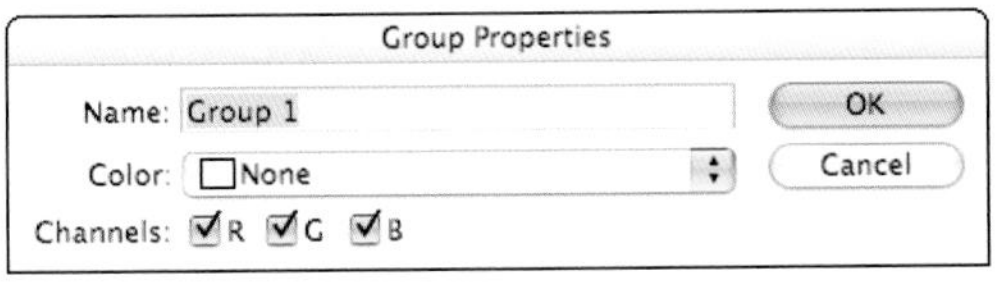

Group Properties	
Name: Group 1	OK
Color: ☐None	Cancel
Channels: ☑R ☑G ☑B	

Locking layers

Layer locks protect specific characteristics of a layer from being edited. There is an icon for each lock at top of the palette, as shown in Figure 1.24. To lock a layer, click the layer to highlight it and click one of the checkboxes. The lock types include:

- **Lock Transparent Pixels:** Protects the areas without pixels or with an opacity value of zero from being edited. If you try to paint on a transparent area, for example, no color will be deposited. The transparency lock works like a mask. The areas that do contain pixels will still respond to any Photoshop operation. Locking transparency does not protect transparent areas from the effect of transformations such as scaling, rotating, or moving.

- **Lock Image Pixels:** Protects the layer from editing functions such as painting, color adjustments, or filters. You can, however, transform or move the content of a layer.

- **Lock Position:** Prevents the layer from repositioning or the application of the Transformation functions such as Scale, Rotate, Distort, and so on.

- **Lock All:** Protects a targeted layer from all editing functions.

Creating new layers

You frequently need to make a new layer, either to add new content to the image or to move part of an existing layer onto a new layer. There are several options for creating new layers.

You can make new empty layers with any of these three methods:

- From the Layers menu, choose Layer ⇨ New ⇨ Layer to bring up the New Layer dialog box. Name the layer and specify its characteristics. Click OK.

- From the Layers palette pop-up menu, choose New Layer to bring up the New Layer dialog box, shown in Figure 1.25. Name the layer and click OK.

FIGURE 1.23

On the top is the original image and on the bottom a layer that has been placed in a Layer Group whose properties allow only the information from the Red and Green channel to be displayed. Combined with the Hard Light blending mode the effect produces a warm saturated look.

FIGURE 1.24

Click the Layer Locks icons to prevent layer content from being affected.

■ Click the New Layer icon at the bottom of the Layers palette. A new layer named Layer 1 appears in the stack immediately above the targeted layer. To rename the new layer, double-click its name and enter the new name in the Name field.

FIGURE 1.25

The New Layer dialog box.

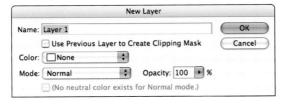

You can also make a new layer by copying a selected area to a new layer. Copying leaves the original layer intact and transfers the selected area to a new layer immediately above it. To copy the contents of a new layer follow these steps:

1. Click the layer you want to copy and highlight it.

2. Select an area of a layer or background.

3. Choose Layer ➪ New ➪ Layer Via Copy. The selected portion of the image is duplicated and moved to the same position on a new layer. By default, the first new layer you copy or cut is assigned the name Layer and the next highest number that hasn't been assigned (see Figure 1.26).

4. Double-click the layer's name to rename the layer, and then press Return/Enter.

FIGURE 1.26

The Layers palette after the content has been copied to a new layer.

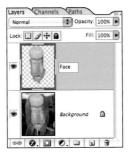

When you cut a selected portion of an image to a new layer, the selected area is either filled with the current background color if it's on the background as in Figure 1.27, or replaced by transparency if it's on a layer as in Figure 1.28. It is transferred to the same position on a new layer immediately above it.

To cut a selected area to a New Layer:

1. Target the layer or Background with the element(s) that you intend to cut.
2. Make selection of the area.
3. Choose Layer ⇨ New ⇨ Layer Via Cut.
4. Double-click the layer's name to rename the layer, and then press Return/Enter.

The Layers palette after the content has been cut from a background to a new layer.

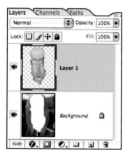

The Layers palette after the content has been cut from a layer to a new layer.

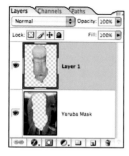

 **TIP** To transfer selected content more quickly to a new layer, press Cmnd/Cntrl+J to copy or Shift+⌘/Ctrl+J to cut selected content to a new layer.

Transferring layer content

Individual layers can be copied from an open source document onto a destination document. The same is true with multiple highlighted layers and selected areas.

Copying individual layers

The entire contents of a layer can be dragged and dropped to an open document.

To drag a layer from a document, follow these steps:

1. Open the source document and the destination document so that they both appear on-screen.
2. In the Layers palette of the destination document, click the layer where you want the copied layers to appear.
3. In the Layers palette of the source document, click a layer or the background and drag it to the Image window of the destination document.

   Alternatively, you can choose the Move tool. Click the Image window of the source document and drag it to the Image window on the destination document.
4. Release the mouse when you see an outline. The new layer appears immediately above the targeted layer on the destination document.

Copying multiple layers

The entire contents of two or more layers can be dragged and dropped to an open document.

To drag a two or more layers from a document, follow these steps:

1. Open the source document and the destination document so that they both appear on-screen.
2. In the Layers palette of the destination document click the layer where you want the copied layers to appear.
3. On the source document click a layer or the background. Shift-click to select additional consecutive layers or ⌘/Ctrl click to select non-consecutive layers.
4. In the Layers palette of the source document, click and drag the layers to the image window of the destination document

   Alternatively, you can choose the Move tool. Click the Image window of the source document and drag it to the Image window in a destination document.
5. Release the mouse when you see an outline. The new layers appear above the targeted layer on the destination document.

Dragging selected content

The contents of a selection can be moved from a source document to a destination document. When you drag and drop selected content, a new layer is automatically created in the destination document and will appear immediately above the targeted layer in the stack.

Here's how to drag and drop layers between two documents:

1. Open the source document and the destination document so that they both appear on-screen.

2. In the Layers palette of the destination document, click the layer where you want the selected content to appear.

3. Target the layer or background on the Layers palette of the source document.

4. Make an accurate selection of the area to be moved.

5. Choose the Move tool. Click and drag the selection from the source document's Image window to the destination document's Image window until you see a rectangular outline. Release your mouse when the outline appears where you want to position the selected content.

Duplicating layers

There are two techniques for creating a copy of a layer. The copy appears directly over the original in the stack and has identical characteristics and content. To duplicate a layer, do one of the following:

- Highlight a layer and then choose Duplicate Layer from the Layer menu or from the Layers Palette Options menu. The Duplicate Layer dialog box appears where you can name the layer and determine a destination document for it in the Destination field. Any currently open document will appear in the list. Then click OK.

- Drag the layer to the New Layer icon in the Layers palette. If you Option/Alt-drag, the Duplicate Layer dialog box, shown in Figure 1.29 appears.

FIGURE 1.29

The Duplicate Layer dialog box.

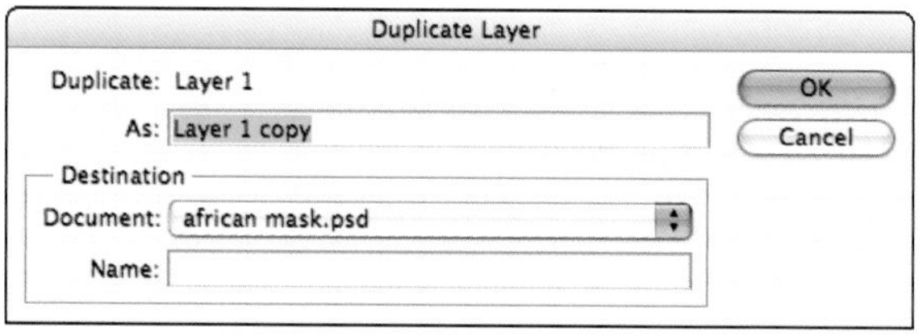

Discarding layers

You can discard individual or multiple layers. To discard a layer, do one of the following:

■ Target the layer or layers to be deleted. Choose Delete Layer from the Layer menu or from the Layers Palette Options menu.

■ Drag the layer or highlighted layers to the trash icon in the Layers palette.

■ Highlight one or more layers and then click the trash icon. The dialog box shown in Figure 1.30 appears.

■ Highlight one or more layers and then Opt/Alt-click the trash icon to delete the layer without the Delete Layer dialog box.

FIGURE 1.30

The Delete Layer confirmation window.

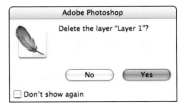

Blending layers

Blending layers is like having two color transparencies on a light table. If you sandwich a red transparent gel between the two transparencies you would have a combination of the bottom transparency and the top slide tinted by the gel. When you blend layers, instead of just the tinted image, you have the ability to sandwich in more complex effects, such as color saturation, which is shown in Figure 1.31.

Blending modes are preprogrammed formulas that affect the color relationships between aligned pixels on two consecutive layers. A blending mode can be assigned to a layer a couple of different ways:

■ Highlight the layer. Click the Mode menu at the top of the Layers palette (directly under the Palette Title tab) to choose the desired blending option.

■ Opt/Alt-double-click the layer name or double-click the thumbnail to display the Layer Style dialog box; see Figure 1.32. From the list on the left, choose Blending Options: Default. In the General Blending area, choose your blending mode and opacity level.

The options in the General Blending area are identical to those in the Mode menu at the top of the Layers palette However, by using the General Blending in the Layer Style dialog, you can save the settings as a style and apply them to a different layer (see Saving Styles later in this chapter).

Applying layer styles

Layer styles are canned effects that simplify the application of enhancements such as shadows, glowing edges, and embossing that used to require labor-intensive channel and layer juggling. Most layer styles affect the edges of the layers content, so the content should be surrounded by transparency. To apply a style, double-click the layer or click the style icon at the bottom of the Layers palette and choose a style from the menu to display the Layer Styles dialog box.

When a layer has been affected by a style, the italic *f* icon appears to the right of its name in the Layers palette. Click the small arrow to the left of the f icon, to display a list of the current layer styles that have been applied to this layer. Clicking (Win)/double-clicking (Mac) any one of these effects displays its controls so that you can make modifications to it.

FIGURE 1.31

The original image on the top and a layer with the Hard Light blending mode applied to increase saturation in the bottom image.

If you want to create, define, or edit a layer style, access the Layer Style dialog box by doing one of the following. If a layer is targeted when you open this dialog, the style you choose will be applied to the layer.

NOTE **You cannot apply a layer style to the Background.**

FIGURE 1.32

The Layer Style dialog box with Blending Options displayed.

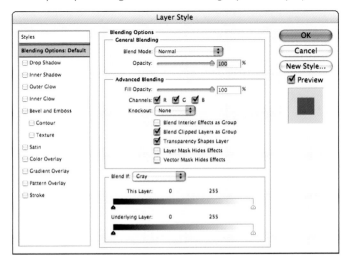

Add a layer style by following these steps:

1. Choose Layer ⇨ Layer Style. Choose a style from the list.

2. Choose Blending Options from the Layers Palette Options menu. Click a layer style from the list to display its controls.

3. Double-click the layer.

4. Click the Layer Style icon at the bottom-left of the Layers palette and drag to a layer style to display its controls.

5. You can choose an effect from the Layer Style dialog box. To display the controls for each effect, click its name. Many of the controls have similarities, and experimentation with a live preview is the best way to see the results.

Each layer style provides a unique and potentially complex set of options. Experimentation with the controls and with combinations of styles is the key to producing the best possible effect.

Saving layer styles

If you've applied one or more styles or blending options to a layer you can save the style to later apply it to a separate layer. To save a style, click the New Style button in the Layer Style dialog box; a window is displayed where you'll be prompted to name your new style.

To apply the style, choose Window ⇨ Styles. Highlight a layer and click the style that appears in the Styles palette.

Consolidating layers

During the editing process, you may accumulate quite a few layers. With each new layer, the size of your file of your document increases depending on the amount of information the layer contains. Or so many layers may be difficult to manage. To work more efficiently, you should periodically merge your layers. Merging layers combines the content of two or more layers into one layer. You can also flatten the image so that all the layers are consolidated into a Background. There are several ways to merge layers all of which can be selected from the Layers menu or the Layers Palette Options menu:

- **Merge visible layers:** This operation merges the content of all the visible layers into one layer. The layer retains the name of the current highlighted layer.
- **Merge layers:** Merges all highlighted layers into one layer. The layer retains the name of the topmost highlighted layer.
- **Merge linked layers:** Merges the content of all the linked layers into one layer. The layer retains the name of the current highlighted layer.
- **Merge down:** Merges the content of the targeted layer and the layer immediately below it into one layer. The layer retains the name of the highlighted layer.

TIP To merge the content of layers into a single new layer press Opt/Alt and choose one of the Merge Options from the Layers menu or Layers Palette Options menu.

Flattening an image

Flattening an image discards all layers and creates a single background from all layer content. Before you flatten an image, make a duplicate version and save the original in PSD or TIFF format; both support layers. Flatten the duplicate because after the image has been flattened, saved, and closed, it cannot be un-flattened. To flatten your image, be sure all your layers are visible. Photoshop discards layers that are not visible. Choose Flatten Image from either the Layer menu or the Layers palette pop-up menu.

Masking Concepts

Masking is presented in detail throughout the book. In this section, I introduce masking briefly because it is such a key component of the Photoshop workflow. Masks provide the means to isolate regions of an image for various purposes. Creating accurate masks is essential to maintaining the credibility of a manipulated image.

When working with Photoshop, several types of masks are used:

■ **Selection masks:** These are regions of an image temporarily defined by Photoshop's selection tools. The selection tools are the primary method of isolating a region for editing (see Chapter 15 for a detailed look at making selections).

■ **Quick masks:** This type of mask is made by clicking the Quick Mask icon on the Tool palette or pressing the Q key. A Quick Mask is a temporary mask that can be edited with the painting and editing tools. Quick Masks are an on-the-fly solution to accurately produce new selections or edit existing ones (see Chapter 16 to learn how to work in Quick Mask mode).

■ **Alpha channels:** Save and store selections for later use. An alpha channel is created by saving a selection to the Channels palette and edited with Photoshop's painting and editing functions. You can also apply filters to Alpha Channels to produce a variety of masks (see Chapter 16 for a closer look at Alpha Channels).

■ **Layer masks:** Attached to a layer, these masks reveal or conceal layer content. They can be edited with Photoshop's painting and editing features (see Chapter 20 to learn how to create Layer Masks).

■ **Clipping masks:** Elements in a layer can be "clipped" to the pixels of the layer beneath it. The content in the top layer takes the shape of content of the lower layer. Transparent areas remain transparent (see Chapter 18 for more on Clipping Masks).

■ **Filter masks:** This new feature that has been added to Photoshop CS3 enables you to block out portions of filtered areas on Smart Objects (Chapter 18 tells you all about it).

■ **Vector masks:** Created from shapes or paths, Vector Masks are similar to Layer Masks except that they are created and edited using the Pen tools and Shape tools (see Chapter 20 to work with Vector Masks).

■ **Type masks:** This typographical feature creates selections that conform to the shape of type characters in a font. Because many effects such as color adjustments and filters cannot be applied to type generated on layers, the Type Mask feature extends the typographical capabilities of Photoshop (see Chapter 22 to learn what Type Masks can do).

Summary

This chapter examines the construction of Photoshop images. You should now be familiar with how Photoshop image elements are assembled.

This chapter introduces many topics, including:

- Distinguishing between vector and raster graphics
- Understanding file formats
- Using the Crop tool
- Working with layers
- Duplicating and discarding layers

In this chapter, I touched on the basic fundamentals to get you familiar with building images. In the next chapter, you find more details on key Photoshop features.

Chapter 2

Exploring Tools, Palettes, and Menus

Fundamentally, image editing is about changing the color of pixels. When you apply many of Photoshop's editing features, what results is a change in color or tonality. Sure, there are many features that enable you to display your image, isolate areas, organize data, and save your images to different formats and locations but the bottom line is all these features are there to assist you in your ultimate purpose — to change how your image looks.

Photoshop's graphic user interface offers a large variety of tools, commands, dialog boxes, filters, and menu items to perform almost any image editing task. But Photoshop's real power comes from your ability to apply combinations and sequences of these operations accurately and creatively, especially when working with channels and masks.

This chapter describes the primary features that you employ in your workflow — how they operate, where to locate them, and when to use them.

Displaying the Image

When you open an image in Photoshop, by default, it fits perfectly in the Image window regardless of its size. During the editing process, you may have to change the size of the screen image so that you can observe details more closely or see changes to the image as a whole. Changing the size of the image display does not affect the physical size of the image or how it prints.

NOTE The percentage at which you see an image in Photoshop depends on the ratio of the image resolution to the monitor's screen resolution. Macintosh monitors have a screen resolution of 72 ppi, while Windows monitors use 96 ppi to display an image. A document with an image resolution of 72 ppi, when viewed at 100 percent, will display at a ratio of 1:1 of its actual height and width dimensions on a Mac and 33 percent larger on a PC. A resolution of 144 ppi (2 x 72) will display an image at twice its print size on a Mac and, again, larger on a PC when displayed at 100 percent viewing size. (See Chapter 1 for more on monitor and image resolution.)

There are several methods for changing the image display that all perform the same basic function — to increase or decrease size of the screen image, so you can accurately select a region or to apply an image editing technique. The method you choose depends on the convenience of the operation and your personal preference. I cover the methods in the following sections.

Using the Zoom tool

The Zoom tool is probably the technique you'll use most frequently simply because it is the most accessible. Click the Zoom tool in the Tools palette to select it or type the letter Z. The Zoom tool's cursor appears by default as a magnifying glass with a plus sign that indicates that the Zoom tool will enlarge the view when you click your mouse. Place the curser on the Image window over the area you want to see more closely and click until you see the view you want. You can continue to click to a maximum view size of 1600%.

The size of the displayed image can be reduced by Option/Alt clicking the image. When you press the key the Zoom tool displays a minus sign to indicate that it will reduce the view with each click all the way down to 1 screen pixel.

Here are a few quick key techniques for efficiently operating the Zoom tool:

- **Restoring the display to a 100% view:** Double-click the Zoom tool icon in the Tool palette.
- **Toggling to the Zoom tool from any tool or dialog box:**
  - Press the ⌘/Ctrl key and the spacebar, click the mouse to zoom in. Release the keys to resume using the tool or dialog box.
  - Press the Option/Alt key and the spacebar, and click the mouse to zoom out. Release the keys to resume using the tool or dialog box.
- **Zooming into an area:** Click and drag the Zoom tool around the area you want to see close up.

Using the View menu

The View menu offers several methods for zooming in and out. Choose a command from the menu or use the corresponding key commands as shortcuts. Table 2.1 describes them.

TABLE 2.1

View Menu Items and Corresponding Key Commands

Command	Function	Keyboard Shortcut
Zoom In	Image appears larger. The Image Window changes size to frame the image size.	⌘/Ctrl +
Zoom Out	Image appears smaller. The Image Window changes size to frame the image size.	⌘/Ctrl -
Fit on Screen	Fits the image in an image window so that all of it appears on screen.	⌘/Ctrl 0
Actual Pixels	Displays image at 1:1 ratio (1 actual pixel to 1 screen pixel) on screen.	Opt/Alt ⌘/Ctrl 0
Print Size	Displays the image at its physical height and width dimensions.	None

Choosing a screen mode

There are three screen modes in which images can be viewed for editing and display. These commands are found in the View menu and are also represented by icons in the Tools palette.

- **Standard Screen Mode:** The default view displays the image Photoshop interface against the operating system's desktop on a Macintosh or against the neutral gray Photoshop desktop in Windows.
- **Full Screen Mode with Menu Bar:** The image is displayed centered against a neutral gray background with menu bars at the top of the screen.
- **Full Screen Mode:** The image appears centered against a black background without menu bars.

 To toggle between display modes, press the F key.

 To conceal all palettes so that you can see an unobstructed view, press the Tab key.

Sizing by percentage

In the lower-left corner of the Image window you can type a precise percentage value to the one hundredth of a percent. Press Return/Enter to commit the display change. The same feature can be found in the lower-left corner of the Navigator palette. (See the section on the Navigator in this chapter.)

Scrolling images

Scrolling tools and techniques move the image around within the window so that you can access various regions for viewing and editing. They work only when the image is displayed larger than the Image window. There are three general techniques for scrolling:

■ **The Hand tool:** Click the Hand tool in the Tools palette or press the H key. Click the image and drag to move the image around.

Press the space bar to toggle to the Hand tool from any tool or dialog box. Click and drag when you see the hand cursor.

■ **Scroll bars:** Scroll bars are to the right and bottom of the image. Click and drag a scroll handle, or click an arrow at the end of a scroll bar to scroll in the desired direction.

■ **Key commands:** There are a few key commands that scroll your images:

■ Press the space bar to toggle to the Hand tool from any tool or dialog box. Click and drag when you see the hand curser.

■ Scroll up or down by pressing the Page Up or Page Down key.

■ Scroll to up or down slightly by pressing the Shift key and the Page Up or Page Down key.

■ Scroll to the left or right edge by pressing the Control key on Windows or Command key on Macs and the Page Up or Page Down key.

The Navigator

It can be difficult to tell exactly what you are looking at when you are looking at the image at a close view, particularly if the image is composed of large areas of similar texture. The Navigator, shown in Figure 2.1, is a map of the image displayed as a thumbnail showing the exact location of what appears in the Image window relative to the entire image.

When you launch Photoshop, the Navigator is displayed by default and offers the following navigational features:

■ **View Box:** The red outlined rectangle on the thumbnail indicates what is currently displayed in the Image window. Click your mouse within the box and drag to scroll around the image.

TIP To change the color of the View box, click the arrow in the upper-right corner of the palette and choose Palette Options. Pick a color from the pull-down menu or click the swatch to choose a color from the Color Picker.

■ **Zoom Slider:** You can zoom in on the image by moving the slider to the right, or zoom out by moving the slider to the left.

■ **Zoom In and Zoom Out Buttons:** The button with the small mountains on the left of the slider zooms out, and the button with the large mountains to the right of the slider zooms in. The buttons use the same predefined increments as the Zoom tool.

■ **Magnification Box:** At the bottom-left of the Navigator palette, you can enter a specific percentage at which to view your image.

FIGURE 2.1

The Navigator palette displays what is visible in the Image window.

Video box

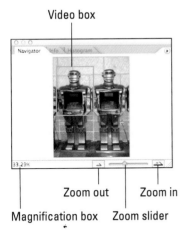

Zoom out   Zoom in

Magnification box   Zoom slider

> **TIP** To resize the Navigator on a Mac, click and drag the lower-right corner of the Navigator box to increase or decrease the size of the Navigator palette and its image thumbnail. In Windows, click and drag from any resizable edge.

Examining the Image Window

Images that you open or create from scratch are displayed in the Image window, shown in Figure 2.2. On a Mac, click and drag the lower-right corner of the Image window to the right and down to enlarge it or to the left and up to reduce its size. In Windows, drag any corner or edge.

To move the window, click the bar at the top of the window and drag. The scroll bars to the right and at the bottom allow you to scroll around images that appear larger than the size of the window. (See the section on scrolling in this chapter.)

The Title bar

The Title bar at the top of the window displays the following information: the document's name, the current view percentage, its color mode, the current layer, the currently highlighted channel or mask, and the images bit depth.

The Status bar

The status bar is located in the lower-left of the Image window (on the Macintosh) or the Photoshop application window (in Windows) just to the right of the percentage field.

FIGURE 2.2

The Image window.

Title bar   Color mode

Name   View %   Bit depth

IMG_0712.JPG @ 16.7% (RGB/8*)

16.67%   Doc: 20.3M/20.3M

Version cue status

Magnification box   Status bar

By default, there are two numbers divided by a slash. These values represent the file size of the image. The number to the left of the slash is the amount of space the flattened file takes up on your disk. The number to the right of the slash indicates the size of the image with the addition of any additional channels, paths, or layers, layer masks or annotations that you may have created. This number best represents the actual file size.

You can quickly view additional information about your document when you click the arrow on the right side of the status bar:

■ **Image Position:** Click the information field to display a diagram of the image as it appears centered on the paper size specified in the Page Setup (see Figure 2.3). Use this diagram to assure that the image will fit on your paper before you print it.

FIGURE 2.3

Click the information field arrow to show the position of your image on the paper size designated in Page Setup.

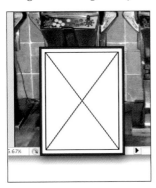

■ **Size and Mode Information:** Opt/Alt-click the status bar to display the image's size, resolution, color mode, and number of channels. (See Figure 2.4.)

FIGURE 2.4

Option-click (Mac) or Alt-click (Win) the information field arrow to show size, resolution, color mode, and channels information.

■ **Tile Information:** ⌘/Ctrl-click the status bar to display the tile sizes of the document. Photoshop uses tiles to display and process images. When you display an image or when the image refreshes, you can sometimes see the image appear progressively as it tiles on-screen. This window tells you how many tiles comprise the image, and is of little practical use to most users.

■ **Status Bar Menu:** The status bar, by default, displays the current size of your document. But if you click the small black arrow at the right end of the bar and then the Show sub-menu, you can select other information to be displayed as in Figure 2.5.

FIGURE 2.5

Click the black arrow next to the status bar and then Show to reveal the status bar menu.

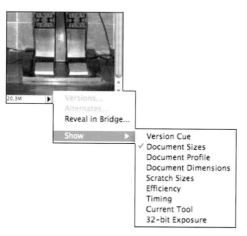

■ **Version Cue:** Version Cue is an Adobe product that organizes and stores related documents. This option displays the status of a document if it is part of a Version Cue project.

■ **Document Profile:** This option displays the name of the color profile embedded in the image. The color profile affects how the image appears on-screen (see Chapter 4 to learn more about color profiles).

■ **Document Dimensions:** The width and height of the document is displayed in the current units specified in the preferences.

■ **Scratch Sizes:** The number to the left of the slash indicates the amount of memory needed to hold all current images open in memory. The number to the right indicates the amount of memory Photoshop has been allocated.

■ **Efficiency:** This option indicates what percentage of the last operation was performed in RAM. If this percentage drops below 80%, you may want to consider allocating more memory to Photoshop or installing more physical RAM.

■ **Timing:** The information field tells you how long the last operation took to perform to the tenth of a second.

■ **Current Tool:** This option displays the name of the currently selected tool.

■ **32-Bit Exposure:** This feature displays a slider that controls the exposure of 32-bit images. Click and drag it left to darken and right to lighten the exposure.

Accessing Menus and Dialog Boxes

The majority of Photoshop's operations can be implemented through the menus at the top of the screen. There are ten windows in the Photoshop Macintosh interface and nine menus in Windows. Some of the menus, such as the Photoshop menu (in Mac) and the File menu, are used to set preferences or save the image. Others such as the Edit menu, the Image menu the Select menu (shown in Figure 2.6), the Layers menu, and the Filter menu apply operations to the image directly or through dialog boxes. The View menu or the Window menu are used to display additional tools or palettes and to change how the image appears on-screen.

FIGURE 2.6

Photoshop's menu bar with the Select menu displayed.

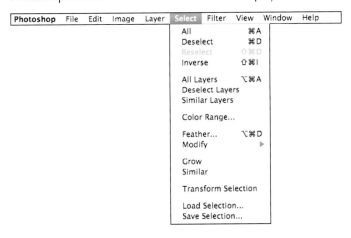

Some commands can be directly applied to an image just by selecting the command from a menu but more frequently, a dialog box is displayed that contains options for a particular operation. When the dialog box is open, you usually cannot perform any other operations until you implement or cancel the command. There are a couple of exceptions. You can access the Zoom tool while a dialog box is open, (see the section on the Zoom tool in this chapter) and you can hide the edges of a selection marquee by pressing Cmnd/Ctrl+H.

The dialog boxes are similar to each other in many respects. Here are general steps to follow in using them:

1. Select a region of an image or highlight a layer.

2. Choose an operation from the menu. The dialog box shown in Figure 2.7 appears.

3. Choose from the displayed options, move sliders or enter values in the value fields.

4. If there is a preview box, make sure it's checked to preview the result of the operation in the Image window before closing the dialog box.

5. Make your changes and commit or abort an operation using these methods:

   ▨ To undo the last operation inside a dialog box, press ⌘/Ctrl+Z.

   ▨ If you've entered values and wish to cancel the operation but keep the dialog box open, press Option/Alt to change the Cancel button to Reset. Click the Reset button.

   ▨ Click Cancel to abort the operation and close the dialog without making any changes or click OK to implement the command.

FIGURE 2.7

The Hue/Saturation command displays a typical Photoshop dialog box.

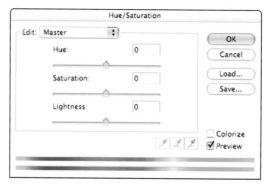

Using Palettes

By default, some palettes appear on the desktop when the program is launched. Photoshop CS3 has 21 palettes that perform a variety of operations. Some of the palettes appear in vertical Palette panes at the left edge of the desktop. This feature has replaced the Palette dock that was in the Options bar. You can perform the following operations on the panes to customize your workspace:

■ **Resize panes:** Place the cursor on the edge of the pane. Then click and drag the edge of the pane to the left to make the pane bigger or to the right to make it smaller. Or click on the resize strip on the left edge of the pane to expand or contract it.

■ **Dock palettes in panes:** To dock a single palette, drag the palette's tab onto the pane. To dock a palette cluster on a pane, drag its title bar. Palettes can be stored at the top or bottom of a pane, between palettes, or to the left or right of palettes. (See Figure 2.8.)

■ **Remove a palette from a pane:** Drag its tab if it's a single palette or title bar if it's a cluster outside the pane.

■ **Rearrange palettes:** Drag the tab or title bar to a new location in a pane.

The Palette pane displays icons that represent palette cluster categories. Click an icon to display the cluster, and then click the palette's tab to display the palette.

 **TIP** **You can access any of the palettes by choosing Window ⇨ and the palette's name.**

The palettes are context sensitive; the image or the program responds directly to edits you make or the preferences you change from within the palettes without having to display dialog boxes. There are palettes that control layers, channels, and paths. Some let you choose color, gather information, display brushes, and create animations and automated processes called *actions*.

FIGURE 2.8

Photoshop's CS3 default workspace palette configuration and palette panes and icon bar.

To hide or display all the palettes simultaneously, press the Tab key.

Palettes provide interactive functionality that many of the dialog boxes lack. Palettes are an easy and efficient way to access many of Photoshop's primary functions. They float on the workspace; they can be accessed immediately because you don't need to open them from a menu. Many palettes are context sensitive, which means that they are synchronized to changes made in the image.

Palettes can be clustered, moved, separated, and reclustered in any combination of your choosing. And with the new palette docking system in Photoshop CS3, they are more accessible than ever. Set up a palette configuration that displays the palettes you most often use for a particular job and then save it as a custom workspace to better utilize space and enhance workflow.

Palette clusters

By default, palettes appear in clusters that can be separated or reconfigured. To separate a palette from a cluster, click its tab and drag it away from the cluster. To place a palette into a cluster, click the palette's tab and drag it into the cluster until a heavy black outline appears. Then release the mouse. The palette repositions itself wherever you release the mouse.

Joining palettes

Two palettes can be joined and moved as a unit. To join a palette to another palette, click the palette's tab, drag it, and place it on the bottom of the target palette. When you see a bold double line, release the mouse; the palette positions itself to the bottom of the target palette. To move the palettes as a group, click the bar of the topmost palette and drag the palettes into position.

Organizing palettes

Palettes can be organized to use the desktop more efficiently. You can reposition a palette or a cluster by clicking and dragging its topmost bar. Reduce the size of a palette by double-clicking the bar at the top of the palette or the palette's nametag.

Restoring and changing palette locations and workspaces

If you've moved the palettes around the desktop and want to reposition them back to their original default locations, choose Window ➪ Workspace ➪ Reset Palette locations.

You can restore default settings such as keyboard commands palette locations you may have changed without having to quit the program and restore preferences. Choose Window ➪ Workspace ➪ Default Workspace.

If you use a particular workspace for a specific type of job, such as painting for example, you may have clustered the Brushes palette, the Color palette, and the Swatches palette or positioned them on the desktop exactly where you like them. You can save your current workspace before you reset the palette locations or the workspace back to the default locations. Not only does this command save palette locations, it also saves menu items, such as dialog box settings you may have altered and keyboard commands you may have changed in the Edit ➪ Keyboard Shortcuts menu. Choose Window ➪ Workspace ➪ Save Workspace. Name the workspace in the dialog box shown in Figure 2.9 and choose the characteristics of the workspace you want to preserve.

FIGURE 2.9

The Save Workspace dialog box.

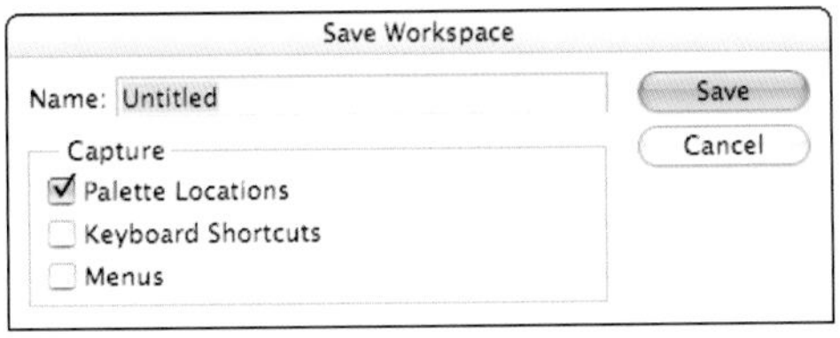

Using the New CS3 Tools

Photoshop CS3's Tools palette displays the icons for 22 different tools in a tall vertical palette (see Figure 2.10). Some of the tool icons expand to access tools that are not visible, bringing the entire number of tools to 58 plus paint swatches, Quick Mask icons, and the view modes. Click the small black arrow on the lower right of the Tool icon to display the additional related tools in a flyout menu, as shown in Figure 2.10.

The Tools palette

The Tools palette is divided into sections that divide the tools into nine general categories. From top to bottom, they are:

- **Adobe On-Line access logo:** Click to connect to the Adobe Website.
- **Selection tools:** Isolates regions of an image.
- **Painting and Editing tools:** Applies color or changes the color of existing pixels.
- **Vector tools:** Draws and selects paths and shapes and creates type.
- **Display tools:** Used for navigation, measurement, and annotations and color sampling.
- **Foreground and Background color swatches:** Displays and chooses colors.
- **Default and Switch foreground background color icons:** Sets colors to the default black and white or reverses foreground and background colors.
- **Quick Mask options:** For entering Quick Mask mode to make and refine selections.
- **Display options:** Displays the image against the desktop, a neutral gray or black background.

FIGURE 2.10

Photoshop CS3 Default Tool palettes with flyouts.

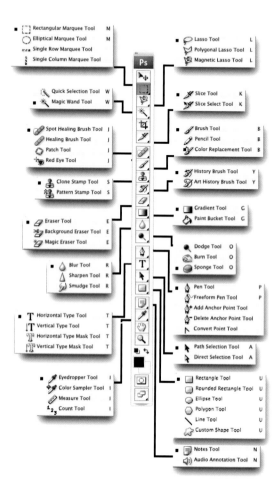

Tool tips

Hover your cursor over a tool and in a few seconds a little yellow label called a *tool tip* appears that identifies the tool, and its shortcut key as shown in Figure 2.11. The tool and shortcuts are also labeled in the flyout menus.

FIGURE 2.11

Hover your mouse over a tool to display a tool tip.

Tool icons

Tool icons represent all the program's manual operations. To choose a tool, click its button on the Tool palette. Drag the cursor where you want to affect the image. Click the mouse or click and drag (depending on the tool) to apply the tool's function to the image.

To access a tool by using its shortcut key press the shortcut letter. For grouped sets of tools such as the three Lassos for example, type the shortcut repeatedly to cycle through the tools in the group.

The Options bar

When you select a tool, its options become visible in the Options bar at the top of the workspace. Here you determine the behavioral characteristics of the tool as shown in Figure 2.12. A tool's performance can vary considerably with different options.

FIGURE 2.12

The Options bar with the Elliptical Marquee tool selected.

Tool presets

Click the tool icon on the far left side of the Options bar to access the current Tool Preset menu (see Figure 2.13). You can save and access tools that you frequently use for which you have created specifications.

FIGURE 2.13

The New Tool Preset menu.

To save a new tool preset, follow these steps:

1. Choose a tool from the Tool palette and set its characteristics in the Options bar.

2. Click the small arrow next to the icon to display the Tool Presets list. Click the New Tool Preset icon in the upper-right of the palette, or click the small arrow at the upper-right side of the palette, to display the pull-down menu.

3. Choose New Tool Preset. The New Tool Preset dialog box shown in Figure 2.14 appears.

4. Name the Tool Preset and click OK. It now appears in the Tool Preset list.

FIGURE 2.14

The New Tool Preset dialog box.

TIP   When naming a preset, remember that descriptive names help you quickly locate a tool.

Summary

I discussed the most frequently used Photoshop features in this chapter. You now know when to use them and how they work.

This chapter covered the following topics:

- Displaying the image
- Accessing menus and dialog boxes
- Using palettes

The following three chapters in Part II cover the fundamentals of working with color.

Part II

The Zen of Color

Chapter 3

Understanding Color Modes

IN THIS CHAPTER

Understanding digital color

Looking at color modes

Converting color modes

Creating colors

Many of the tools in Photoshop's graphic user interface are designed to simulate real-life studio or darkroom techniques, and indeed, almost any effect that can be created on paper, canvas, or film can be created virtually in Photoshop.

No matter what technique you choose, the numerical values of the image pixels are altered to simulate these effects. The values are transmitted through a video card to a monitor that instantaneously displays the changes to the colored pixels on its screen.

Ultimately these effects modify the core data of the color channels, and this is why understanding how channels work is so essential. This chapter is about digital color, how it can be configured, and how each configuration offers a different means of control.

Understanding Digital Color

We take a lot for granted when we use a computer to edit pictures. How does the mechanical movement of your hand touching a key or clicking and dragging a mouse translate into the changing luminous image you see on your screen? Digital color, in this regard is enigmatic, and the technology that makes it happen is miraculous.

The tower or laptop that you perform these miracles on is a super calculator that implements calculations with incredible speed. Think how long it would take you to calculate the changes to all the pixels in one square inch of an image destined for printing (300 ppi x 300 ppi). That would be 90,000 calculations! A computer can perform that many calculations in a fraction of a second.

The coprocessor and the memory of the computer and, of course, Adobe Photoshop create a path for these calculations to be performed accurately and consistently. Photoshop uses algorithms or preprogrammed mathematical formulae to apply operations and effects to the on-screen image. When you paint with the Brush tool, for example, the size, color, hardness, transparency, and color mode you specify program the formula so that the pixel colors of the image change relative to the numerical values of the brush as you click and drag over them. The computer uses a series of microcircuits to pass these numerical values on as electrical impulses to its memory, where they are temporarily stored as positive and negative magnetic charges. When you save changes to the image, all the numerical values are again deposited through microcircuits to your hard disc and again, stored in the form of magnetic charges until you make changes to the image.

Light capturing devices

Of course, this process of editing an image really begins at the image capture device. Digital images are a compilation of data that is captured by a device such as a scanner or digital camera. A digital camera or a scanner collects information when waves of light strike its sensor, usually a Charged Couple Device (CCD) or a Cadmium Metal Oxide Semiconductor (CMOS). Sensors are composed of a grid of photoreceptors with red, green, or blue filters covering individual cells. The filters separate the light into its component colors by letting only one color pass through the filter onto each cell (see Figure 3.1). The information collected by the sensor is processed and assembled by the scanner's software or the camera.

FIGURE 3.1

A sensor is composed of a grid of photoreceptors covered by red, green, or blue filters.

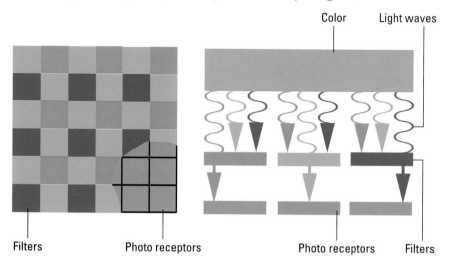

Turning colors into numbers

Each red, green, and blue pixel is assigned a numerical value based on the strength of the color that strikes the photoreceptors. When the image is opened in Photoshop, it is configured into three separate color channels — a red, a green, and a blue, with the information distributed in a grid of pixels. Photoshop processes the information in each channel as an independent grayscale image representing the values of its component color and assembles a component RGB channel that displays the image in full color.

These numerical values can remain in RGB or translate into specific color systems that distribute numerical information differently and provide access to different aspects of color. For example, the three-channel RGB system is often used as a working mode and to display images on-screen, but the four-channel CMYK color system is used to organize the information into color separations for printing on paper.

Choosing Color Modes

Photoshop gives you the flexibility to choose a specific color system to fit your needs either during the image editing process or for preparing an image for print or the Web. Some of these systems are called color modes. Color modes include bitmap, grayscale, duotone, indexed, RGB, CMYK, lab, and multichannel, in which color information is organized into channels with specific characteristics. HSB (Hue Saturation and Brightness) is not a color mode; rather, it is a model. In other words, it doesn't have a specific channel configuration. It is used to determine color in the Color Picker, Color palette, and in the Hue Saturation command to alter relative color. It is supported as a convenient method to determine or locate specific colors based on their individual characteristics. There is one other color system that Photoshop supports, and it is actually an offspring of the Indexed color mode called Web color also known as hexadecimal color that is used for, you guessed it, creating colors for Web pages.

Bitmap mode

Bitmap mode images (not to be confused with the Bitmap file format) are the simplest form of a true black-and-white graphic image. They contain only one channel with two types of pixels, literally black or white, and are used to create line art and digital halftones. Bitmap images contain only 1 bit of information per pixel, so their file sizes are small. Bitmap mode is very limited in the Photoshop features that it supports. Bitmap doesn't support layers, nor does it support alpha channels, and you can't apply filters or perform transformations. If you want to edit a bitmap image you should convert it to grayscale first. Although it is limited, it is useful for converting color images to line art or digital halftones.

Bitmap Notes

Bitmap mode can be used as an intermediate step for creating special graphics effects. Because an image is divided into black or white pixels several interesting effects can be achieved. Diffusion Dither, for example, looks like an old fashion mezzotint and has a soft, silvery look. The Halftone option can produce a course halftone effect by using a 10 or 20 line halftone screen. You can produce a comic book effect by superimposing it over a posterized image that resembles the work of American pop artist, Roy Lichtenstien. The Bitmap option enables you to experiment with different line screen frequencies and different shaped halftone screens.

The Threshold option in the Bitmap dialog box divides the image into black and white areas which is very useful for creating line art; however, it doesn't offer the control that the Threshold command (Image ⇨ Adjustments ⇨ Threshold) provides, which is preferable.

When using the Pattern Dither option, experiment with different size patterns to achieve the best results. Larger patterns may dominate the image and obliterate the detail whereas smaller patterns produce a more refined configuration of dots that can create some very interesting Graphic effects.

To create a bitmap image, follow these steps.

1. Open a color image.
2. Choose Image ⇨ Mode ⇨ Grayscale to convert the image to grayscale.
3. Choose Image ⇨ Mode ⇨ Bitmap. The Bitmap dialog box appears (see Figure 3.2).

FIGURE 3.2

The Bitmap dialog box lets you choose an output resolution and a method for converting grayscale images to images that contain black-and-white pixels.

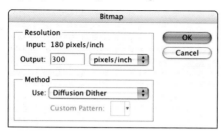

4. Type a resolution for your image.

TIP

The resolution will profoundly affect the quality of the image. Choose higher resolutions for more refined halftone dots lines and patterns.

5. Choose a method from the menu. The Bitmap dialog box offers the following options:

- **50% Threshold:** Replaces all pixels in the grayscale with values from 0 to 127 with black and all pixels with values of 128 to 255 with white as in Figure 3.3.

- **Pattern Dither:** Applies a preprogrammed pattern to the bitmap as in Figure 3.4.

FIGURE 3.3

50% Threshold method.

FIGURE 3.4

Pattern Dither method.

- **Diffusion Dither:** Creates a pattern of pixels that produce what looks like a traditional mezzotint. It creates more pixels in darker areas and fewer pixels in lighter areas, as shown in Figure 3.5.

- **Halftone Screen:** Choose this function, click OK, and another dialog box is displayed as shown in Figure 3.6. Type a halftone frequency that determines the density of screen in lines per inch (see the section on halftones in Chapter 1). Type an angle in degrees. The angle determines the direction of the horizontal and vertical matrices of the screen.

FIGURE 3.5

Diffusion Dither method.

FIGURE 3.6

The Halftone Screen dialog box.

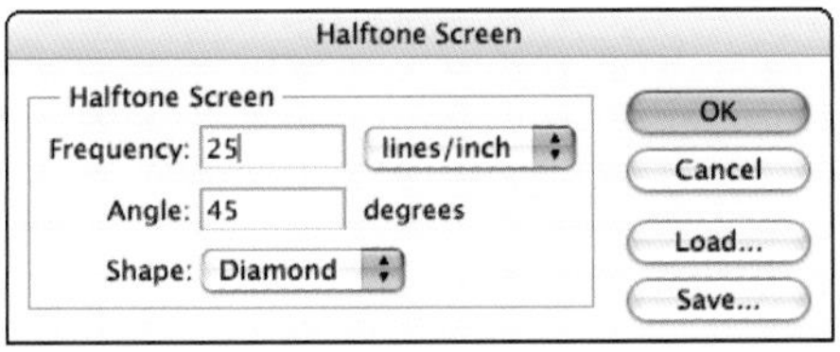

6. If you chose Halftone Screen, choose a shape for the halftone dot. You can choose from the following:

   ▪ **Round:** Uses square pixels to create round-shaped halftone dots (see Figure 3.7).

   ▪ **Diamond:** Uses square pixels to create diamond-shaped halftone dots.

   ▪ **Ellipse:** Uses square pixels to create elliptical-shaped halftone dots.

   ▪ **Line:** Uses lines that vary in width to create tonality.

   ▪ **Square:** Creates square-shaped halftone dots resulting in blocky tonality.

   ▪ **Cross:** Uses square pixels to create cross-shaped halftone dots.

7. If you chose Custom Pattern a dialog box is displayed (see Figure 3.8). Specify a resolution and choose a pattern from the pattern list to apply to the bitmap as in Figure 3.9.

FIGURE 3.7

Halftone screen option.

FIGURE 3.8

The Custom Pattern dialog box.

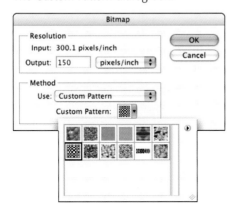

FIGURE 3.9

Custom Pattern.

Grayscale mode

Grayscale is a mode that displays what we traditionally think of as a black-and-white image (see Figure 3.10.) A grayscale image is composed of one channel with 256 possible shades of gray. Pixels have brightness levels ranging from 0 (black) to 255 (white). Sometimes grayscale pixels are measured in percentages of black ink from 0% (white) to 100% (black).

When you convert a flattened color image to grayscale by choosing Image ⇨ Mode ⇨ Grayscale, a caution box asks you if you want to discard color information as in Figure 3.11. Click OK and the hue and saturation information is eliminated and the brightness values remain intact.

FIGURE 3.10

A grayscale image.

The Discard Color Information caution box.

If you are working on a layered image the caution box warns you that changing modes can change the appearance of layers, and then directs you to Flatten, Cancel, or Don't Flatten the image. You usually want to preserve the content layers but it's not a bad idea to merge adjustment layers before converting to grayscale (see the section on merging layers in Chapter 1).

CROSS-REF Converting an image directly from color to grayscale can often produce images with less than a perfect tonal range. There are several methods for converting a colored image into a grayscale to produce the best possible results. Chapter 9 walks you through methods that give you many more choices for converting your color images to grayscales.

Indexed Color mode

Indexed Color mode produces 8-bit color images with anywhere from 2 to 256 colors on one channel to display images. The fewer the potential number of colors in the image, the smaller the file size. Indexed color documents are often used for saving files in GIF format for use on the Web or as multimedia images because of their smaller file sizes.

As with bitmap documents, Indexed Color documents are limited in editing capabilities. They don't support layers, filters, or color adjustments. Only grayscale and RGB images can be directly converted to indexed color. You can save indexed color documents in PSD, BMP, GIF, Photoshop EPS, (PSB), PCX, Photoshop PDF, Photoshop Raw, Photoshop 2.0, PICT, PNG, Targa, or TIFF formats.

When you convert an image to Indexed Color, you can choose a specific palette to display the image to match the colors as closely as possible to the original. When you convert an image, a color look-up table (CLUT) is created which Photoshop uses to store the colors of the image. If a color in the original image does not appear in the table, the program chooses the next closest color or dithers available colors to simulate it. Choose Image ➪ Mode ➪ Indexed Color; the dialog box (see Figure 3.12) displays the following options:

- **Palette:** The Palette menu items represent specific CLUTs used to best represent your image.

- **Exact:** This option produces a palette using the exact color values from images that contain between 2 to 256 colors.

- **System Mac OS:** Select this option to use the Mac OS system palette.

- **System Windows:** Select this option to uses the Windows system palette.

- **Web:** This option converts the image to 216 Web colors.

- **Uniform:** Use this to sample for two to six colors from each of the RGB color channels. Photoshop can sample up to six evenly spaced color values each of red, green, and blue, to produce a palette of 216 colors ($6^3 = 216$). The total number of colors in the image will be the value of the nearest perfect cube that is less than the current value currently in the Colors value box (8, 27, 64, 125, or 216).

- **Local (Perceptual):** Creates a CLUT prioritizing color combinations that are most natural and pleasing to the eye.

- **Local (Selective):** The Local option creates a CLUT similar to the Perceptual color table but that favors large regions of continuous color and preserves Web colors.

- **Local (Adaptive):** This option creates a CLUT by sampling the colors from the most common colors in the image. An RGB image only composed of reds and yellows produces a CLUT made primarily of reds and yellows. You can control the palette with more precision if you select an area of specific color range before converting the file to indexed.

- **Master (Perceptual):** You can create a master palette in ImageReady to apply to group of GIFs or PNG-8 images. You can then use the Master palette in Photoshop when converting files to Indexed color. When you include the Master palette with a batch of images, all images display using the same colors. Master Perceptual creates a CLUT from the Master palette by prioritizing color combinations that are most natural and pleasing to the eye.

- **Master (Selective):** Master creates a CLUT from the Master palette similar to the Perceptual color table that favors large regions of continuous color and preserves Web colors.

- **Master (Adaptive):** This option creates a CLUT by sampling the colors from the most common colors in the image and converting them to similar colors in the Master palette.

- **Custom:** A custom palette is created using the Color Table dialog box (see Figure 3.13). By default, the CLUT displays the current Adaptive palette, which is useful for previewing the colors most often used in the image. You can edit the color table by clicking on any swatch to display the Color Picker, or click the eyedropper icon, release the mouse and drag over the image. Click to sample a color. You can save the color table for later use and load it when you need it.

- **Previous:** Uses the Custom palette from the previous conversion.

- **Colors:** You can determine the exact number of colors in the image from 3 to 256 by typing a value. The bit depth of the image does not change. It remains an 8-bit image but the fewer the colors the smaller the file size.

- **Forced:** Use this option to force specified colors to be included in the conversion. From the menu choose Black and White to force black and white onto the color table. Choose Primaries to add red, green, blue, cyan, magenta, yellow, black, and white; Web adds the 216 web-safe colors, and Custom lets you sample colors from the image.

FIGURE 3.12

The Indexed Color dialog box.

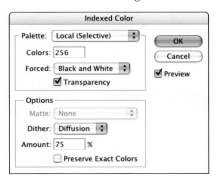

FIGURE 3.13

Create a custom palette.

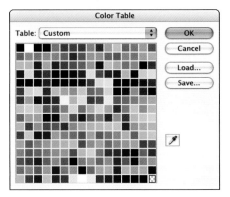

- **Transparency:** Checking the Transparency box preserves the transparent areas of the image during conversion and adds a transparency swatch to the CLUT. If unchecked the transparent areas of the image will be filled with the specified matte color or white when no matte color is chosen.

- **Matte:** The image must contain transparent areas for Matte to be enabled. Choose a matte color from the menu or click custom to display the Color Picker. Matte fills anti-aliased edges in transparent areas of the image with color to better blend them with a Web background. When Transparency is selected, the matte is applied to edge areas to blend the edges with a Web background. When Transparency is deselected, the matte is applied to all transparent areas.

■ **Dithering:** If you reduce the number of colors to less than 256, the image may not contain all the colors in the color table. Dithering the colors simulates the missing colors by mixing the pixels of the available colors. Choose a dither option from the menu and enter a percentage value for the dither amount. Choose from the following dither options:

■ **None:** Posterizes the image by creating sharp transitions between shades of color.

■ **Diffusion:** Produces a random structured dither. This is useful for preserving fine details and text on Web images.

■ **Pattern:** Uses a halftone-like square pattern to dither colors.

■ **Noise:** Reduces seam patterns along the edges of slices. Choose this option if you plan to slice the image for positioning in an HTML table.

■ **Preserve Exact Colors:** Protect colors in the image that are in the color table from dithering.

Duotone mode

Duotones are images that have been separated into two ink colors. They are frequently used to extend the tonal range of images when printing on an offset lithographic press or to add a sepia or other colored tint to an image. Before you can convert a colored image into a duotone you must first convert it to a grayscale. Then choose Image ➪ Mode ➪ Duotone. The dialog box (shown in Figure 3.14) enables you to choose type — Monotone (images with one color of ink), Duotone, (two colors), Tritone (three colors), and Quadtones (four colors). By clicking on the color swatch, you can choose colors from the custom color books. Click the Color Picker's Color Libraries (see the "Working with the Color Picker" section later in this chapter). Then click the Curve swatch to adjust the distribution of ink. The color ramp at the bottom of the dialog box displays a simulation of the ink combinations. Duotones are detailed in Chapter 9.

FIGURE 3.14

Select duotone options.

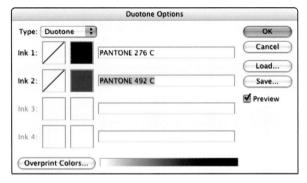

RGB Color mode

Color scanners and digital cameras are RGB devices. They collect and separate light into its red, green, and blue primary components. A monitor is also an RGB device that combines and displays the information as a full color image. The RGB color mode is called a *device dependant* color mode because it represents the three colors created by RGB devices.

RGB consists of the three primary colors red, green, and blue in three 8-bit color channels. Each color channel can contain 256 brightness values. The brightness values of each channel are assigned numbers that vary from 0 (black) to 255 (white) with all intermediate values in between. There is also a composite RGB channel that combines the color information into a full color image. RGB can produce a total of 256^3, or 16,777,216, possible colors.

RGB is an additive color mode; the more light that is added, the brighter the color becomes. Lighter colors are produced by pixels with high numerical values. Pixels with red, green, and blue values at their highest extreme (255) produce white on the composite channel. Darker colors are produced by pixels with low numerical values. Pixels with red, green, and blue values of 0, the lowest extreme, produce black. If the pixels are composed of equal proportions of red, green, and blue, they produce gray.

Mixing paint or ink is a *subtractive primary mode*; the more pigment you add, the darker the color becomes. In RGB, you mix quantities of colored light which is an *additive primary mode*. The more color you add the lighter the color becomes. If you are used to mixing paint or ink, mixing RGB colors can produce unexpected results. When you mix full intensity red and green together you get yellow or the complete absence of blue. When you mix full intensity green and blue together, you get cyan or the absence of red. Blue and red produces magenta, the absence of green. Mix red, green, and blue at their strongest intensities and white is produced. Mix all three colors at their lowest intensity and you get black. As you work in Photoshop you will use these concepts in some of the dialog boxes when you are adjusting color on an image. RGB is one of Photoshop's primary working modes for the following reasons:

RGB is one of Photoshop's primary working modes. Images can be edited in RGB and later converted to CMYK for output to four-color process color separations. The advantage of working in RGB mode is that it contains a large color range (gamut) and only three color channels that produce more colors and smaller file sizes, unlike CMYK with its limited color gamut and four color channels.

Another reason to work in RGB is that several of the filters and adjustments work only in this mode. The disadvantage is that when you convert from RGB to CMYK there may be considerable loss in color intensity when the colors are remapped to the CMYK gamut (see the section on converting color modes in this chapter).

CROSS-REF Because RGB is one of the primary editing modes in Photoshop, it is important to understand how 24-bit color is compiled and how RGB channels are accessed. More information on RGB color mode can be had in Chapters 1 and 6.

CMYK Color mode

CMYK is the universal color system for printing full color images. Cyan, magenta, yellow, and black (CMYK) are ink colors used in offset lithography and on inkjet printers. By printing tiny dots of ink of the four process colors on white paper, a large range of color can be represented. Because the dots on a printed image are so small, the eye mixes them together (see Figure 3.15). The relative densities of groups of colored dots produce variations in color and tonality. CMYK is referred to as a *subtractive* color system. The more ink you add to a CMYK image, the darker it becomes; conversely, using less ink produces lighter colors, and the absence of ink produces white.

Cyan, magenta, and yellow are the opposites of red, green, and blue. RGB colors are additive primaries. Added at full strength they produce white. In theory, full strength CMY being the subtractive primaries should produce black but in practice they don't. Mixing CMY pigments together produces not black but a muddy brown color. This is because CMY is composed of pigments with impurities. To compensate for this problem black is added to the mix to heighten the details and darken shadows.

In Photoshop, CMYK is a color mode used to display the color components of an image before it is printed. CMYK contains four channels one each of cyan, magenta, yellow, and black that represent CMYK color separations. The channels can be viewed separately or together to assess how the printed plates or images will look. There is also a composite color channel that displays the full color image.

CROSS-REF Photoshop's Selective Color command is designed primarily to adjust images in CMYK mode. It targets the individual color channels and enables you to alter their relative content. Learn more about this and other adjustment features in Chapter 5.

Lab Color mode

RGB images have three channels that divide the color information into brightness levels of red, green, and blue. RGB images reflect the characteristics of the RGB devices such as the scanner or the digital camera that captures them, and the RGB monitor that displays them. In other words, RGB images are dependant on devices for their appearance. An image that has been converted to Lab Color mode is very different. Lab Color mode is the most complete color model used conventionally to describe all the colors visible to the human eye. It was developed for this purpose by the International Commission on Illumination (*Commission Internationale d'Eclairage*) and is sometimes referred to as CIELab.

FIGURE 3.15

A close up of dots of CMYK ink printed on white paper.

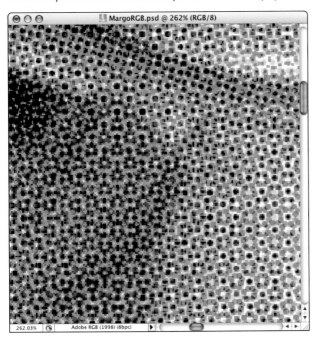

Lab Color is device independent, meaning that the color model is based on the perception of the human eye rather than a mechanical ink or light system. Lab images contain three color channels and a composite channel with the information being divided up differently than in RGB mode. Lab images have a lightness or the L channel and two color channels — a and b. The *L* channel represents the lightness of a color where a value of 0 indicates black and a value of 100 equals white. The *a* channel is magenta and green where negative values between 128 and -1 indicate green while positive values between 0 and 127 indicate magenta. The *b* channel is blue and yellow where values between -128 and -1 indicate blue and positive values between 0 and 127 indicate yellow (see Figure 3.16).

Working in Lab mode is advantageous because having access to the lightness information separate from the color information enables you to control each independently. As a color model, Lab can be used to independently adjust luminosity and color. Photoshop uses Lab as an interim color space when converting files from one color mode to another. Many professionals swear by CIELab mode in its ability to increase color intensity, heighten detail, reduce noise and moiré patterns, and sharpen images.

FIGURE 3.16

A diagram of the Lab Color mode.

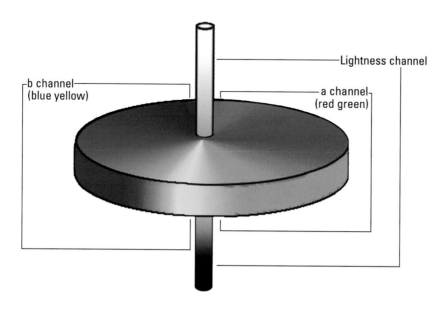

b channel
(blue yellow)

Lightness channel

a channel
(red green)

CROSS-REF Lab Color is rapidly becoming the pro's choice as a working mode and indeed, many doors will open if you understand how it works. Lab can perform miracles on lackluster, soft, grainy, and otherwise broken images. Lab techniques are covered in detail in Chapter 11.

Multichannel mode

The channels in Multichannel mode are independent of each other. When you convert an image to this mode, the core color information is divided into spot color channels. The number of channels produced depends on the number of channels in the source image before it was converted (see Figure 3.17). Each channel supports 256 shades of gray and represents a specific spot color. The pixel values in the new grayscale channels are based on the values of the pixels in each channel before the conversion.

Converting a CMYK image to Multichannel creates cyan, magenta, yellow, and black spot channels. Converting an RGB image creates cyan, magenta, and yellow spot channels. Although RGB can convert to spot CMY, these are not true CMY separations that are press-ready; they are simply the theoretical subtractive opposites of the additive original. If you delete a channel from an RGB, CMYK, or a Lab image, the file is automatically converted to Multichannel.

FIGURE 3.17

The Channels palette displaying a Multichannel image.

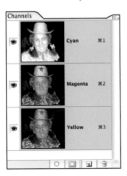

Multichannel does not contain a composite channel. You can see the combination of the channels on-screen by assuring they are all visible in the Channels palette, but there is no single channel entity that compiles the combined information and therefore you cannot print a color composite of a Multichannel document.

Multichannel mode is quite useful for converting duotone images into separate color channels for the purpose of analyzing the color information. Most export file formats do not support Multichannel. However you can save a Multichannel file in DCS 2.0 file format for the purpose of exporting files into a desktop publishing program for printing color separations.

HSB color model

HSB is not a color mode. You can't create images whose data is exclusively organized in HSB channels. Instead, the HSB *color model* defines color by its three basic characteristics. It is used by the Color Picker and the Color palette to create colors in Photoshop and by the Hue/Saturation and the Replace Color dialog boxes to alter relative color (see the section on choosing color in this chapter). Each color is divided into the following characteristics:

- **Hue:** The color of light that is reflected from an opaque object or transmitted through a transparent one. Hue in Photoshop is measured by its position on a color wheel, from 0 to 360 degrees.

- **Saturation:** Sometimes referred to as chroma, it is the intensity of a color as determined by the percentage of the hue in proportion to gray from 0% to 100%. 100% saturation produces a color at its maximum intensity. Zero percent saturation means that the color is entirely gray.

- **Brightness:** Also called luminosity or value, it is the relative lightness or darkness of a color, measured from 0 to 100%. Zero percent brightness produces black no matter what the saturation or hue.

Converting Color Modes

When you convert images from one color mode to another, you alter the core information on the color channels. The results of conversions vary depending on the modes you start and end with. It's entirely possible that layers and effects will be discarded, file sizes may increase or shrink, color information may be lost, and colors may radically shift. It's also possible that the conversion will not affect the appearance of the image at all. Nevertheless it is always prudent to duplicate a file before you convert it to assure that you can access the original data. Choose Image ⇨ Duplicate Name the new file and then convert it to the new mode.

NOTE When you see an ellipses (three periods) after a menu item, it signifies that a dialog box will appear.

Converting from RGB to Lab or Lab to RGB displays no visual difference because there is no loss of data, only a reconfiguration of color and lightness information. Layers are maintained and there are no radical color shifts. Converting RGB to CMYK, however, can be problematic. CMYK has a smaller color gamut and many of the RGB colors, especially the more saturated ones, are not reproducible in CMYK.

CAUTION Don't convert CMYK mode back to RGB. The re-conversion remaps the colors based on the CMYK values and does not restore the original RGB data. You end up with an image that has been degraded from the original.

When you convert an image to CMYK you may expect to see significant changes in how the image appears on-screen so it's a good idea to preview the image in CMYK mode and experiment with adjusting the image prior to actually converting it. To preview an RGB image in CMYK, follow these steps.

1. Choose Edit ⇨ Color settings and choose an CMYK profile.
2. Choose Image ⇨ Duplicate... to make a copy of the image.
3. Use the Zoom tool or the Navigator to reduce the display size of each image so that the original and the copy both appear on-screen for comparison.
4. Click on the duplicate image to activate it.
5. Choose View ⇨ Proof Setup ⇨ Working CMYK.
6. Choose View ⇨ Proof Colors. The image is displayed as if it were converted.
7. Choose Select ⇨ Color Range. The Color Range dialog box appears, as shown in Figure 3.18. In the Select pop-up menu scroll down to Out of Gamut.
8. Click OK to select the out of gamut colors.
9. Experiment with making modifications with the Adjustment features such as Hue Saturation or Curves to the areas within the selection to more closely match the RGB image.

NOTE Although you may improve the image you will most likely be unable to perfectly match the RGB image.

10. When you're satisfied with the adjustment, choose Image ➪ Mode CMYK to convert the image to the CMYK mode.

CROSS-REF Photoshop has several features that assist in the conversion to CMYK. Chapter 13 gives you the scoop on these techniques and how to get optimal color when you prepare files to print to color separations.

CAUTION Although inkjet and large format printers print in CMYK, don't convert your files before printing them. Leave them in RGB mode. The printer or software RIP (Raster Image Processor) converts the color in your files to automatically match the printer's color gamut. If you convert to CMYK they will automatically be converted back to RGB first and then again to the printers CMYK profile resulting in a significant loss of color.

FIGURE 3.18

Experiment with color range adjustments.

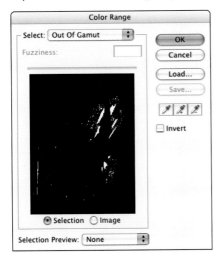

Creating Colors

There are several ways to choose color in Photoshop. You can

- Create color by visually picking a color from a Swatch palette or the Color Picker.
- Type specific values for a mode or model in the Color palette or Color Picker.
- Drag dynamic sliders in the Color palette to specify the color you want.
- Sample colors from any open image.

The two color swatches near the bottom of the Tools palette represent the current foreground and background colors. The swatch on the upper left is the foreground color that is applied to an image directly by any of the painting tools. The default foreground color is black. The background color on the right is applied with the Eraser tool or by deleting or cutting a selected portion of an image on the background layer. The default background color is white.

To reverse the foreground and background colors, click the curved arrow to the upper right of the swatches or press the X key. To restore the colors to the default black and white, click the icon at the lower left of the swatches or press the D key.

Sampling colors

Sometimes you'll want to sample a color directly from the image and paint with it or fill a selection with it. To sample a color, choose the Eyedropper tool from the Tools palette. Click and drag over the image while observing the foreground color swatch in the Tools palette. When you see the color you want click the mouse and that color becomes the current foreground color. To specify a background color press the Opt/Alt key as you drag. If you are painting with the Brush or Pencil tools and you want to sample a color from the image, press the Opt/Alt key. The curser displays the Eyedropper tool. Click the mouse to sample a color. Release Opt/Alt to resume painting with the new foreground color.

Working with the Color Picker

To choose a foreground or background color, click the appropriate swatch on the Tools palette. The Color Picker appears as shown in Figure 3.19. The Color Picker lets you choose from five methods of defining color: HSB, RGB, Lab, CMYK, and Web Colors. The Color Picker's default model is Hue. Your primary tools in the Color Picker are a vertical slider and a large color field and boxes with radio buttons that contain numerical values.

FIGURE 3.19

Choose the appropriate method for defining color.

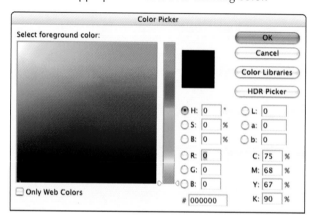

Hue

When the radio button to the left of the H is selected, the vertical slider displays a ramp of the available hues. The top and bottom of the ramp is red. If you drag the slider to the extreme top or bottom of the color bar, the values in the Hue text box are the same; 0 degrees. This number represents red's position on a color wheel. The vertical ramp is actually a color wheel that has been cut at the 0 degree position and straightened. Drag the slider anywhere on the bar. The hue value changes to a number between 0 and 360 degrees. As you move the slider, the field to the left changes color.

Saturation

By default, the color field on the left determines the saturation and brightness of the hue. Saturation is the intensity of color and is represented by the X, or horizontal axis in the color field. If you drag the slider horizontally, the numbers in the S box change between 0%, the minimum saturation and 100% the maximum intensity of color. If the value in the Saturation box is 100%, or if the circle on the color field is to the far right, the color will be at its maximum intensity. If the value in the Saturation box is zero, or if the circle is at the far left of the field the color will be gray.

Brightness

The brightness of a color is controlled by the Y, or the vertical axis in the color field. Brightness, sometimes called luminosity, is the lightness or darkness of a color. Lower values at the bottom of the color field represent darker colors, with 0% equaling black. Higher values at the top of the color field, up to 100%, produce brighter colors.

Picking color

To choose a color, drag the slider on the color ramp to establish a hue or enter a number between 0 and 360 degrees in the H field. Click anywhere on the color field to control saturation and brightness or you can enter values between 0 and 100% in the H and S fields. You can tweak the color by dragging the hue slider and the small circle in the color field.

Active parameters of color

The Color Picker can be configured for HSB, RGB, Lab, and CMYK active parameters by clicking a radio button next to the desired model. The vertical bar then represents the selected characteristic in the selected model. When the S radio button is active, for instance, the active parameter of the Color Picker shifts to Saturation mode and the vertical bar becomes a Saturation slider. The color field now displays hue and brightness variations. If you click or drag in the field, to the left or right, you affect the hue; if you click and drag up or down, you affect the brightness.

When the B radio button is checked, the active parameter of the Color Picker shifts to Brightness and the vertical bar becomes a Brightness slider. The color field now displays hue and saturation variations; clicking in the field or dragging the circle to the left or right affects the hue, and dragging it up or down affects the saturation.

Choosing RGB color

In the case of RGB, when a color channel's radio button is selected, the vertical slider displays the variations of color within that channel, and the color field becomes the other two color channels, one represented horizontally and the other represented vertically. You can also type numerical values in the RGB values between 0 and 255 to produce color. If you enter any three equal numbers between 0 and 255 in the fields you can create 256 variations of gray.

Choosing Lab color

When Lab color is the active parameter you can choose any of the three channels in which to configure the color ramp. If you click the L radio button the lightness values are displayed in the color ramp and the a channel (magenta and green) is displayed as the horizontal axis and the b channel (yellow and blue) is displayed in the color field. When the a radio button is checked, the a channel is represented by the color ramp, the b channel is represented by the horizontal axis, and the L channel is represented by the vertical axis. When the b radio button is checked, the b channel is represented by the color ramp, the a channel is represented by the horizontal axis, and the L channel is represented by the vertical axis.

You can also type numbers in the value fields between 0 and 100 for Lightness and between -127 through 128 for both the a and b channels.

Specifying CMYK colors

CMYK colors do not have radio buttons. You specify CMYK values by typing percentages into the CMYK value fields. Or you can click on any of the radio buttons and drag the slider on the color ramp and the color field's circular indicator and the values will change to produce the equivalent CMYK color.

The CMYK gamut warning

The CMYK gamut is smaller than RGB or Lab. So small that some colors, especially highly saturated ones, cannot be produced at all. If you choose a color in HSB, Lab, or RGB that is outside the printable gamut of CMYK a gamut warning next to the current color swatch appears. The small swatch below the icon represents how the color will print. If you click on this swatch the current color swatch will display the in-gamut color equivalent. Some CMYK colors, especially highly saturated ones, can vary significantly from their RGB counterparts. If you get a warning, you may want to specify a different color for a closer match, or be prepared to accept considerable variation of the color on the printed piece.

Specifying Web colors

In HTML colors are coded with a combination of six characters or *hexadecimal* numbers so that Web browsers can read and display them. Not all browsers can display all colors. You can use the Color Picker to assure that the colors you use are browser-safe by specifying Web colors.

Check the Only Web Color checkbox at the bottom left of the of the Color field to limit the color bar and color field to the 216 Web-compatible colors, as shown in Figure 3.20. When you click any variation, the color's six-character hexadecimal characters appear in the # box. The character pairs represent the Red, Green, and Blue channels. You can choose a hue saturation and brightness from the ramp and color field or if you know the hexadecimal equivalent type in the # box. The equivalents of Web-safe hexadecimal colors are sometimes represented by numbers and sometimes by letters. Table 3.1 defines what these numbers and letters indicate.

TABLE 3.1

Hexadecimal Equivalents

Characters	Grayscale value	Color
ff	255	White
cc	204	Light Gray
99	153	Medium Light Gray
66	102	Medium Dark Gray
33	51	Dark Gray
00	0	Black

FIGURE 3.20

Choose only Web-compatible colors.

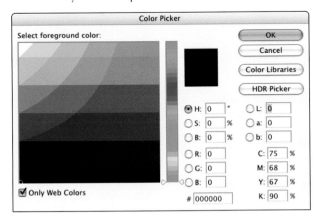

Controlling exactly how colors are seen on browsers is very difficult. A lot depends on the quality and age of the viewer's monitor, the current system palette, and how the brightness and contrast controls are set. The Only Web colors feature lets you choose colors that will not radically change when viewed on other monitors of the same quality and calibration as the one you are working on. They also produce dither-free solids.

As with CMYK colors, Web colors have a limited gamut compared to RGB. When the Only Web Colors box is cleared, the Color Picker displays a Web Color Gamut Warning next to the lower color swatch in the Color Picker. The small swatch below the warning shows how the color will be seen on Web browsers.

It is not absolutely necessary to use the Web-safe palette when creating graphics for the Web because the limited gamut can reduce color options and overall image quality. The option is there in the event that some viewers may not be able to view more than 8-bit color with older video cards and monitors. However, though the image may look slightly better to these users, overall it would appear less than marvelous to the majority of users capable of viewing 24-bit color. As the curve of technology improves with time, and older equipment declines in use, this becomes less and less of an issue.

Specifying color from Color Libraries

Color Libraries let you choose color from a list of solid spot color inks. The PANTONE Matching System of inks for example, is universally recognized. You can specify a color by its number and it can be matched anywhere in the world. Photoshop supports spot color ink libraries such as the PANTONE Matching System and other color libraries such as ANPA, DIC, Toyo, Focoltone, HKS, and TRUMATCH (a CMYK computer color-matching system).

These colors are applied as spot colors used to produce rich solid areas on an image printed on a printing press. They are also used as CMYK spot color equivalents. You can specify these inks from within the Color Picker.

To specify a spot color from a color library, follow these steps:

1. Click the Foreground or Background color swatch to display the Color Picker.
2. Click the Color libraries button to display the Color Libraries dialog box (see Figure 3.21).
3. From the Book pop-up list, choose the desired matching system.
4. Enter the color's number using the keypad. You can, instead, scroll through the color list using the slider; when you find the color you want, click it.
5. Click OK.

CROSS-REF Spot colors can be tricky because they are channel operations. There are several methods used to create them. If you're interested in preparing files for one, two, or three color print jobs with solid color inks, or high-end CMYK plus spot color, Chapter 15 shows you how.

FIGURE 3.21

The Color Libraries option in the Color Picker.

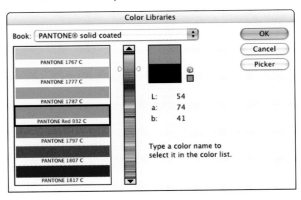

Using Color palettes

The interface in the Color Picker displays the RGB, LAB, and CMYK color modes and the HSB color model in one integrated field. Unfortunately it is not context sensitive. A context-sensitive palette responds immediately to your commands without having to click an OK button. For speed and convenience, you may want to utilize the context-sensitive Color and Swatches palettes that float on the desktop.

The Color palette (is in the palette cluster with the Swatches and Styles palettes. Choose Window ➪ Color or press the F6 key. By default, the Color palette displays the RGB color model but you can choose HSB, Grayscale, CMYK, Lab, or Web Color sliders from the Palette Options menu. Click a swatch in the upper-left corner of the palette to designate whether you want to specify a foreground or background color.

The position of the dynamic color sliders on the gradient bars determines the color. The color corresponds to the swatches on the Tools and Color palettes as you drag the sliders. You can also enter specific numbers for each component of any color model in the value boxes to the right of the sliders.

The most efficient way to specify a color is to click either swatch in the Color palette to determine foreground or background color. Click within the color ramp at the bottom of the Color palette to designate an approximate hue. Release the mouse and the color appears in either color swatch in the Tools palette. Drag the sliders until you get the exact color you want.

The Swatches palette

To display a group of color swatches, choose Window ➪ Swatches. Or press the F6 key and click the Swatches tab on the palette cluster. You can choose from predefined colors, or add and save new colors. Table 3.2 provides useful swatch techniques.

TABLE 3.2

Swatch Techniques

Technique	Operation
Choose a foreground color from the Swatches palette	Click a color in the Swatches palette.
Choose a background color from the Swatches palette	Press the ⌘/Ctrl key while clicking a color.
Adding the foreground color to the Swatches palette	Place your cursor in the blank space below the color swatches. The cursor changes to a paint can. Click your mouse, name the color in the Color Swatch Name dialog box
Delete a color from the Swatches palette	Option/Alt click a swatch on the palette.
Saving a Swatch palette	From the Swatches Palette Options menu, choose Save Swatches. Designate a folder in which to store your palette.
Loading swatches	From the Swatches Palette Options menu choose Load Swatches.
Resetting swatches to the default	Choose Reset Swatches from the Swatches palette option menu.
Naming a swatch	Double-click the swatch and type the name in the Swatch Name dialog box.

Summary

This chapter serves as an introduction to understanding digital color. I guided you though figuring out how to use the correct technique to achieve your intended result.

Specifically, this chapter covered:

- Choosing color modes
- Converting color modes
- Creating colors

In the next chapter, I discuss color management in greater detail.

Chapter 4

Managing Color

Much of your editing depends on your perceptions of the on-screen image. You depend on what you see on your monitor to be able to assess the color and contrast relationships of an image. But the color your monitor displays is affected by several variables and, therefore, can be problematic when making decisions about color.

How can you be sure that what you see onscreen will match what your printer will print? And how can you be sure that what you see onscreen will match what another computer displays? These are the questions that color management attempts to address. Color management is a critical factor in maintaining the quality of an image and producing optimal color. This chapter looks at color management and its numerous variables. It will help you to prepare files for output to print media and digital display.

Understanding Color Working Space

When you manage color, you create an environment in which to view your work, known as a *Color Working Space* (*CWS*). The CWS is based on the type of output device you will use to publish your image. The CWS is independent of the display and can be chosen by the user. When you manage color in Photoshop or in other Adobe Creative Suite software, it is possible to scan, save, edit, and store an image with an embedded CWS as part of the file. When the image is saved and reopened, its appearance will display the characteristics of the CWS.

ICC profiles

An image embedded with a CWS contains an *ICC (International Color Consortium) profile* that describes the images color characteristics. The ICC profile can describe the characteristics of a particular RGB output device, such as a monitor or inkjet printer, or a device that prints CMYK color separations similar to an imagesetter. When viewed on any calibrated computer display, it will appear the same or it will print consistently with predictable results on a specific device. The CWS describes color characteristics so that processing is more reliable and the resulting images are aligned with the environment in which they are output.

The glass window

To grasp the concept of CWS, imagine looking through a window at a painting. Maybe the window is not perfectly transparent; perhaps it is slightly tinted or light is reflecting off the surface causing the colors to appear slightly muted. How is the painting illuminated? By a 100-watt light bulb? Maybe it's lit by florescent light or by a light with a tinted gel?

In fact, monitors really behave as a window between us and our images, modifying the "reality" of the actual image and showing us something that is appropriate to the display's abilities, but not always the actual qualities of the image.

A monitor's profile is a document that describes the monitor's ability and limitations to display pure red, green, and blue as bright, clear color components of an image. In the digital arts, pure RGB colors and the millions of possible variations when mixing these colors together are used. This color information is stored in the form of color channels. For Photoshop to display an image correctly, it must know the characteristics of the monitor you are using and it must also be able to show you what the image might look like if printed or displayed on a particular device. This way, when you work on your image you can make informed decisions about color.

Calibrating Your Monitor

The first step in color management is to create a display profile for your monitor. The display profile is "ground zero"—all other management operations are dependant on the display characteristics of your monitor. Therefore, you *calibrate* the monitor to run at its optimal performance. The easiest method is to make a visual calibration of your display using a software program, such as Adobe Gamma (bundled with Photoshop for Windows) or found within the Mac OSX operating system preferences.

There are a few general rules that apply to using calibration software. First, allow your monitor to warm up for at least 30 minutes before calibrating. Calibrate in low or no ambient light and, if possible, wear black or dark gray clothing to prevent colored reflections from distorting the color on the screen. To use the calibration software in Windows, open the Control Panel and launch Adobe Gamma. On a Mac, you can find the Mac OSX calibration software in the Apple Menu ⇨ System

Preferences ⇨ Displays ⇨ Color ⇨ Calibrate. Then follow the step-by-step instructions. The introductory screen is shown in Figure 4.1. Calibration software instructs you to adjust the brightness and contrast settings of your monitor. It helps you eliminate any color cast that might be displayed, and it has you choose a gamma and white point. Finally, you name and save the profile. As part of the name, you should date the profile for example, "monitor_profile 08-22-06" so that you have a record of your last calibration. Then, calibrate frequently, perhaps once a month.

FIGURE 4.1

The introductory screen for Mac OS calibration software.

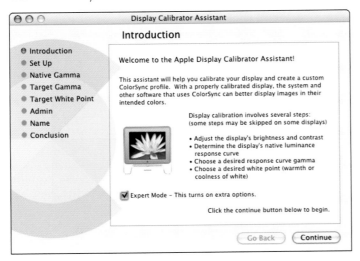

Windows and Macintosh calibration software are visual calibration systems. Their settings are based on the subjective perceptions of the viewer. A visual calibration system can only create a very generalized profile. Precision calibration of a display can be achieved with device called a *colorimeter*. A colorimeter is a worthwhile investment if accurate color is critical to your work. For example, if you are doing a significant amount of color correction for output to color separations or high-end RGB or inkjet prints, working in a predictable color environment from session to session is essential.

A colorimeter attaches to the screen with suction cups in the case of CRT monitors. On LCD panels, it rests on the screen. The device automatically measures the temperatures of variations red, green, blue, gray, white, and black to eliminate any color casts and to establish luminance curves for the gamma, and the white point of the monitor. It sends the collected data to a software program that constructs a monitor profile. Its aim is to create an environment where white is optimally displayed at the appropriate temperature and the monitor's gray tones are neutral.

Choosing the right working space

Calibrating your monitor is the first step in color management. With a calibrated monitor, you can be sure that the image is being displayed with the optimal color that the monitor can produce. The next part of the process involves choosing a color working space that reflects the characteristics of your output goals.

Deciding which color working space to use

The color working space is independent of the monitor display. Go to Edit ➪ Color Settings. In the default Color Settings dialog box, shown in Figure 4.2, there are seven RGB CWSs, including your monitor's display profile plus six commonly used spaces. If you choose More Options from the dialog box, there are quite a few more to choose from those that are designed to display specific working environments. Each has a combination of characteristics, including its color temperature, gamma, and white point. The default workspaces include:

- **sRGB IEC61966-2.1:** Of the color spaces available, sRGB (the s stands for *standardized*) is the smallest. This means that it puts serious limitations on the colors available in your Color palette in Photoshop. The sRGB space was designed by Microsoft and Hewlett-Packard and has a limited color gamut. It is suitable for output to low-end desktop printers or when developing images for display on the Web. For photographic and graphic arts uses it's better to use a working space with a larger color gamut.

  sRGB is the default color working space in Photoshop. You can change this setting, of course but most people don't realize that it is important to do so. The JEIDA trade association, a group of manufacturers (Japan Electronic Industry Development Association) that make consumer digital cameras, standardized the sRGB as the default color space for many consumer digital cameras. Opening an image from virtually any of the many consumer digital cameras is best done into the sRGB space. Professional digital cameras do not suffer from the sRGB limitations, usually supporting one or more of the larger color gamut profiles.

- **Adobe RGB (1998):** This important CWS is large enough to accommodate graphic arts images and most scanned images, and allows for good representation on most high-quality displays. Adobe RGB (1998) has a white point of 6500 Kelvin, the approximate color temperature of midday outdoor ambient light, which is commonly used as the temperature in which to view images printed to white paper. Its gamma is 2.2. Adobe RGB (1998) and is also able to accommodate conversions to CMYK for printing with good results because very little of the CMYK color is clipped or remapped in the process.

  Adobe RGB (1998) is a pretty good choice for most images that are going to be converted to CMYK. There may be some clipping in the highly saturated greens and blues however.

If you are printing to a specific device many manufacturers include profiles with their drivers that show up in the RGB Working Space menu when you choose More Options from the Color Settings dialog box. You can open the image into the Adobe RGB working space which has an ample color gamut, duplicate the file, convert it to the device's profile, and then color correct it (see the section "Converting and Embedding Profiles" in this chapter).

■ **Apple RGB:** The first "graphic arts" display monitor was the Apple 13-inch RGB monitor. It provided color previews to millions of users from 1988 to about 1995, when it was replaced by larger and much better displays. Almost all the stock photos made between 1988 and 1995 were made with computers and scanners connected to Apple 13-inch monitors, and although the quality of displays have improved substantially since then, that profile still represents the colors of the era. This Apple RGB working space uses 6500 K color temperature for white and a 1.8 gamma, which is relatively flat in appearance, appropriate to print applications but its limited gamut renders it somewhat useless by today's standards.

■ **ColorMatch RGB:** The Radius PressView monitor was, for years, the viewing standard of the graphic arts. Almost all professional color work was created on monitors in this class. Although it is no longer manufactured, ColorMatch RGB represents a good gamut of colors, a 1.8 gamma, and a 5000 K white point, which causes some images to turn a sickly yellow color. Use this profile if it causes the colors on your screen to look good while maintaining a pleasant white. If your images turn yellowish on-screen, switch to Adobe RGB (1998) that has characteristics that will deliver a cooler white and a more attractive appearance on most displays. ColorMatch RGB does include most of the CMYK colors and it doesn't contain the highly saturated colors of Adobe RGB 1998. Some prepress professionals use it because it loses fewer colors when converted to CMYK.

■ **Color Sync RGB — Generic RGB Profile:** This matches the current color profile set in the in the Control Panel in Windows or System Preferences on a Mac. From this control panel you can choose from a list of ICC display profiles that are found in the ICC profiles list in the Directory (Win) or Library (Mac).

■ **ProPhoto RGB:** This profile has a very large color gamut that encompasses a wide range of papers and ink sets and is well suited to images destined to be printed to extended gamut (six or more ink colors) dye sub and photo inkjet printers. Use this profile if you are planning to print to a high-end inkjet printer that has an ink set with multiple cyans, magentas, and blacks on high-quality glossy or matte photo paper.

■ **Monitor RGB:** This profile sets the CWS to the current display profile (the profile you created with the calibration software or colorimeter) or choose from the display control panel. Use this working space if other programs you will use to view the image do not support color management.

The Color Settings dialog box showing the default RGB color working spaces.

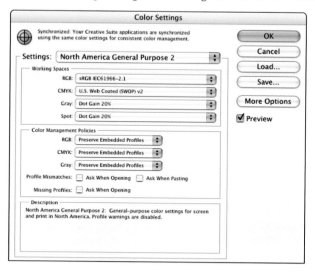

Converting and embedding profiles

When you scan your image or capture it with a digital camera, and you open it into a specific working space, the existing colors are remapped, that is to say, the numerical values of pixels on the color channels change to conform to the limitations of the profile used in the color working space.

There are numerous other RGB spaces available for profiles of specific displays, laptop computers, printers, or other RGB devices. You can save and load specific profiles from other sources, too. Or you can make your own using Adobe Gamma, a colorimeter, or a spectrophotometer and the associated software (see the section "Creating Custom Profiles" in this chapter).

You'll often prepare multiple versions of the same image for specific output conditions. Let's say, for example, you are going to print an image to an archival inkjet printer, and another version is destined for a Web page. Apply and embed different profiles to images by following these steps:

1. **Before opening the image choose Edit ⇨ Color Settings.**
2. **In the Working Spaces field under RGB, choose Adobe RGB (1998).**
3. **Open the image and duplicate it. (Choose Image ⇨ Duplicate.)**

    Name it so that you can identify it as the printed image.
4. **Choose Edit ⇨ Convert to Profile.** The Convert to Profile dialog box shown in Figure 4.3 appears. In the Destination space field, click the choose ProPhoto RGB from the menu. Click OK.

5. Click the original image. Duplicate it again.

6. Choose Edit ⇨ Convert to Profile. Click the Profile radio button and choose sRGBIEC61966-2.1 from the menu. Then click OK.

7. Save both images with the embedded profiles. Choose File ⇨ Save As. Click the Embed Color profile check box.

FIGURE 4.3

The Convert to Profile dialog box.

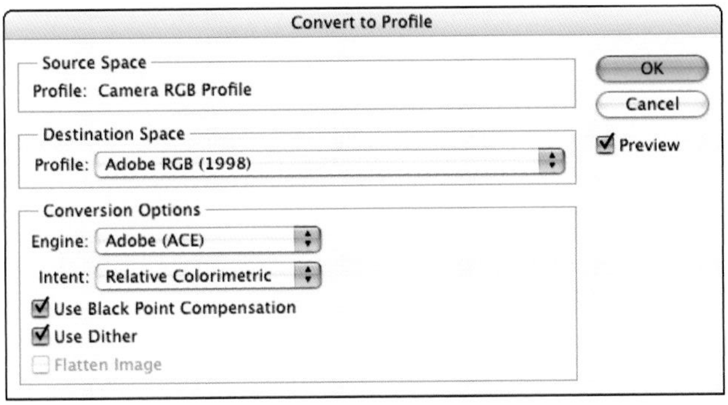

Using Basic Color Settings

The settings you select for color handling can make a huge difference in the appearance and repro-duction of color. When you access the Color Settings dialog box, you can apply a color working space to an image and preview it on-screen. You can also program the image with several options that dictate when color settings are applied to untagged images and images with profiles other than the working space.

Choose Edit ⇨ Color Settings to access the dialog box. You should configure color settings prior to opening a document or creating a new document according to your output goals. You can choose a set of global settings from the Settings menu at the top of the window. The default settings include an RGB, CMYK color space, and gray and spot color that controls dot gain on monochromatic images or images with spot color channels. The settings also include the default Color Management Policies. The Color Management Policies control what happens when Photoshop opens an image that either has no embedded profile or has one that is different from the current CWS.

If you are unsure about what to assign, a good place to start is with *North American Prepress 2* which includes the Adobe RGB (1998) color space and frequently used CMYK color space; U.S. Web Coated (SWOP) v2. This is a good space for both RGB and CMYK colors, and will cause little, if any, harm to images handled by the program (see "Advanced Color Settings" in this chapter for more on the CMYK color space).

Any change to these defaults settings creates a Custom setting. You can save your custom settings with a new name by clicking on the Save button, and load them at another time by clicking the Load button.

Color Management Policies

Color Management Policies determine how Photoshop deals with color profiles when opening a document. You can specify how Photoshop will treat documents that have no embedded profile, or whose profile differs from those specified in the Color Settings dialog box.

If you open a file using the same color working space specified in the Color Settings dialog box, the file will open without interruption. But if we move the file to another machine with different Color Settings, or we open an image that has a different embedded Color Settings, Photoshop puts on the brakes, and displays a dialog box that says, in effect, "Not so fast! This file does not fit in the current working environment. What should I do with it?" This assigns the responsibility for controlling how files are opened to the user. Photoshop asks you to set one of the policies for each type of file we might be opening, RGB, CMYK, and Grayscale. The policies are as follows:

- **Off:** When a file type's Color Management Policies option is set to Off, documents with unknown profiles will be opened with color management turned off. This causes Photoshop to behave more like Photoshop 4 (before color management), where the display's CWS gamut limits the available colors in the image.

- **Preserve Embedded Profiles:** When this option is chosen, images automatically keep their embedded CWS profile when opened. This is a safe approach to opening files with embedded profiles, as it will allow these images to be opened without making any modification to the image's CWS.

- **Convert To Working RGB/CMYK/Grayscale:** This option remaps all the color values in the image to the current CWS when the image is opened. This conversion can cause changes in the colors and is the preferred method for converting files to the current working space.

- **Profile Mismatch/Missing Profile check boxes:** There are two check boxes for profile mismatches: *Ask When Opening* and *Ask When Pasting,* and one for missing profiles: *Ask When Opening.* Selecting these boxes further controls the behavior of Color Management Policies. In either case, if any of these boxes are checked, a dialog box appears when the image is opened. You can then instruct Photoshop on how to proceed. It is a good idea to select each of these boxes so that you can decide, on a case-by-case basis, how to deal with these variables when they are presented to you.

Opening images with mismatched profiles

When you open or paste from an image with a profile that does not match the current working space, the Embedded Profile Mismatch dialog box shown in Figure 4.4 appears, indicating the name of the embedded profile and the working space currently assigned in the Color Settings dialog box. You can then decide how to proceed.

In the What would you like to do? field you can choose one of the following options:

- **Use the embedded profile (instead of the working space):** Opens the image in its embedded working space.

- **Convert document's colors to the working space:** Discards the embedded working space and assigns the one specified in the Color Settings dialog box.

- **Discard the embedded profile (don't color manage):** Applies the current monitor's profile to the image.

The Embedded Profile Mismatch dialog box.

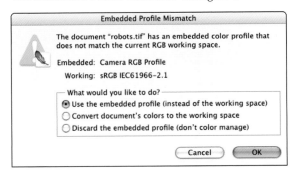

Opening images with missing profiles

When you open an image with no profile, Photoshop displays the Missing Profile dialog box shown in Figure 4.5 where you can choose from these options.

- **Leave as is (don't color manage):** The image will not be color-managed and will display in the monitor's current display profile.

- **Assign working RGB:** The image will be assigned to the current RGB profile chosen from the Color Settings dialog box.

- **Assign profile:** The image will be assigned a profile that you select from the menu.

- **And then convert to the working RGB:** If you select this check box, the image is converted to the working space you choose and then converts it to the working RGB when saved. This will result in the image taking on the embedded profile of the current working space when it is saved. The net effect is to assign the colors to a working space that you think is the correct one for the original image, then convert it to the current working space so its embedded profile will be adequate for the reproduction plans you have.

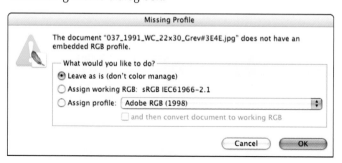

FIGURE 4.5

The Missing Profile dialog box.

Of course, there may be circumstances under which you would want all images whether RGB, CMYK, or Grayscale with mismatched or missing profiles to be mapped to your current working space. If, for example, you are batch-processing images, you may not want to deal with the Mismatch or Missing profile dialog boxes each time an image opens. If this is the case, you can set the working space in the Color Management Policies menu. Choose Convert to RGB, CMYK, or Grayscale and then clear the Profile Mismatches check box. The image converts to the current working space. If you change this setting for processing a batch of images, be sure to put it back to *Ask when opening* after you have finished.

NOTE Whenever Photoshop opens an image in a working space other than the current working space, it will mark the title bar with an asterisk to indicate that it is not using the current working space.

CMYK color working space

If you plan to convert your image from RGB mode to CMYK to print to color separations, you can choose a CMYK color working space. If you have a four-color (CMYK) profile for a printer that prints color separations, for example, or a printing environment that you normally use, you can select it if it's on the CMYK list. If you don't have a custom profile to use, there are several "generic" CMYK profiles you can load. For North America, you can use the U.S. Web Coated (SWOP) v2, U.S. Sheetfed Coated v.2, or U.S. Sheetfed Uncoated v.2 profiles provided by Adobe. These profiles take into account specific standardized printing practices that include ink and paper type and dot gain. If you are outside North America, choose either Eurostandard (coated or uncoated) or the Japan Standard profiles as appropriate to your location. The image will be remapped to these CMYK profiles when you convert to CMYK with the Mode ➪ CMYK or Edit ➪ Convert To Profile commands.

Working with Advanced Color Settings

Clicking the More Options button in the Color Settings dialog box displays two sets of additional settings, as shown in Figure 4.6 — Conversion Options and Advanced Controls. In the Conversion Options field, the Engine setting sets the color conversion "engine." Depending on the options available on your computer, those options range from a selection of two to six or more.

Color management engines

Adobe has its own color management engine (in the parlance of the industry it is called a CMM, or color management method): Adobe Color Engine (ACE). Other CMMs you might encounter include Apple ColorSync, Heidelberg, Kodak, Imation, or Agfa.

FIGURE 4.6

The More Options Color Settings dialog box.

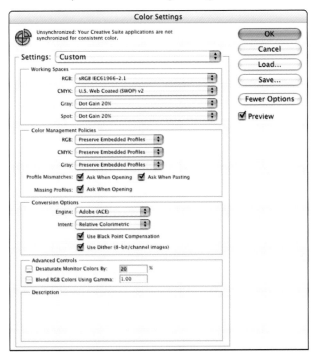

Which engine should you choose? Each company suggests that its CMM uses a superior method of polynomial voodoo to convert color. A good suggestion is to use a CMM that is available in all the applications you use to manage color. This ensures that color is being converted similarly between applications. In reality the net effect of a color management engine is essentially the same. Even experts can discern only very subtle differences, so it's not worth a lot of worry. You are certainly welcome to try various combinations of engines and rendering intents and decide for yourself.

Conversions with rendering intent

The next item under Conversion Options is cryptically named *Intent* (see Figure 4.7). The ICC has established a set of four rendering intent settings under which color conversions can be made. Each has a purpose, and each can be used to maximize the quality of your images for a specific outcome. Rendering intents modify color while it is being converted into a new working space. These modifications can appear as subtle changes or shifts that make color images appear very odd. The five Intent options are:

FIGURE 4.7

The Intent Conversion options.

■ **Perceptual:** This option is a rendering intent designed to make photos look pleasing to the eye when converted to a new color space. The Perceptual rendering intent remaps colors, maintaining their relationships to achieve pleasant appearance. At the expense of color accuracy, the appearance of the image will generally follow the appearance of the original scene. Most photo applications default to Perceptual rendering, and Photoshop uses the Perceptual rendering intent in many of its default color settings.

■ **Saturation:** This option is used primarily for images with solid colors. Best used when converting graphs, charts, and other business presentations, Saturation rendering will result in bright, fully saturated colors in solid areas, and fairly strong contrast applied to color variation. Saturation rendering sacrifices color accuracy for sharp contrast and saturation.

If you convert images from Postscript illustration programs such as Adobe Illustrator, the Saturation rendering intent will result in a better-looking image after conversion than the other intents.

■ **Relative Colorimetric:** You can use this rendering intent when you prefer color over saturation. It produces a more accurate conversion of colors into the new color space. This rendering intent is recommended by Adobe's experts and many prepress professionals for most color conversions. Relative Colorimetric moves the whites in the image to the white point of the working space, usually resulting in (as they say in the ad biz) "whiter whites and brighter brights" than in the source image. Always select the with Black Point Compensation box when you use Relative Colormetric or shadow detail will fill in, because the black points in the conversion may not be correctly remapped.

- **Absolute Colorimetric:** This option is similar to Relative Colormetric except in the way it renders whites. Whites remain the same as in the source image resulting in an image that can be used effectively for proofing print printing on nonwhite or off-white papers (such as newsprint). Absolute Colorimetric is a rendering intent that is used for a very specific purpose. If you don't have these specific goals in mind, you should avoid it.

- **Black Point Compensation/Dither:** Of the two check boxes under the Conversion Options: *Use Black Point Compensation* and *Use Dither (8-Bit/Channel Images,* Black Point Compensation is usually selected; it is used to maintain saturation of solid black in conversions (it remains composed of proportions of cyan, magenta, yellow, and black) where the normal behavior of a conversion would desaturate blacks. When converting RGB images to CMYK for print for example, if we leave this box unchecked and make a conversion (Image ⇨ Mode ⇨ CMYK), the darkest blacks are often remapped to the closest color that is within the gamut of the destination profile, which might include an adjustment for dot-gain. This adjustment can desaturate the solids to keep their value below the total ink coverage number, but will result in some washed-out colors where a solid would be better. Black Point Compensation corrects this problem.

  The Use Dither checkbox causes 8-bit per channel images to be *dithered* when converted to 8-bit per channel images of another color mode. Dithering is a blending method using pixels of other colors to create smoother gradations.

Advanced controls

Though recommended for "advanced users only," the Advanced Controls settings can improve the accuracy of the images that you see on your monitor. The following two settings are available in the Advanced Controls field:

- **Desaturate Monitor Colors By:** This setting tells Photoshop to desaturate colors by a specified percentage when displayed on the monitor. You can check this option when viewing the full range of colors in images with color gamuts larger than that of the monitor profile. For example, you might check this box if you're viewing an image with a Wide Gamut RGB embedded profile on a calibrated monitor. Because the gamut in Wide Gamut is larger than the monitor display, this function may simulate the tonality of the image — even though the monitor can't display the actual color beyond the range of its profile.

CAUTION Using this feature can cause errors between what is displayed on-screen and the colors of the printed image.

- **Blending RGB Colors using Gamma:** This setting controls the blending of RGB colors on-screen. When the option is selected, RGB colors are blended using specified gamma between 1.0 (which has no effect) and 2.2, which creates slightly higher-contrast edge transitions. When the option is not selected, like most other applications, RGB colors are blended in the document's color space.

Creating custom profiles

A custom profile, either configured in the Color Settings dialog box or made with color management software, often provides more precise color than any of the more generic profiles available in Photoshop. Custom profiles can often be obtained from the manufacturer of the better quality inkjet printers. Custom profiles can also be made with profiling hardware and software such as GretagMacbeth's Eye One Spectrophotmeter and ProfileMaker Pro (www.gretagmacbeth.com).

A *spectrophotometer* is a device that measures the wavelength of colors off of a reflective surface. The calibration process includes making a print of a target image of a grid of colored squares from your inkjet printer. Each paper or substrate has different absorption and reflective qualities, so you need to make a profile for each type of paper that you use. Scan the printed target image with the spectrophotometer. The raw data that the device gathers is sent to software that constructs a profile. You can then load the profile in the Color Settings dialog box and be assured that you have an accurate profile of your printer.

This is the preferred method of creating printer profiles but, unfortunately, the hardware and software can be pricey ($1,200 to $3,000). Another cheaper alternative is to contact a company on the Web that creates custom profiles. It will send you a digital target image, which you will print on your inkjet printer. You need to make a print on each paper that you use. Then you mail the print(s) back to them. They scan it and send you a profile for your specific device and each type of paper.

Printing Your Image

After you've completed your image, assigned RGB profiles to it, and converted it (or not converted it, depending on the circumstances), you can print it. The majority of desktop inkjet printers use the RGB information to convert the image to CMYK (or CcMmYKK) on the fly.

CAUTION When printing to an inkjet printers it is not advisable to convert the image to CMYK because the printer handles this conversion internally.

Inkjet printing results can vary dramatically from model to model because of the different color gamuts of each type of printer. If you have the printer's profile provided by the manufacturer, or even better, created with a spectrophotometer, the results will be more predictable. If you don't have the profile of a specific printer, you can improve the results on inkjet printers by printing the image in RGB and letting the printer software do the conversion on the fly. You can then use the print as a proof to recalibrate your display (using Adobe Gamma or the Mac OS calibration software) to display the image as close to the proof as possible. Save the calibration settings to be used specifically for editing images printed on the target printer. Make your adjustments to the image based on the on-screen display and save the image as a separate file, identifying it for the specific printer. This is a funky, trial-and-error way to match the printed image to the display, but it works if you're willing to pull a number of prints and tweak adjustments to get as close of a match as possible.

Using the print dialog boxes

Several dialog boxes offer similar functions for ultimately printing your image. They are Page Setup, Print With Preview, Print, and Print One Copy. Print One Copy automatically prints the image on the default printer. Print brings up the printer's dialog box (see Figure 4.8) in which you can designate a printer, the number of copies, and other printer-related presets depending on the printer you choose.

FIGURE 4.8

The Print dialog box.

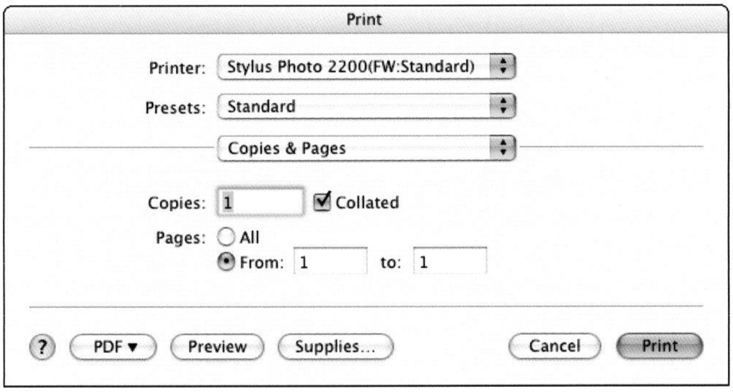

Page Setup

Choose File ➪ Page Setup (see Figure 4.9) to determine the paper size, orientation, and scale of the image. The dialog box includes different options depending on your installed printer, sometimes including some of the same options found in the Print with Preview dialog box.

FIGURE 4.9

The Page Setup dialog box.

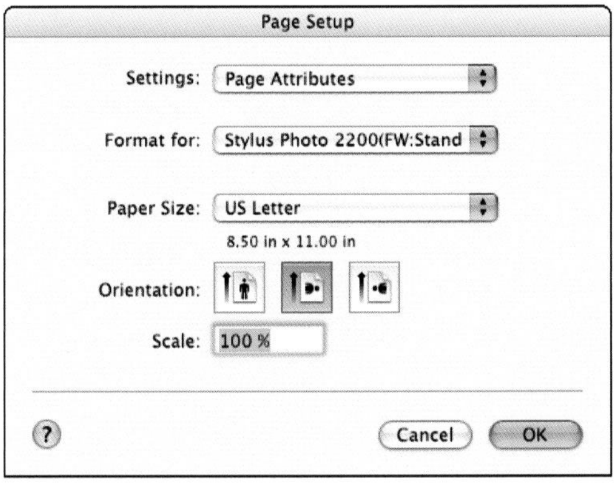

Print

When you choose File ➪ Print, the Print dialog box shown in Figure 4.10 appears. It displays a preview on the left side of the screen that shows the image's size in relation to the paper. It offers the following options:

- **Printer:** Choose a printer from the pop-up menu.
- **Copies:** Type a number in the text box to print the number of copies that you want.
- **Position:** Specifies the location of the printed image on the current paper size.
- **Scaled Print Size:** Lets you increase or decrease the image size while maintaining the image's constrained proportions.
- **Scale To Fit Media:** Select the check box to size the image to fit the current paper.
- **Show Bounding Box:** Select the check box and manually scale the preview by dragging the corner points.
- **Colormatch Preview:** Matches the image to the
- **Print Selected Area:** If you have an active selection, you can select this check box to print only that part of the image.

Check the More Options box to expand the dialog box. In the expanded area, a menu offers two sets of settings, Output and Color Management.

FIGURE 4.10

The default Print with Preview dialog box.

Output options

Output options let you specify a number of printing functions and also create labels, registration, and crop marks. The options include:

- **Background:** Choose a color from the Color Picker for the area surrounding the image.
- **Border:** Enter a value from 0.00 to 10.00 points in points, inches, or millimeters to produce a black border around the image.
- **Bleed:** Enter a value from 0.00 to 0.125 inches to specify the width of the bleed. When printed, crop marks will appear inside rather than outside the image.
- **Screen:** Enter values for screen frequency, angle, and shape for the halftone screens or individual color separations.
- **Transfer:** This function is designed to compensate for poorly calibrated printers. If a printer is printing too dark, for example, adjust the curve to lighten the image to achieve better results.
- **Interpolation:** Select this check box to automatically reduce the jagged edges that would be created when a low-resolution image is resampled up for printing.
- **Calibration Bars:** Selecting this option produces an 11-step grayscale wedge for measuring dot densities with a densitometer. On CMYK images, a gradient tint bar is printed on each separation.
- **Registration Marks:** These marks, including bullseyes and star targets, are used to register color separations.
- **Crop Marks:** These marks show where the page is to be trimmed.
- **Captions:** Prints text entered into the File Info box.
- **Labels:** Prints the file name on images.
- **Emulsion Down:** Prints the emulsion side of the image down so the type is readable when it is on the back of the film. Most plate burners in the United States use emulsion-down negatives.
- **Negative:** Prints a negative image. Most printers in the United States use negative film to burn plates.

Color management options

These options control color management directly before printing.

Under the print area there are two:

- **Document:** This option uses the current color settings as a profile for the printed image.
- **Proof:** This option uses the current proof settings.

The Color Handling menu offers six:

- **No Color Management:** Ignores embedded profiles.

- **Let Printer Determine Colors:** Uses the printer's software to determine the colors of the printed image.

- **Separations:** Prints color separations from CMYK, Duotone, and Multichannel images. Separations does not print a composite.

- **Let Photoshop Determine Colors:** By default, this uses the embedded working space or lets you choose a profile and rendering intent from the menu.

- **Rendering Intent:** Lets you choose a rendering intent from the pop-up menu that will be used when the file is converted to CMYK.

- **Description:** Displays a verbal description of any item in the Color Management options field.

Printing composites, separations, channels, and layer content

You can print an entire full-color composite, color separations, individual color or alpha channels, and individual layer content.

Composites

Printing a color composite is easy; follow these steps:

1. **Choose a color printer from the Page Setup dialog box.**

2. **Set the specifications for number of copies and the orientation and click OK.**

3. **Choose any of the print options: Print One Copy, Print, or Print with Preview.**

4. **If you choose Print With Preview, set the specifications for the print.**

5. **Click the Print button.** The Print dialog for the specific printer appears where you can determine additional settings for the print. Click the Print button.

Separations

To print separations the image must be in CMYK, Duotone, or Multichannel mode. Follow these steps:

1. **Choose Print With Preview.**

2. **Choose Output from the menu.**

3. **Select the Registration Marks, Labels, and Negative checkboxes.**

4. **Choose a Color Management from the menu.**

5. **In the Color Handling menu choose Separations.**

6. **Click the Print button.**

Individual channels or layers

You can print individual color, alpha, or spot color channels. The printer prints what is visible in the image window. If you want to print the contents of any specific color, alpha, or spot color channel simply conceal all other channels by clicking on their visibility icons in the Channels palette. You can print combinations of channels the same way. The same is true with printing layers or combinations of layers. When the layer content is visible in the image window, choose one of the print dialogs and output the image.

Summary

Determining if what you see onscreen will translate to the printed image, or if what you see on your screen will display the same on someone else's screen requires an understanding of color management.

In this chapter, you found out how to

- Manage your Color Working Space
- Calibrate your monitor
- Work with advanced color settings
- Print an image

Now that you've learned how to manage color, you're ready to move on to fine-tuning your image. Techniques to improve your images appearance are covered in Chapter 5.

Chapter 5

Adjusting Color

Pick up a copy of any glossy, commercially published magazine and notice that the images on the cover and within are always bright, crisp, and clear. In fact, a picture rarely appears in a commercial publication that is not, well. . .picture perfect. Tonality, color, contrast, and focus are always at their best, and the images pop off the page.

Virtually every photograph that finds its way into commercial print media whether it is scanned, copied from a Photo CD, captured with a digital camera, or downloaded from the Web has been processed and adjusted to improve its appearance.

Images need color adjustments for several reasons. Image contrast could be too low. Areas can be over or under exposed. The focus might be soft. Color can be flat or inaccurate. Photographic techniques, such as lighting, exposure, shutter speed, or depth of field can cause color aberrations in images. Image capture devices such as scanners and digital cameras can also contribute to the changes in color and tonality. Most commonly, the conversion from one color mode to another can also be responsible for color distortion.

This chapter is about the tools and commands in Photoshop that are best suited to correcting and improving the color. It reveals methods for recognizing color deficiencies beyond what you see on the screen and the basic solutions for correcting these problems. Mastering these techniques can help you improve the color of your images and like the images in glossy magazines, make them pop.

Understanding Adjustment Dynamics

Virtually all of Photoshop's color adjustment tools perform in the same way. They assess the information in the color channels and alter it. In other words, the color adjustment tools transform the numerical value of pixels. Each of the 22 adjustment features alters the values through a different interface that enables you to target and modify specific aspects of color. Many color adjustment features are capable of performing subtle or radical transformations. Some of the adjustments concentrate on improving the overall contrast of the image, and some eliminate colorcasts. Adjustments can focus on a specific range of color or radically alter an image's entire color scheme.

Before you begin modifying color you should analyze the factors that contribute to color deficiency. Photoshop provides several tools to help you assess colors in an image.

Recognizing color deficiencies

When you open an image, carefully scrutinize it to determine what the colors you see represent. If you read Chapter 4, you know that there can sometimes be a difference between what you see on-screen and the image's actual colors. If you are going to correct color, calibrate your monitor using calibration software or a hardware device to create an accurate on-screen image. Then look at the image's histogram to assess its tonal values.

Viewing histograms

To view the histogram palette, choose Window ➪ Histogram (see Figure 5.1). A *histogram* is a graph composed of lines that show the relative number and distribution of tonal values within an image. In the default composite histogram, there are a potential total of 256 lines. You can view the histogram in an All Channels View and see a total of 256 lines for each channel. The height of a line represents the relative quantity of pixels of a particular brightness. The taller the line, the more pixels there are at that brightness level. The histogram often looks like a mountain range because the lines are so close together that they create a mountainous shape.

The left side of the histogram represents dark pixels with low values called shadows. The right side of the graph represents light pixels or highlights. The central areas of the graph represent the image's midtones. An exclamation point icon on the graph is a warning that the Histogram palette is displaying a cached histogram, which is an assessment of the screen image and may be different than the actual image. Click the icon to display the more accurate uncached histogram.

The Histogram palette has features that enhance the display of brightness information. By default, the compact view of the histogram is displayed showing a graph of the global brightness information. Choose Expanded View from the Palette Options menu to display numerical data about the image.

Displaying the full palette with all of the colored channels allows quick access to specific channel information so you can determine which channel is deficient. Then, using the Levels or Curves dialog boxes you can make specific channel adjustments to correct the problem.

> **NOTE** The Levels dialog box also displays a histogram. The difference is that the Histogram palette is context sensitive, it responds to any adjustment by reconfiguring the graph and the data displayed. The Levels histogram is not context sensitive.

Choose All Channel View from the Palette menu to expand the palette to view the histogram of each channel individually. Choose Show Channels in Color to display the histogram of each channel in its corresponding color, as shown in Figure 5.1. If the image has multiple layers, you can choose to view the histogram of the entire image, a specific content layer, or the data on an adjustment layer by clicking the desired option from the source list.

> **NOTE** The New Curves Dialog box in Photoshop CS3 displays an interactive Histogram on the surface of it's Graph. As the curve is adjusted the histogram changes to reflect the changes.

FIGURE 5.1

The Histogram palette, expanded and showing the channel information in color.

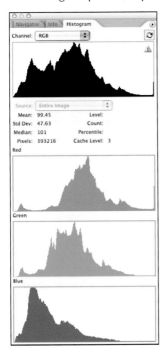

The Histogram palette is context sensitive. When you edit to the image, it instantaneously displays an updated histogram, superimposed over the previous histogram for comparison.

The numbers below the graph to the left represent statistical data about the image's tonality. The numbers in the right column indicate values about a specific level or range. To view data about a specific level, place your cursor on the graph and click your mouse. To display data about a range of pixels, click the graph and drag to the left or right to define the range and display information in the data field. Table 5.1 shows how the data is organized:

TABLE 5.1

The Histogram Data Field

Value	Description
Mean	The average brightness value of all the pixels in the image from 0–255
Std Dev	*Standard Deviation*, or how widely brightness values vary
Median	The middle value in the range of brightness values
Pixels	The total number of pixels in the image or in a selection
Level	The specific pixel value, between 0 and 255, of the position of the cursor if you place it on the graph
Count	The total number of pixels in a specific level
Percentile	The percentage of pixels equal to and darker than the level
Cache Level	The current image cache setting

The histogram palette is often the first thing you preview when you open a document. By previewing the histogram, you can determine the overall color and brightness relationships of an image. With a little experience you can determine what the image characteristics are and what corrections you need to be made to achieve optimal contrast and rally make that image pop.

From a histogram you can derive information about the tonal characteristics of an image. For example, a histogram where the majority of tall lines are clustered on the left side of the graph and short lines are on the right side indicates that the image is dark, or, in the parlance of graphics professionals, a low key image (see Figure 5.2).

A histogram where the tallest lines cluster on the right side of the graph indicates that most of the pixels are in the highlight range or are light in color. This is referred to as a high key image (see Figure 5.3).

FIGURE 5.2

The majority of the lines in the histogram are in the darker range of the image indicating a low key image.

 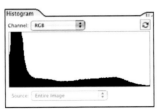

FIGURE 5.3

In this histogram, most of the lines are on the right or within the highlight range, indicating a high key image.

A histogram such as the one shown in Figure 5.4 where the majority of the tallest lines are clustered in the center of the graph indicates that the image is primarily composed of midtones — this is called a medium key image.

FIGURE 5.4

This histogram has most of its values in the center or midtone range indicating a medium key image.

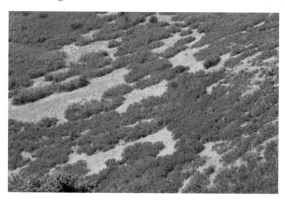
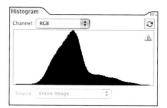

Just as important, histograms indicate tonal deficiencies. A histogram devoid of lines on both the left and right ends of the graph indicates that most of tones are in the midtone range but the image is devoid of highlight and shadow. Therefore, the image lacks contrast (see Figure 5.5).

FIGURE 5.5

The absence of lines in the shadow and highlight range represents an image with insufficient contrast.

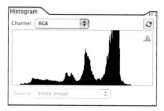

A histogram that has large gaps between the lines could mean that the image is lacking color detail, in that the full and continuous range of colors is not represented (see Figure 5.6). This could be a product of an image that was photographed in poor light, scanned improperly, or contains excessive dithering.

FIGURE 5.6

Gaps in the graph could indicate that there is insufficient color detail in the image.

Measuring color by using the Info palette

You can accurately measure the color of a single pixel or a group of pixels using the Info palette. Then you can mark these areas for comparison when you make adjustments to the image. To access the Info palette, choose Window ➪ Show Info. By default, the upper left of the Info palette displays the Actual Color information in the current color mode of the image. In the field to the right it displays the CMYK information. The x and y coordinates show the position of the cursor, and the height and width of the selection (see Figure 5.7).

The Info palette is context sensitive. If you drag any cursor across the image, the numerical values change to reflect the data that the curser is sampling.

Click one of the eyedroppers in the palette to display an options menu. You can configure the options to display CMYK, RGB, HSB, Grayscale, Lab, Total Ink, or Opacity information. Table 5.2 describes the Info palette settings and what the numbers indicate.

The default Info palette of an RGB image.

Info Palette Settings

Setting	Explanation
Actual Color	Color levels of the current mode of the image
Proof Color	Color after conversion to the ICC CMYK profile designated in the Color Settings dialog box
Grayscale	Percentage of black ink that would be deposited if the image were printed in black and white
RGB	Color of the numeric brightness values, from 0 (black) to 255 (white) of each of the red, green, and blue channels
Web Color	RGB hexadecimal equivalents of the sampled color
HSB	Hue, saturation, and brightness values of the sampled color
CMYK	Percentages of cyan, magenta, yellow, and black that would be output to process color separations
Lab	Lightness (L), green–red (a), and blue–yellow (b) values of a CIE Lab Color image
Total Ink	Cumulative percentage of ink densities of the combined CMYK separations in a four-color process print
Opacity	Cumulative level of opacity on the visible layers of an image
8, 16, 32-bit	Shows pixel values of images of 8, 16, and 32-bit depths

Choosing Palette Options from the Info Palette options menu lets you configure the modes for color readouts, mouse coordinates, and status information (see Figure 5.8).

The Info Palette Options dialog box.

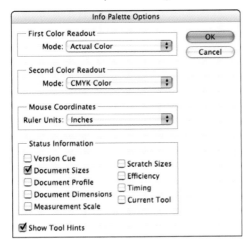

Using the Eyedropper tool

The Eyedropper samples pixel color. If you drag over an image, the color information appears in the color readouts in the Info palette. If you click your mouse on a color it appears as the foreground color swatch in the Tools palette. Option/Alt click to sample a background color.

It is often more accurate to measure an average of a group of pixels than a single pixel to get a better idea of the tonality of a specific area. You can configure the Eyedropper tool to sample an average value. The readings in the Info palette, or in any other operation that uses the Eyedropper tool to sample color, reflects the new configuration.

In the Eyedropper tool Options bar, choose Point Sample to sample a single pixel, 3 By 3 Average to sample the average color of a 9-pixel square, or 5 By 5 Average to sample the average color of a 25-pixel square. You will usually get the best results by averaging a 3 By 3 square on lower resolution images and 5 By 5 on high-resolution images greater than 300 pixels per inch.

Colors can be selected from outside the image window or even outside of the Photoshop. To select a color from a Web browser window, an application or the desktop wallpaper, click and hold the Eyedropper tool inside the image window, and then drag the tool to any point outside the Image window. The color of any screen pixel that your curser touches will appear as the current foreground color swatch — releasing the mouse selects that particular color.

Using the Color Sampler tool

The Color Sampler tool marks areas of the image for before-and-after comparisons of color adjustments. Prepress professionals often find this tool useful to adjust images to target CMYK values.

To place a color marker, click the Eyedropper tool in the Tools palette to display the flyout menu. Choose the Color Sampler. Drag the cursor on the image and click your mouse where you want to identify the color. The cursor leaves a marker, and the Info palette expands to display the data for that particular marker, as shown in Figure 5.9.

 TIP   **Press the Shift key with the Eyedropper tool to convert it to the Color Sampler tool.**

FIGURE 5.9

An image with Color Sampler markers (left) and the expanded Info palette showing color readouts for areas marked with the Color Sampler tool (right).

The Color Sampler tool records up to four colors in the Info palette. To change the color mode of a marker, click the arrow next to the Eyedropper icon in the Info palette and drag to the desired color model in the pull-down list.

You can move a marker you've already placed. With the Color Sampler tool selected, click and drag the marker to a new location. To delete a marker, choose the Color Sampler tool and drag the marker off the Image window, or press Option/Alt and click the marker. The Clear button on the Options bar also deletes all Color Sampler markers with a single click.

The Color Sampler readouts are context sensitive. The Info palette displays two numbers for each value, divided by a slash, as shown in Figure 5.10. The number on the left is the numeric value of the sampled color prior to the adjustment, and the number on the right represents the new values of the color after the adjustment. As you apply a color adjustment to an image, the numbers change. You can compare these values and, with a bit of experience reading these numeric color relationships, determine the effect the adjustment will have on the targeted area.

FIGURE 5.10

An image with Color Sampler markers and the expanded Info palette showing color readouts for before and after an adjustment.

Using Auto Adjustments

Using the auto adjustment feature can speed color correction at the expense of control. You can use them to perform fast adjustments and correct simple, common problems. The drawback is that by using the automatic adjustment features, you give the control of how your image looks to Photoshop, and it is not always the best judge of the aesthetic qualities of your image. So look carefully at the results especially in the shadow and highlight areas to be sure that details have not been lost. These adjustments are well designed, and they apply preprogrammed color ranges to your pixel values and can be useful as a starting point. You can go in later with the heavy artillery such as curves or levels and refine the adjustment. The biggest drawback of auto adjustments is that often they produce color casts which you need to remove with a feature that offers more control.

Applying auto adjustments

There are three fully automatic adjustments. Select an area or target a layer. Choose Adjustments ➪ Auto Color, Auto Contrast, or Auto Levels and Photoshop does the rest. Figure 5.11 compares the results of the Auto Correction features. Here are what these operations do:

■ **Auto Levels:** Photoshop converts the lightest pixel in each color channel to white and the darkest pixel to black. All the other pixels are proportionally distributed in between the extremes. By default, the Auto Levels command ignores the lightest and darkest 0.5% extremes when choosing the lightest and darkest colors so as to choose more representative colors.

CAUTION Observe the image carefully. Auto Levels can potentially introduce color casts that dull the highlight areas.

- **Auto Contrast:** Adjusts the overall contrast relationships in an image. As with Auto Levels, Auto Contrast maps the lightest highlight to white and the darkest shadow pixel to black. Unlike Auto Levels, Auto Contrast maintains the color balance by remapping the color to a specific brightness curve. By default, the Auto Contrast command clips the lightest and darkest 0.5% of the light and dark extremes so as to choose more representative colors.

- **Auto Color:** Auto Color, for an automated tool, is effective — some of the time. Auto Color corrects the image's contrast by mapping the brightest highlight to white and the darkest shadow to black and eliminates color casts by mapping gray colors to equal parts of red, green, and blue. All other values fall between these key neutrals.

FIGURE 5.11

The original image (top left), the image after Auto Levels (top right), Auto Contrast (bottom left), and Auto Color (bottom right) have been applied.

Controlling clipping

You can control the clipping range of the auto adjustment features. Open the Levels or Curves dialog box and click the Options button. The Auto Color Correction dialog box appears (see Figure 5.12), enabling you to more precisely control the highlight and shadow clipping of the auto adjustments. The dialog box lets you choose from these options:

■ **Enhance Monocromatic Contrast:** This option is the default Auto Contrast algorithm. It clips all channels by the same amount, which preserves the color relationships while lightening highlights and darkening shadows.

■ **Enhance Per Channel Contrast:** The default Auto Levels algorithm, it produces the maximum tonal range in each channel for more dramatic results. Each channel is adjusted individually, sometimes eliminating or introducing color casts.

■ **Find Dark and Light Colors:** The default Auto Color algorithm, it finds the average lightest and darkest pixels in the image for maximum contrast and minimal highlight and shadow clipping.

■ **Snap Neutral Midtones:** Another default Auto Color algorithm. Click the check box to find an average nearly neutral midtone color and then adjust its values to make the color neutral.

■ **Target Colors & Clipping:** Enter percentages in the Clip text boxes to specify percentages of how much to clip from the black and white extremes. A value between 0.0% and 1% is recommended.

NOTE By default, Photoshop clips the black and white pixels by 0.1%. It ignores the first 0.1% of the highlight and shadow extremes when identifying the lightest and darkest pixels in the image.

■ **Color Swatches:** To assign color values to the darkest, neutral, and lightest areas of an image, click a color swatch to display the Color Picker.

■ **Save as Defaults:** Click the check box and then click OK. When you click the Auto button in the Levels or Curves dialog box, the current settings will be applied. The new default clipping percentages are applied by the Auto Level, Auto Contrast, and Auto Color commands.

TIP Often automatic tools may actually perform *alterations too well,* creating an over-adjustment. You can modify an over-adjustment with the Fade command. After you've performed the adjustment choose Edit ⇨ Fade to tone it down to a level between the original and the auto-adjusted image creating a more smoother more natural look.

FIGURE 5.12

The Auto Color Correction Options dialog box.

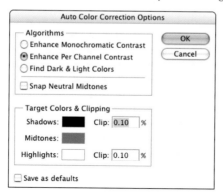

Adjusting brightness and contrast

Brightness/Contrast performs global adjustments of brightness or contrast to a selected area or to the entire image. When you choose Image ➪ Adjustments ➪ Brightness/Contrast, the top slider (see Figure 5.13) controls how dark or light the image appears, by pushing the pixel values lower when you move the slider to the left or higher when you move the slider to the right. The slider on the bottom increases or decreases the contrast by changing the pixel values toward the midtone range when you move the slider to the left, or toward the highlight and shadow ranges when you move the slider to the right. Check the Preview box to see the results. Brightness and contrast is very limited in that it has only two correction options.

TIP Due to the limited control of the Brightness/Contrast command, professionals rarely use it for major color corrections. Levels and even more so, Curves applied on adjustment layers (see the section on adjustment layers in this chapter)are more the choice of professionals who want comprehensive control of the brightness range of their images.

FIGURE 5.13

The Brightness/Contrast dialog box.

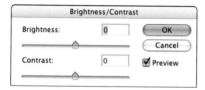

Working with Levels

Levels is also an essential color and contrast correction tool that gives you much more control than any of the aforementioned auto adjustments. The Levels dialog box displays a histogram and initially offers three points of adjustment: highlights, midtones, and shadows. If you access the channels menu you can target a specific channel and adjust its highlights, midtones, and shadows bringing the total to 12 points of adjustment for RGB and Lab images (each color channel plus the composite channel), and 16 points of adjustment for CMYK images.

Input levels

When you choose Image ⇨ Adjustments ⇨ Levels you see a histogram with three sliders along the bottom of the graph that you use to visually adjust the image's tonal range or its *input levels* (see Figure 5.14).

The black slider on the left determines the numerical value that will be converted to the black point, or the darkest level in the image. The white slider on the right determines the *white point* or the lightest level. The number field below the sliders indicates the numerical value of the levels that will be converted to the tonal extremes. All the values in between the white and black points remap to encompass the entire range of tonality from white to black. Click and drag the black and white sliders inward to adjust the shadow and highlight extremes. When you drag the black slider to the right the numbers in the shadow field increase and the image darkens. When you drag the white slider to the left the number decreases and the image lightens. The middle or gamma slider determines the median value between the black and white points. Drag the slider to the right to decrease the median value, darkening values lower than the median, or to the left to increase it, lightening all values higher than the median.

FIGURE 5.14

Use the Levels dialog box to adjust an image's tonal range.

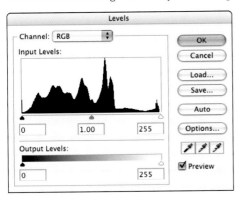

Output levels

Input Levels increase contrast and Output Levels do the opposite; they reduce contrast. Click and drag the white slider to the left or the black slider to the right to reduce the range of contrast in an image to eliminate the extremes of highlight and shadow in your image. Printers frequently do this to control ink coverage in preparing files for the press. For example, if the black arrow is moved from 0 to 12 (approximately 5% of the tonal range), values between 100% (black) and 96% ink coverage print as a 95% halftone dot value.

Reassigning pixel values

When you perform a Levels adjustment, you are actually reassigning pixel values. For example, suppose that you have a low-contrast image similar to the photograph in Figure 5.15. You can redistribute the brightness values in the image so that there is much wider tonal representation and consequently improved color and contrast.

Follow these basic steps to increase the contrast in this picture:

1. Choose Window ⇨ Histogram to display the Histogram palette. From the Palette Options menu choose Expanded View.

2. Choose Image ⇨ Adjustments ⇨ Levels. The Levels dialog box displays an identical histogram. There is a deficiency at the right and left extremes of the histogram, where the absence or shortness of lines indicates that there are few dark and light pixels.

3. Move the white slider toward the center until it is aligned with the lines on the right of the graph.

4. Move the black slider toward the center until it is aligned with the lines on the left of the graph. The context sensitive Histogram palette displays the new histogram superimposed over the previous one.

5. Click OK to commit the adjustment, or click Cancel to cancel it.

FIGURE 5.15

This picture is deficient in contrast as you can see by its appearance and its histogram.

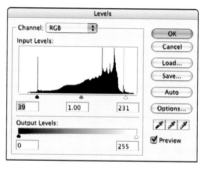

The brightness range in the histogram has been redistributed to encompass the length of the entire graph. The lines that had a value of 39 now have a value of 0 (black), and the lines that had a value of 231 now have a value of 255 (white) (see Figure 5.16).

FIGURE 5.16

The picture and the histogram palette after the levels adjustment.

 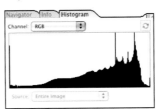

> **TIP** To reset the Levels adjustment, press the Option/Alt key. The Cancel button now reads *Reset.* Click to begin again. Note that this cancels all the operations that you have performed in the dialog box. To cancel only the last operation, press ⌘/Ctrl+Z.

Adjusting channel levels

Adjusting the levels of individual channels extends your capabilities to make more precise adjustments. Because you have so many more points of adjustment, you triple or quadruple the power of the Levels command. Here's how to adjust the levels of individual channels:

1. Display the Histogram palette. Choose All Channels View from the Histogram Palette menu to individually preview the results to each channels histogram. Choose Show Channels in Color to display the histogram of each channel in its corresponding color.

2. Choose Image ⇨ Adjustments ⇨ Levels to open the Levels dialog box.

3. From the Channels pop-up menu, choose a color channel.

4. Click and drag the white and black sliders toward the center until they point to the part of the histogram where the larger lines begin.

5. Repeat the process on each channel.

6. If the image has developed a color cast, target the first channel levels again. Drag the midtone slider to reduce the color cast and even out the color. Repeat as necessary on each channel.

7. Click OK to commit the adjustment.

Determining and setting white and black points

The Levels control lets you assign specific values to the darkest shadow areas and the lightest highlight areas of an image and then redistribute the brightness information based on the light and dark extremes that you specified. Prepress professionals frequently use this technique to determine CMYK values for highlight and shadow areas based on the characteristics of their printing presses.

You can determine a specific RGB value for the white point of the lightest pixels. When you determine the white point, use the lightest printable area of the image that contains detail, not a specular white (255,255,255) that when printed contains no ink. The black point is the lowest value that is not absolute black (0, 0, 0). To set a black or white point, do the following:

1. Click the Color Sampler tool in the Tools palette. In the Options bar, set the sample to 3 By 3 Average.

2. Open the Info palette. From the Options menu, choose RGB as the first color readout. Scroll around the lightest areas of the image until you see the highest numbers in the readout. Then click your mouse to deposit a sample point. The Info palette displays the numerical values for sample point #1.

3. Scroll around the darkest areas of the image until you see the lowest numbers in the readout. Then click your mouse to deposit a sample point. The Info palette will display the numerical values for sample point #2.

4. Choose Image ➪ Adjustments ➪ Levels.

5. Double-click the white eyedropper. The Color Picker appears. Enter values for the white point to. Enter these recommended RGB values if you are printing on white paper: 240R, 240G, 240B. The grayscale density is a 6% halftone dot (you can determine the highlight density by subtracting the Brightness value, B, in the Color Picker from 100). Because the RGB values are all the same, the highlight will be neutral.

NOTE The RGB values will vary depending on the RGB color space you are working in. I'm working in Adobe RGB (1998) as a color setting. No matter what the color space, you're aiming for about a 4% to 6% neutral gray.

6. Double-click the black eyedropper. The Color Picker appears. Enter RGB values for the black point. Use these recommended values if you are printing on white paper and working in the Adobe RGB (1998) color space: 15R, 15G, 15B. The Grayscale density is a 95% halftone dot.

7. Click on the white eyedropper in the Levels palette. Click on sample point #1 on the image. The sample point changes to the specified color and all the values on all the channels in the image are remapped relative to that highlight value.

8. Click on the black eyedropper in the Levels palette. Click on sample point #2 on the image. The sample point changes to the specified color and all the values on all the channels in the image are now remapped proportionally to the highlight and shadow values.

A variation of this technique is to determine the black and white point individually on each channel. Choose a color channel from the channel menu. Perform the same steps as above on each channel. After you corrected for white point and black point you may have to adjust the midtone sliders for each channel to correct for color casts.

Saving and loading levels

If you've made a correction to an image, you can apply the same settings to other images. To save and load a setting, follow these steps:

1. Choose Save from the options on the right side of the Levels dialog box.

2. Choose a folder in which to save the settings, name them, and click OK. Click OK again to close the Levels dialog box. Now that you've saved them, you can reload them at any time.

3. To load the settings, choose Load from the options on the right side of the Levels dialog box.

4. Locate the folder where the settings were saved, and click Open to open the settings.

NOTE You can save and load settings from both the Levels and Curves dialog boxes.

Adjusting Curves

Curves are indispensable for professional retouching and color correction because they are Photoshop's most powerful and versatile adjustment feature. Curves can target and adjust virtually any brightness value in your image. You can adjust an image's brightness curve to produce an overall lighter or darker image, improve its contrast, or even create wild color relationships. You can lock-down a curve to target and adjust a specific range of color and you can target individual channels and adjust their brightness values individually.

The default Curves dialog box displays a 16 cell grid (see Figure 5.17). The Photoshop CS3 improved version of Curves displays a histogram behind the grid. The horizontal axis of the graph represents the *input* levels or the colors of the image before the adjustment. The vertical axis represents the *output* levels or the color of the image after it has been adjusted. By default, for RGB images, dark colors are represented by the lower-left corner, and light colors are represented by the upper-right corner of the graph. The diagonal line running from the lower left to upper right is the image's brightness curve. The horizontal brightness bar below the graph represents the direction of the values of the graph. Adjustments are made to the image by bending the line.

Click the arrow to expand the dialog box to display the Curve Grid Options where you can set additional options. The options include:

- **Show amount of: Light or Pigment/Ink%:** This option lets you configure input and output values to display light values between 0 to 255 or ink coverage between 0% and 100%.

- **Grid icons:** Click the Grid icons to display either the 16 cell grid (4 by 4) or a 100 cell (10 by 10) graph. You can also Option/Alt-click anywhere on the graph to change the grid pattern.

- **Show:** If the boxes are checked in this field, channel overlays, baseline, histogram, and intersection lines are displayed on the graph.

FIGURE 5.17

The Curves dialog box with the new curve grid options displayed.

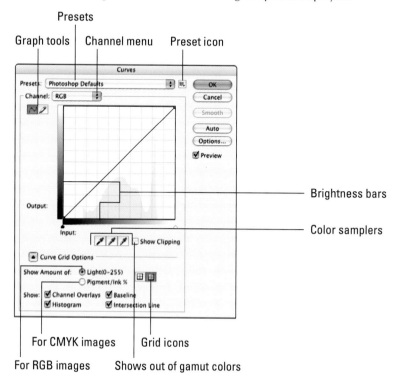

Presets

Graph tools | Channel menu | Preset icon

Brightness bars

Color samplers

For CMYK images | Grid icons

For RGB images | Shows out of gamut colors

Basic curve adjustments

Figure 5.18 through 5.21 provide an illustration of the power of curves. The unaltered photograph (Figure 5.18) lacks contrast and color depth. Click and drag the center of the diagonal line toward the upper-left, to lighten the image, as in (Figure 5.19). If you bend it toward the lower-right, you will darken the image as in Figure 5.20. If you perform either of these operations, you alter the position of the midtones. Bending the curve into an S shape, as shown in Figure 5.21, increases the contrast of the image by darkening the shadows and lightening the highlights. A rollercoaster curve pushes the pixel values all over the graph and creates wild color effects as shown in Figure 5.22

Using the Presets

At the top of the new Photoshop CS3 dialog box, the pop-up menu contains several useful curve settings that quickly adjust the curve to predefined settings. Choose these settings as a beginning adjustment and then manually bend the curve to better adjust your image.

FIGURE 5.18

The unaltered image lacks contrast.

FIGURE 5.19

The image can be darkened by dragging the curve to the lower right.

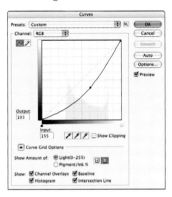

FIGURE 5.20

Lighten the image by dragging the curve to the upper left.

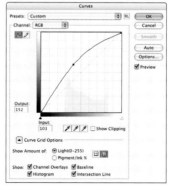

FIGURE 5.21

An S curve produces more contrast.

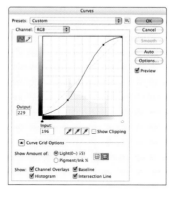

Using the Brightness bar

The horizontal Brightness bar below the graph represents the brightness values of the graph. On RGB images, the lighter values are on the right and the darker values are the left. When you click the Pigment/Ink% radio button the bar reverses and the input and output values read as percentages of ink coverage. This information can be of use to printers who want to adjust an image to exact ink coverage specifications.

FIGURE 5.22

A roller coaster curve radically redistributes color.

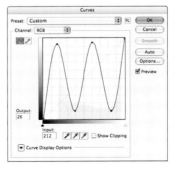

Choosing Graph tools

The Graph tools can be selected from the icons in the upper left of the Curves dialog box. Use them to edit the brightness curve. The Point tool is selected by default. Click the diagonal line of the default curve to deposit anchor points. The points can be moved by clicking and dragging them with your mouse. As you drag, you can see the changes to your image if the Preview box is checked.

Choose the Pencil tool by clicking its icon. Click and drag on the curve to draw freeform lines. It performs very much like the Pencil tool in the Tools palette. If you want to draw a straight line, click once, press Shift, and click elsewhere.

Changing Input and Output values

When you click and drag the cursor anywhere on the curve, the Input and Output values change to reflect its position relative to the horizontal and vertical axes of the graph. You can click on the curve itself or a point on the curve and type new values in these boxes, which results in the bending of the curve and a change in the brightness values in the image.

Adjusting channels

If you perform a Curves adjustment on the composite channel, you affect all the image's color channels simultaneously. As with levels, you can work with more precision by adjusting the channels individually. To choose a specific channel in which to work, click the Channel menu and choose a channel. A colored histogram for the channel will appear behind the grid. You can then adjust the curve just as you would the composite channel — by clicking and dragging it.

Making a lock-down curve

A *lock-down curve* lets you affect specific areas on the curve and leave other areas unaffected when you make an adjustment. A lock-down curve stabilizes the curve and prevents it from bending. To make a lock-down curve, follow these steps:

1. Choose Image ➪ Adjustments ➪ Curves. The Curves dialog box appears.

2. Click the Curve Grid options arrow and then the 100 cell grid icon.

3. Click anywhere on the diagonal line exactly where the horizontal and vertical grid lines intersect.

4. Click each intersection point along the diagonal line, as shown in Figure 5.23.

5. Choose Red from the Channel pop-up menu. Repeat the process.

6. Repeat the process for the Green and Blue curves so that you can lock down a curve for a specific channel.

7. Click the Preset icon, choose Save Preset, and specify a location for the lock-down curve. Name the curve lockdown_curve.acv and save the file. You can now load the curve on any RGB document in any channel at any time.

FIGURE 5.23

A lock-down curve stabilizes the line so that you can affect specific colors.

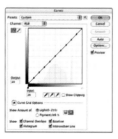

Making a spot adjustment

You can pinpoint the exact location of a color on the curve. You can then place an anchor point and make a precise spot adjustment to a small range of colors.

To determine the location of a color, follow these steps:

1. Choose Image ➪ Adjustments ➪ Curves to display the Curves dialog box.

2. Click the Preset icon and click Load Preset to load the lock-down curve that you made in the previous step-by step exercise.

3. Choose a channel from the Channels menu.

4. Click and drag across the image. Observe the circle on the graph as you drag your cursor across the image. Press your Cmnd/Ctrl key and click the mouse to deposit a point on the curve.

5. Click the new point and drag straight upward.

The targeted color intensifies because you've increased its brightness value. The other colors in the image are left at their original values because you locked them down (see Figure 5.24).

NOTE For most color corrections, less is more with the amount you drag. Dragging too much can produce radical transformations of color and dithering.

FIGURE 5.24

Adjusting a channel specific lock-down curve.

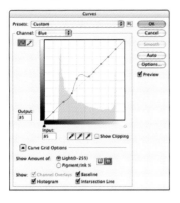 

Balancing Color

Color casts can result from a number of factors including poor lighting, aging, or incorrect scanner or camera settings. You can correct color casts with Levels or Curves but it might be more efficient to use the Color Balance command for your RGB images and Selective Color for your CMYK images. Both of these features are designed for "tweaking "images. In other words, they are not normally used for radical transformations but instead to push the image into balance where the whites, grays, and blacks are neutral and all the other colors look as they should.

Using the Color Balance command

Before you access Color Balance make sure that the composite channel is targeted in the Channels palette, and then follow these steps:

1. Click on the Color Sampler tool in the Tools palette. In the Options bar, set the sample to 3 By 3 Average.

2. Open the Info palette. From the Options menu choose RGB as the first color readout. Click on a very light gray or white area of the image. The Info palette will display the numerical values for sample point #1.

3. Click on a middle gray area of the image. The Info palette will display the numerical values for sample point #2.

4. Click on a dark gray or black area of the image. The Info palette will display the numerical values for sample point #3.

5. Choose Image ⇨ Adjustment ⇨ Color Balance to display the Color Balance dialog box shown in Figure 5.25.

6. If necessary click the Midtones radio button (it is already selected by default) to select the tonal range to focus your adjustment.

7. Check Preserve Luminosity to maintain the tonal balance of the image and affect only the colors.

NOTE Each color slider represents two color opposites. By increasing the amount of a specific color by moving the slider toward its name, you, in effect, decrease its opposite.

8. To increase the amount of a color in an image, drag the slider toward it. To decrease the amount of a color, drag the slider away from it. Observe the Info palette readout #2 as you drag the sliders. In the second column of numbers, try to produce equal numerical values of red, green, and blue.

FIGURE 5.25

The Color Balance dialog box.

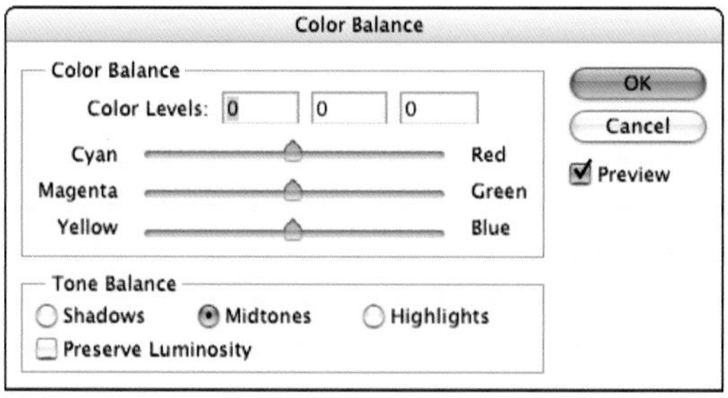

If necessary, click the shadow and highlight radio buttons and repeat the process to eliminate casts in those tonal ranges. You may change the midtone values if you do this and it may be impossible to neutralize all tonal ranges. Try to reach a happy medium with all three tonal ranges, but in general the most important one to balance is the midtone range.

Using Selective Color

CMYK colors use various proportions of the four *process colors*, cyan, magenta, yellow, and black, to produce full-color images. Selective Color is designed to adjust ink proportions on CMYK images, however, you can use it to balance RGB images, too. Selective Color determines the amount of process colors that will be used to create a predefined color range by altering the density of each color within each of the four CMYK channels. This is especially useful for reducing color casts within a targeted range of color. Prepress professionals use Selective Color to control ink densities on color separations.

Follow these steps to use this command:

1. Target the composite channel in the Channels palette.

2. Choose Image ➪ Adjustments ➪ Selective Color to display the Selective Color dialog box (see Figure 5.26).

FIGURE 5.26

The Selective Color dialog box.

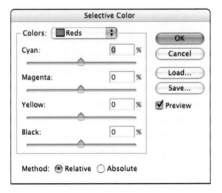

3. From the Colors menu, choose the color range you want to affect. The list shows reds, yellows, greens, cyans, blues, magentas, whites, neutrals, and blacks.

4. Choose a method:

   ▪ **Relative** changes the existing quantity of process color by a percentage of the total. For example, if you start with a pixel that is 80% cyan and add 10%, 8% is added to the pixel (10% of 80 = 8), for a total of 88% cyan. You cannot adjust specular white with this option, because it contains no color.

   ▪ **Absolute** adds color in absolute values. If, for example, you start with 30% cyan in the pixel and add 10%, you end up with a pixel that is 40% cyan.

5. Drag the CMYK sliders to determine how much of each process color the target color will contain. Drag the sliders to the right to increase the amount of the process color component in the selected color by a percentage value. Drag to the left to decrease it. (Some colors may not contain any of the process color, so they will not be affected.)

Remapping Color

Unlike the color correction features that are normally used to enhance color relationships, the color mapping features can radically alter existing colors in an image — *color mapping* operations that go beyond brightness and contrast adjustments and simple color fills. These features can alter the basic characteristics of color while maintaining image detail. You can use these commands to change the entire color scheme of your image or target individual colors and replace them. The color mapping features affect the image by changing the color relationships between the channels. These features also have the capability of affecting the saturation and brightness values of the image.

Altering Hue and Saturation

The Hue/Saturation command is used for altering relative color. Image ➪ Adjustments ➪ Hue/Saturation, displays the dialog box. There are three sliders (see Figure 5.27). Each slider *remaps* a different color characteristic.

FIGURE 5.27

The Hue Saturation dialog box.

The Hue slider affects the relative color relationships of an image, selection, or layer. You can produce some really beautiful and unexpected color combinations. With this command you'll find that it's easy to change the hum-drum green reality of an everyday landscape into a fauvist work of art as in Figure 5.28.

The Hue/Saturation feature can alter the entire color scheme of an image.

When you drag the Hue slider, you reposition the color's hue values on the color wheel expressed in degrees. Values in the Hue box reflect the amount of rotation from the original color. Moving the slider to the right, or a positive value, indicates a clockwise rotation of the color wheel. Moving it to the left indicates a negative value, a counterclockwise rotation.

The color bars at the bottom of the palette are a graphic indicator of how the colors change as you move the Hue slider. By default, the color bars are aligned. The top color bar represents a color wheel that has been cut at the 180-degree point, or blue. As you move the Hue slider, the top color bar remains in place and represents the entire range of colors prior to the change. But the bottom color bar is dynamic. It moves as you drag the Hue slider and realigns with the colors on the top bar to reflect the relative change of colors.

Affecting specific colors

The Hue/Saturation command enables you to precisely control the range of colors that you alter. The Edit menu at the top of the dialog box (see Figure 5.29) features a list of colors that are divided into basic color ranges of 90 degrees each, including the *overlap* (the amount that the colors adjacent to the target color on the color wheel are affected). The Master option (the default range) permits the entire spectrum of color to be affected when you move the Hue, Saturation, or Lightness sliders. Table 5.3 describes the capabilities of the other options:

TABLE 5.3

The Hue/Saturation Edit menu

Edit Option	Target Color with Overlap (on the Color Wheel)
Reds	Affects colors from 315 to 360 degrees counterclockwise and 0 to 45 degrees counterclockwise
Yellows	Affects colors from 15 to 60 degrees ccw and 61 to 105 degrees cw
Greens	Affects colors from 75 to 120 degrees ccw and 121 to 165 cw
Cyans	Affects colors from 135 to 180 degrees ccw and 181 to 225 cw
Blues	Affects colors from 195 to 240 degrees ccw and 241 to 285 cw
Magentas	Affects colors from 255 to 300 ccw and 301 to 345 degrees cw

Choosing a color from the Edit list enables you to control the changes to a specific range of hues. An adjustment slider appears between the two color bars, indicating the extent of colors that are being affected. Dragging left or right increases or decreases the range of hues to be affected. You can control the range of colors and the overlap with these techniques:

- To change the range of color to be affected, drag the dark gray horizontal bar to move the entire adjustment slider.

- To extend the range of color and the amount of overlap, drag the light gray horizontal bars.

- To change the range while leaving the overlap unaffected, drag the white vertical bars.

- To adjust the overlap while leaving the range fixed, drag the white triangles.

FIGURE 5.29

With the Hue/Saturation Edit menu you can change specific ranges of color.

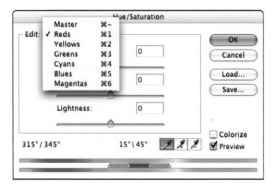

Sampling with the eyedroppers

The eyedroppers in the Hue/Saturation dialog box are used to pick specific colors to be adjusted. Their performance is controlled by the presets made to the Eyedropper tool in the Options bar: Point Sample, 3 By 3 Average, or 5 By 5 Average. Choose the Eyedropper tool that best suits your purposes:

- **The Eyedropper:** Samples a pixel or set of pixels, depending on the options selected for the Eyedropper tool in the Options bar.
- **The Plus Eyedropper:** Adds to the sample range by dragging over pixels in the Image window.
- **The Minus Eyedropper:** Subtracts from the range by dragging over pixels in the Image window.

When you sample a color from an image with an eyedropper, the Edit menu list will produce an additional category, titled Reds 2 or Blues 2, for example. The new category includes the 90-degree range of default color categories with the specific, sampled hue at its center.

After sampling the color on the image with an eyedropper, drag the Hue, Saturation, or Lightness sliders to affect that color.

Adjusting saturation

The intensity of the colors in an image can be increased or decreased by dragging the Saturation slider. The default saturation value on the center of the slider is 0, which represents the current saturation of the color. You can click and drag the slider to the right to a maximum of +100%, where the colors will be intensified producing intense neon colors. Drag the slider to the left to –100%, where the colors will be completely desaturated, or gray.

Most of the time, your values will fall between the two extremes. You can enhance a color and make it "pop" by pushing the Saturation slider between +20% and +40%. On the other hand, if you're interested in muted pastel colors, drag the slider –20% to –40% to the left to diminish saturation.

> **TIP** You can perform a quick, total desaturation of an image or a selection by choosing Image ➪ Adjustments ➪ Desaturate. This operation accomplishes the same thing as moving the Saturation slider to –100 in the Hue/Saturation dialog box.

Adjusting lightness

Click and drag the Lightness slider to the left to darken the image, selection, or layer or to the right to lighten it. The 0 point marks the current input lightness value of the image. The extremes are +100% lightness, which produces white, and –100% lightness, or black.

> **TIP** If an area is very light and you find that adjusting the Hue and Saturation sliders has no effect on it, darken it a little by dragging the Lightness slider to the left. Then drag the Hue and Saturation sliders. The light areas will begin to change to a color.

Colorizing an image

You can modify black and white images and add color to all or part of them with the Hue/Saturation command. You must first convert your grayscale images to a color mode such as RGB, CMYK, or Lab. The appearance of the grayscale image will be unaffected by this conversion.

When you colorize an image or selected area, you convert gray pixels to colored pixels by altering their values on the color channels. Gray pixels have RGB values that are equal. When you colorize a group of pixels, you shift the red, green, and blue components to disparate values.

> **TIP** If you are dissatisfied with the results of your first attempt, you can reset the Hue/Saturation and other dialog boxes to the default, at any time, by pressing Alt/Option and clicking the Reset button, or press ⌘/Ctrl+Z to undo just the last operation.

Click the Colorize checkbox. The Hue and Saturation sliders change to represent absolute values instead of relative ones. The default hue that is produced is the current foreground hue. The Hue slider reads from 0 degrees on the left to 360 degrees on the right, and the current foreground color's position on the color wheel is displayed. Click and drag the slider until image or selection changes to the desired color. You can also type it's the numerical value in degrees in the Hue value field. The Saturation slider reads from 0% to 100% and defaults at 25%. Move the slider to the right to increase saturation or to the left to decrease saturation. The default lightness of the pixels does not change from the original image, displaying relative values between −100 (black) and +100 (white). When you colorize you shift color to the image without affecting the brightness of the individual pixels, thereby maintaining the image's detail.

Here is the step-by-step breakdown of colorization:

1. Open a grayscale image.
2. Choose Image ➪ Mode ➪ RGB. If your image is layered you'll be presented with a dialog box asking if you want to merge the layers before you change mode. Choose Don't Merge.
3. Click the Default Color icon on the Tools palette, or press the D key, to restore the foreground color to black and the background color to white.

> **NOTE** The default foreground color, black, is actually pure red hue, 0 degrees on the color wheel, with 0% saturation and 0% brightness.

4. Make a selection, target a layer or colorize the entire image.
5. Choose Image ➪ Adjustments ➪ Hue/Saturation.
6. Click the Colorize box. The image takes on a red hue.

7. Click and drag the Saturation slider to 90% to increase its intensity (see Figure 5.30).

8. Click OK to commit the edit.

NOTE The Hue/Saturation command can be assigned to an adjustment layer to keep the editing process dynamic. For more about adjustment layers see the section in this chapter.

FIGURE 5.30

The black and white image is converted to RGB and a selection is made (top left), the Hue/Saturation dialog box with the settings (top right), and the colorized image (bottom left).

Creating Adjustment Layers

Applying color adjustment feature such as Levels, Curves, or Hue/Saturation to an image directly affects the information on a layer or on the background. Changing these operations can present problems down the road. Photoshop's adjustment layers assign the alterations of the adjustment to a separate layer that can be re-edited at any time during the imaging process.

Follow these steps to create an adjustment layer:

1. Choose Layer ⇨ New Adjustment Layer and select the type of adjustment layer from the submenu. The New Layer dialog box appears.

2. Name, color-code, and set the opacity and blending mode of the layer, if desired, and then click OK.

3. An Adjustment dialog box appears. Make the adjustment and click OK. The new adjustment layer appears on the Layers palette.

4. The adjustment layer has an attached layer mask which lets you selectively conceal portions of the adjustment. (See Chapter 18 for more on Layer masks.)

By default, an adjustment layer affects all the Layers below it in the stack. You can clip the adjustment layer to the layer immediately below it, as shown in Figure 5.31. Option/Alt-click the line that separates the two layers.

You can also group a layer by clicking the Group With Previous Layer check box in the New Layer dialog box.

FIGURE 5.31

A Hue/Saturation adjustment layer is clipped to the layer immediately below it. The Levels adjustment layer affects all of the layers in the stack.

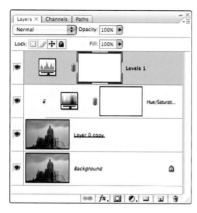

Summary

Producing glossy, magazine quality images can be achieved. In this chapter, I discussed techniques for adjusting color to get a perfect image.

Specifically, I covered several topics including:

- Understanding color adjustment dynamics
- Using auto adjustments
- Adjusting curves
- Balancing color

Now you can move on to finding out about how to use color channels in Part III.

Part III

Color Channel Techniques

Chapter 6

Exploring the Channels Palette

W hen you look at a full-color photograph on a monitor, you see subtle variations of colors blending together to form what appears to be a continuous tone reality. Of course looking more closely at the image reveals that it actually contains pixels, and within each pixel is color information. Color channels store and display color information. Having access to this information enables you to perform powerful modifications and corrections to the appearance of your image.

Alpha channels are masks that store the selections you've made. Color and alpha channels reside in the Channels palette. This chapter takes a detailed look at this important Photoshop feature and demonstrates how to incorporate the Channels palette into your workflow.

Opening the Channels Palette

To open the Channels palette, choose Window ➪ Show Channels. Figure 6.1 shows the Channels palette. By default, the Composite channel at the top of the palette is labeled with the image's color mode — RGB, CMYK, and so on. The individual color channels representing the image's color information are immediately below the color mode. If you've saved any selections you'll see them in the form of alpha channels. And if the image has any layer masks or if you are in Quick Mask mode you will see thumbnails representing these masks.

TIP You can press F7 to display the Layers/Channels/Paths cluster and click the Channels tab.

FIGURE 6.1

The Default Channels palette of a full-color image.

Concealing and revealing channel content

The channels are stacked in a column displaying the thumbnails and names of each channel. Visibility icons are located to the left of the thumbnail — the little eye-shaped graphic. Clicking a visibility icon displays, conceals, or reveals a channel's contents in the Image window.

Each color channel is a separate transparent color overlay consisting of colored pixels. You can view the contents of individual color channels or combinations of channels by clicking on the visibility icons of the other channels to conceal them (see Table 6.1 for other viewing options). For example, click once on the visibility icons of the Green and Blue channels to conceal their contents and to view the contents of the Red channel.

Looking at color channels

By default, when you look at an individual color channel, you can see that it appears as a grayscale image in the Image window (see Figure 6.2). When you view two or more color channels superimposed on each other you see that image in specific color combinations. When all the channels are visible, you see the image in full color.

When you scan an image in RGB color mode for example, or take a picture with a digital camera, the color information is recorded into red, green, and blue components. Photoshop configures this information into three color channels plus a composite RGB channel. When an image is scanned in 8-bit color for example, (see Chapter 1 for a complete description of bit depth), each channel can potentially contain a total of 256 possible shades each of red, green, or blue. Photoshop processes the information in each channel as an independent grayscale image. Each pixel is assigned a specific numerical gray value, where black equals 0 and white equals 255.

Color channels are the core of an image's color composition. Their accessibility in the Channels palette enables you to edit them individually or together. Their colors can be swapped, mixed, or adjusted to enhance the color and color and contrast of an image. Inside many of Photoshop's dialog boxes, color channels can be individually targeted for specific color adjustment.

An individual color channel viewed as a grayscale in the Image window.

Working with Alpha Channels

Alpha channels share similarities with color channels. They are grayscale images that support 256 shades of gray, from black to white. Unlike color channels, alpha channels do not contain information that directly affects the appearance of the image. Instead of representing tonality or color, an alpha channel is a graphic representation of a mask. Black areas of an alpha channel indicate areas of opacity, gray areas indicate semi-transparency, and white areas indicate transparency.

In the Channels palette, alpha channels are always located below the color channels, as shown in Figure 6.3. As with color channels, alpha channels appear as thumbnails, labeled with their names with the visibility icons in a column to the left. They can be viewed and concealed by clicking on their visibility icons.

An alpha channel in the Channels palette.

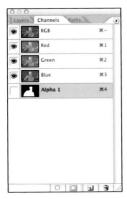

Saving selections as alpha channels

Every image presents unique problems in isolating regions for editing. The selection making process can sometimes be quite labor intensive requiring the employment of several techniques. Photoshop has many features that enable you to accurately select regions of an image under almost any circumstance. After you make a selection you can create an alpha channel that stores the selection to the Channels palette where you can access it when you need it.

Think of an alpha channel as a tool that you create, store, and use to select a region of your image so that ultimately a tool or command can be applied. Save a selection as an alpha channel if the selection is complex, if you need to refine it, or if you are going to use it more than once.

You can save a selection as an alpha channel by following these steps:

1. Make a selection with one of the selection tools.
2. Choose Select ⇨ Save Selection. The Save Selection dialog box appears, as shown in Figure 6.4. In the Destination field, choose from the following specifications:

FIGURE 6.4

The Save Selection dialog box.

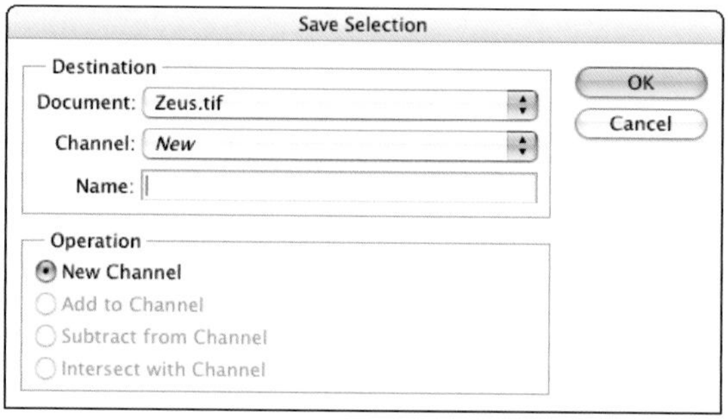

- **Document:** Lets you pick a document in which to save the alpha channel. You can save an alpha channel to the document where the selection was made or to any open document that has the same height, width, and resolution dimensions. The document names that conform appear in the Document list. If you choose New, a new document with no color channels and one alpha channel will appear in the Channels palette.

- **Channel:** Makes a new channel. By choosing New the selection is saved to the Channels palette. You can type a name for it in the Name field or if you don't name it, it will be labeled Alpha 1, 2, etc. If you choose the name of an existing alpha channel, from the Channel list, the new channel will replace it.

3. If you have an active selection on the image and you choose a channel name to write over, that selection, the Operation field presents you with the following four options as shown in Figure 6.5 (click the radio button next to the operation).

   ■ **Replace Channel:** Discards the original mask channel and replaces it with an entirely new alpha channel.

   ■ **Add to Channel:** Adds the new selected area to the alpha channel.

   ■ **Subtract from Channel:** Removes the new selected area from the alpha channel.

   ■ **Intersect with Channel:** Creates an alpha channel of the area where the original channel and the new selection overlap.

4. Click OK to save the selection.

TIP You can quickly create a new alpha channel by clicking the Save Selection as Alpha Channel icon in the Channels palette. It will be named Alpha 1, 2, and so on. If you want to rename it, double-click its name and then type the new name.

FIGURE 6.5

The Operation options in the Save Selection dialog box.

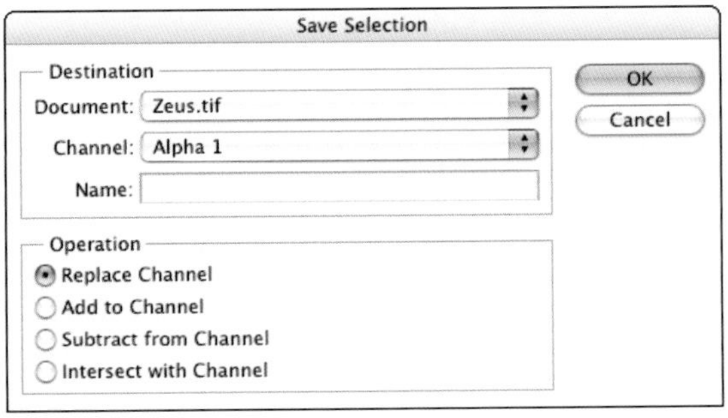

Loading selections

After you save an alpha channel to the Channels palette, you can load it as a selection. Loading a selection surrounds the area with a selection marquee, (sometimes referred to as "marching ants") just as if you outlined it with a Selection tool.

To load an alpha channels as a selection, follow these steps:

1. Choose Select ➪ Load Selection. The Load Selection dialog box appears with options that are similar to the Save Selection dialog box (see Figure 6.6).

2. From the Document list, choose the name of the document where the channel was made. This list displays all alpha channels from all open documents that are the same height, width, and resolution.

151

3. Choose a channel from the Channel list. The Channel list displays all alpha channels and layer masks from the current document. The Invert box loads an inversed selection of the mask.

4. If you have an active selection on the image, the Operation area presents four choices:

   ■ **New Selection:** Loads a new selection on the image, replacing any currently selected area if there is one with the selection derived from the alpha channel.

   ■ **Add to Selection:** Increases the size of the existing selection area to include the loaded selection.

   ■ **Subtract from Selection:** Omits the loaded selection area from an active selection marquee.

   ■ **Intersect with Selection:** Loads the area where the loaded selection and an active selection marquee intersect.

5. Click OK to load the selection.

> **TIP** To quickly load a selection, drag its icon to the Load Channel As Selection icon at the bottom of the Channels palette. Or you can press ⌘/Ctrl and click the channels icon.

FIGURE 6.6

The Load Selection dialog box.

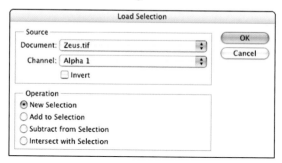

Changing Channel Preferences

As with many of Photoshop's features, the Channels palette is customizable so that you can configure its display features. By default, individual color channels are displayed in grayscale. A grayscale representation of the channel can be quite useful to the imaging process because the subtle variations in contrast can be observed when looking at the channel in black and white. If you desire, however, you can see the independent color channels in color.

To change the display of the color channels from grayscale to color follow these steps:

1. Choose Window ➪ Channels.

2. Choose Edit ➪ Preferences ➪ Display & Cursors. The Display & Cursors preferences dialog box, shown in Figure 6.7 appears.

3. Click the Color Channels in Color checkbox.

4. In the Channels palette, the thumbnails are displayed in color, as shown in Figure 6.8. Click the thumbnail of the red, green, or blue color channel to display that color component of the image on-screen .

FIGURE 6.7

The Display & Cursors Preferences with the Color Channels in Color option checked.

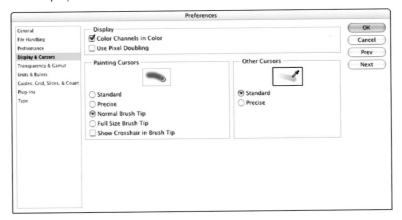

FIGURE 6.8

The Red channel displayed in color in the Image window.

You can change the thumbnail size of the channels in the palette to aid in the identification of channels. This can be particularly helpful when you've added several alpha channels to the image.

To view the thumbnails in the Channels palette at a larger or smaller size or to turn off the display of thumbnails, follow these steps.

1. Click the arrow located in the upper-right corner of the Channels palette.
2. Choose Palette Options from the bottom of the menu. The Channels Palette Options dialog box is displayed.
3. Click the radio button next to one of the four thumbnail size choices.
4. Click OK. The channel thumbnails are displayed at the size you chose.

Performing Channel Operations

Sometimes you need to see the contents of an individual channel in the Image window to assess its brightness and contrast values or to see how an edit changes it. You may also need to duplicate, split, delete or combine channels to perform many of the advanced operations described in this book. Some of these basic channels operations require a simple change in how the channels are seen and some require a radical change to the image's color information.

Viewing channels

To display or conceal the contents of a color or alpha channel, click the first column to the left of its thumbnail, or press one of the keys displayed in Table 6.1.

TABLE 6.1

Key Commands for Viewing Channels

Mode	RGB	CMYK	Lab	Grayscale & Indexed	Multichannel
⌘/Ctrl-~	Composite RGB	Composite CMYK	Composite Lab	Gray/Index	Cyan
⌘/Ctrl-1	Red	Cyan	Lightness	Gray Channel	Cyan
⌘/Ctrl-2	Green	Magenta	A	Alpha 1	Magenta
⌘/Ctrl-3	Blue	Yellow	B	Alpha 2	Yellow
⌘/Ctrl-4	Alpha 1	Black	Alpha 1	Alpha 3	Black
⌘/Ctrl-5	Alpha 2	Alpha 1	Alpha2	Alpha 4	Alpha 1

Viewing alpha channels

You can view an alpha channel as an overlay. To see the colored overlay, at least one other color or alpha channel must be visible. Click the visibility icon to the left of the channel's thumbnail. By default, the channel appears as a red translucent area of color superimposed over the image (see Figure 6.9). The colored regions represent the areas of the mask that are protected. The areas that are clear are the selected areas. Areas that are lighter in color such as the edge of a feathered selection, for example, represent areas that are partially selected. By default, the overlays are 50% red, which is designed to resemble Rubylith, a traditional masking film used in the graphic arts industry.

FIGURE 6.9

A visible alpha channel in the Image window superimposed on the image.

 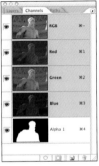

CAUTION If two or more alpha channels are visible at the same time you may not see the mask clearly defined. It's not a bad idea to apply a different color to each alpha channel in the Channel Options dialog box to distinguish between them (see "Specifying the Channel Options" later in this chapter).

A saved alpha channel can be viewed independently in the Image window. It appears as a grayscale image, as shown in Figure 6.10. The black regions of the channel represent the masked areas, and the white areas represent the selected areas. Areas of gray represent partially selected areas. To display the grayscale representation, all other channels must be concealed.

1. Click in the box to the right of the alpha channel's thumbnail to make it visible.

2. Click the eye next to the composite channel at the top of the palette to conceal the color channels.

3. If there are additional alpha channels in the document, conceal them.

TIP To quickly view the alpha channel as a grayscale image, press Option/Alt and click the alpha channel's thumbnail or name. Or press ⌘/Ctrl and the appropriate number key (see Table 6.1).

FIGURE 6.10

A visible alpha channel seen as a grayscale image.

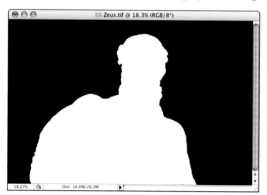 

Specifying the Channel Options

You may have to specify a different color or opacity of an alpha channel overlay if you are looking at more than one channel at a time or if the content of the image too closely resembles the default red color of the overlay. Display options are set in the Channel Options dialog box (see Figure 6.11). The radio buttons in the Color Indicates field let you choose masked areas or selected areas to be displayed as color overlays, or if the image contains spot colors, you can designate the color representation for the a Spot Color channel's mask.

FIGURE 6.11

The Channel Options dialog box.

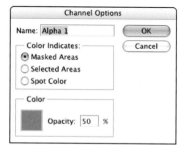

Always check the Channel Options dialog box to see if masked areas or selected areas are represented by color. Look at the alpha channel in the Image window by clicking on the visibility icons next to all other channels to conceal them (see Table 6.1 for additional methods of revealing and concealing channels). When a color represents the masked areas, the masked area appears black and the selected area appears white. The reverse is true when color represents selected areas.

To specify the color of a mask:

1. Click the Alpha channel in the Channels palette to highlight it.

2. Choose Channel Options from the Palette Options menu or double/right-click the channel thumbnail to display the Channel Options dialog box.

3. Click the swatch to bring up the Color Picker.

4. Choose a color and click OK.

5. Specify the opacity of the mask from 0% to 100%.

6. Click OK.

Duplicating channels

When you duplicate a selected channel, a copy is produced and appears in the Channels palette. Duplicate a channel if you want to invert it, modify it by painting, or apply a filter effect, or any other editing function. Click the arrow in upper-right corner of the Channels palette and scroll down to the Duplicate Channel command.

NOTE Because you can duplicate only one channel at a time the Duplicate Channel option will be dimmed if the composite channel is targeted.

TIP To quickly duplicate a channel, drag it to the New Channel icon at the bottom of the Channels palette.

Deleting channels

A targeted channel can be removed from the document by choosing Delete Channel from the Palette Options menu. Deleting an alpha channel maintains the integrity of the image, when you delete color channels, however, the image's color mode converts to Multichannel (see the "Converting to Multichannel" section later in this chapter) and its mode changes to CMYK. For example, if you delete the Red channel of an RGB image, the remaining color channels will convert to magenta and yellow. The composite channel cannot be deleted.

TIP A fast way to delete a channel is to drag it to the Delete Current Channel icon (the trash icon) at the bottom of the Channels palette.

Other channel operations

Other operations can be performed within the Channels palette that modifies a document's color information. Some of these operations change the color mode and some distribute the channels into multiple new documents or consolidate multiple documents into a single document.

CAUTION Due to the radical changes to the color information, I recommend that you to make a copy of the document before executing these channel operations. To duplicate a document, choose Image ➪ Duplicate.

Splitting channels

Photoshop can divide a document's channels into independent Grayscale documents. The title of each window is automatically appended to the channel's name as a suffix in the image title bar at the top of the window. For example, an RGB document with one alpha channel titled Zeus.tif will be divided into three channels: Zeus.tif.Red, Zeus.tif.Green, Zeus.tif.Blue, and Zeus.tif.Alpha 1 (see Figure 6.12). Each channel will be converted to an individual Grayscale document. Splitting channels is a useful first step in redistributing channel information. This is probably not a process you'll frequently use, unless you're a prepress professional who needs to isolate the color information or if you have a very specific need to isolate channel information.

To split a channel, first flatten the image (see the section on layers in Chapter 1). Choose Split Channels from the Channels palette pull-down menu. When you perform this operation, the original document is automatically closed.

CAUTION Splitting channels does not automatically save the document, so you should save them to your hard drive.

FIGURE 6.12

An RGB document with an alpha channel was split into four individual grayscale documents with the Split Channels command.

Merging channels

Individual grayscale images can be merged into a single Multichannel document. The images must be open and be the exact same height, width, and resolution. When you choose Merge Channels from the Channels Options menu, the Merge Channels dialog box, shown in Figure 6.13, appears where you can assign a color mode to the image, based on the number of images open. Three open images produce an RGB, Lab, or Multichannel image. Four open images produce a CMYK or Multichannel image. Click OK and another dialog enables you to determine the distribution of the color channels, as shown in Figure 6.14. You can create some rather surprising color distortions by switching color information between channels.

Prepress professionals use this command to recombine an EPS DCS 1 or DCS 2 file that has no composite preview file that links color separations together. A new EPS DCS file can be created that includes the composite preview file and the high-resolution separations.

FIGURE 6.13

Assign a color mode

FIGURE 6.14

The Merge Channels dialog boxes combine open grayscale images into a single document.

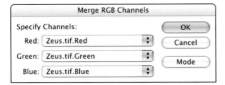

Converting to Multichannel

An image's channels can be converted into a series of separate channels with no composite channel. When you choose Image ➪ Mode ➪ Multichannel, the new channels lose their color relationships to each other and appear as individual Grayscale channels within a single document (see Figure 6.15). This can be useful if you want to separate the color information of a composite channel such as a Duotone, Tritone, or Quadtone and view the color information of each ink color separately. Multichannel conveniently names each channel with its specific ink color. Multichannel converts the red, green, and blue channels on RGB images into separate cyan, magenta, and yellow channels within the same document.

FIGURE 6.15

Multichannel converts color channels into a series of separate channels with no composite channel.

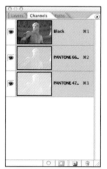

CROSS-REF Duotones can be tricky — see Chapter 9 for more information. Duotones are both a science and an art. They are frequently used to enhance the quality of monochromatic images when they are printed in more than one ink color on an offset lithographic press. Different colored inks can be superimposed over each other to increase the tonal range of the print or to produce a fine colored tint. If you are a graphic designer planning to print monochromatic images, you should know how to prepare duotones for print. Chapter 10 walks you through this powerful channels technique.

Mixing channels

The Channel Mixer is a Photoshop feature that enables you to adjust the color information of each channel from one control window. You can establish color values on a specific channel as a mixture of any or all of the color channels' brightness values. The Channel Mixer can be used for a variety of purposes, including:

- Creating a perfect grayscale image from an RGB or CMYK file
- Making a high-quality sepia tone from a CMYK or RGB file
- Converting images into alternative color spaces
- Swapping color information from one channel to another
- Making creative color adjustments to images by altering the color information in a specific channel

To learn how to use the Channel Mixer, see Chapter 8.

CROSS-REF Swapping color information can be useful for producing interesting color combinations, enhancing color relationships, and correcting color. Chapter 7 demonstrates a few very cool techniques for mixing channel color.

Looking at Other Types of Channels

Occasionally you use the Channels palette to access other types of channels. Spot Color channels are created from within the Channel Options menu but layer masks and Quick Masks appear automatically in the Channels palette when you've created them in another mode. Although they can be accessed from the Channels palette, they are usually seen as indicators that they are currently targeted or active.

Spot Color channels

Spot colors are solid or tint values of a single color of ink. The inks can be independently printed, or combined with a black and white or CMYK image. Each spot color requires a plate of its own. Spot Color channels appear in the Channels palette (see Figure 6.17). Spot Color channels are independent of the color mode of the image and are not part of the composite channel in a grayscale, RGB, CMYK, or LAB image. Spot Color channels are also independent of layers — you cannot apply spot colors to individual layers. Spot Color channels are unlike color channels because, by default, they print separately from the rest of the image.

1. To create a spot color, first make a selection.
2. In the Channels Palette Options menu, choose New Spot Channel. The Spot Color Options dialog box appears (see Figure 6.16).
3. Click the color swatch. The Color Picker appears.
4. Click the Color Libraries button.
5. Choose a color swatch from the color list or type the desired color on the keypad.
6. Click OK on each dialog box. The Spot Color channel appears in the Channels palette and on the image where it was selected.

FIGURE 6.16

The Spot Color Channel Options dialog box.

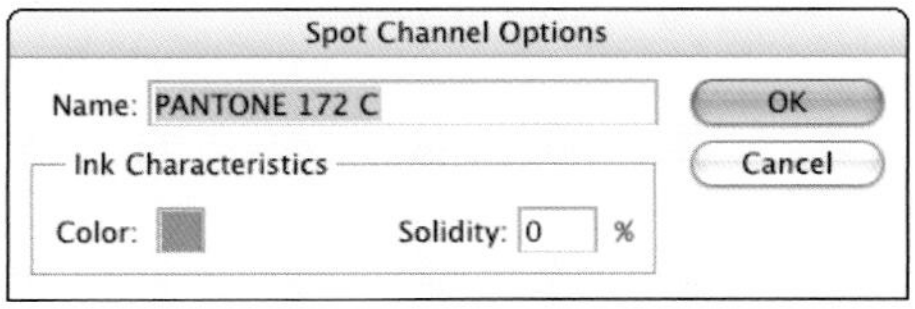

161

FIGURE 6.17

Spot color appears on the image in the area where it was selected. The Spot Color channel appears in the Channels palette labeled with its ink color.

Layer masks

A layer mask conceals and reveals regions of the image. Layer masks reside both in the Layers palette and the Channels palette. They look similar to alpha channels, but the difference is distinct. Where alpha channels are stored selections, layer masks conceal and reveal portions of an image. The iconography of a layer mask is similar, too. On an alpha channel, black represents areas that are protected, white represents areas that are selected, and gray represents areas that are partially selected. On a layer mask, black represents areas that are concealed, white represents are that are visible, and gray represents areas that are partially visible. Layer masks are usually created with the painting and editing tools.

CROSS-REF   **With Layer masks you can perform visual miracles. Layer masks can determine the visibility, translucency, and opacity of specific regions on a layer. You can use them to create seamless composites and beautiful overlays. To experience their awesome power, see Chapter 18.**

Quick Masks

A Quick Mask is a convenient temporary mask that you create on the fly. You usually create a Quick Mask by selecting an area and clicking on the Quick Mask icon in the Tool palette or by pressing your Q key on the keyboard. You can then refine the selection by painting with the Brush tool. When you work in Quick Mask mode, a Quick Mask thumbnail appears in the Channels palette.

A Quick Mask looks exactly like an alpha channel. The default red colored overlay is identical as is the Quick Mask Options dialog box. The difference is that Quick Masks are not automatically saved. After you've created a Quick Mask with the paint tools, you must first click the Edit in Standard Mode icon in the Tool palette or again press the Q key to convert the Quick Mask into a selection. You can then save the selection as an alpha channel (see Chapter 21 for a comprehensive look at this feature).

Summary

This chapter presented information about color channels. You found out that you can make severe modifications to your images.

I covered the following:

- Working with alpha channels
- Performing channel operations
- Specifying channel options

Turn to the next chapter to find out how to mix color channels so that you can configure your image for a specific purpose.

Chapter 7

Mixing Color Channels

A s you've seen in other chapters, the color information in a Photoshop image is nicely separated into channels so that you can independently access and control each color component. The ability to change the image into different color modes lets you configure the image for a specific purpose. You can apply channel specific adjustments, filters, or other Photoshop operations to target color channels. You can also swap or blend color channels to create interesting color relationships. With channel juggling techniques, you can combine the best parts of multiple images, emphasize detail, balance highlights, and create 3D effects.

In this chapter, I show you a few not-so-obvious techniques that use the information inherent within color channels to modify and improve color relationships.

Swapping Color Information

The most direct method of channel juggling entails copying the content from one color channel and pasting it into another. Depending on the image, this method can produce odd, but colorful results as shown in Figure 7.1. You can try this for fun and as a means to understand how color channels work. Remember, as with all color manipulations, you are simply changing the numerical composition of the channel information. The results vary considerably depending on your choice of source and destination channels. Here is a basic method for swapping color information:

1. Open the Channels palette by choosing Window ➪ Channels.

2. Click one of the color channels to target it.

3. Press ⌘/Ctrl+A to select its contents.

4. Press ⌘/Ctrl + C to copy its contents to the clipboard.

5. Click one of the other color channels to target it.

6. Press ⌘/Ctrl+V to paste the contents of the clipboard into the channel.

7. Click the composite channel to see the results.

In the example shown in Figure 7.1, I copied the contents of the Red channel from the original (left) and pasted it into the Blue channel. If you try this in CMYK mode the results will be quite different, as you can see in Figure 7.1 (right) where the Magenta channel has been pasted into the Cyan channel.

This technique swaps all the channels' information and is of little practical use unless you're trying to produce creative color relationships. There are more sophisticated methods of exchanging color information that offer more control, such as the Channel Mixer and the Apply Image command covered later in this chapter.

The ability to mix color information one of the most powerful features Photoshop has to offer. There are several other methods for mixing channels that are covered in this chapter and various places throughout this book. They include:

- The Channel Mixer, which directly swaps color values from one channel to another and also enables you to create perfect black and white monotones.

- The Apply Image command, which mixes color information from one document to another.

- The Blend If sliders in the Layer Styles dialog box that mixes includes or excludes color information from two consecutive layers.

- The Calculations command, which mixes the brightness values of two channels to create a third alpha channel.

CROSS-REF   The Calculations dialog box appears quite formidable, but its bark is much worse than its bite. Learn more about it in Chapter 22.

FIGURE 7.1

The original image (top left), Red channel values pasted into Blue channel (top right), Magenta channel values pasted onto cyan (bottom left).

Working with the Channel Mixer

The Channel Mixer swaps color information from one dialog box. You can specify values on a color channel as a percentage derived from the values of another color channel.

The Channel Mixer can be used for a variety of purposes, including:

- Refining color relationships by swapping color information from one channel to another.
- Adjusting color by modifying the color information in a specific channel.
- Creating an optimal monochrome image from an RGB or a CMYK file (see Chapter 8).
- Creating images with interesting color relationships.

The Channel Mixer does not add or subtract actual color. Instead it combines the numerical values from each channel with those of the target channel. The effect is similar to copying the Red channel, for example, and pasting it on the Blue channel, but with the greater ability to control the degree of the effect.

Here is how you use the Channel Mixer:

1. Target the composite channel in the Channels palette.
2. Access the window by choosing Image ➪ Adjustments ➪ Channel Mixer to display the Channel Mixer dialog box.
3. Target the channel to be affected by choosing a channel from the Output Channel menu.
4. Click and drag the color sliders to modify the color relations between channels.

Swapping colors within channels

You can make a selection which affects only the area within the selection outline or you can globally affect the entire target channel. When you target a channel from the Output Channel menu (say you choose red), the value within the corresponding Source Channel's value box defaults to 100%, or the total amount of red in the image. The values can be increased to 200% or decreased to −200%.

The effect of adding or subtracting color depends on the color composition and mode of the image. When working on an image in RGB mode, increasing the numeric value shifts the selected color toward the color of the selected channel. Decreasing the value shifts the color toward its compliment as shown in Figure 7.2. The limits of these changes are expressed in percentage values between 200% and −200%. You can decrease the value of red if you target the Red channel and move the red slider to the left, which shifts red toward cyan, its complement on the color wheel. Targeting the Green channel and moving the green slider to the left shifts the color toward magenta. Targeting the Blue channel and moving the blue slider to the left shifts the color toward yellow.

FIGURE 7.2

The Red, Green, and Blue channels were modified in the Channel Mixer to change the color scheme of this image.

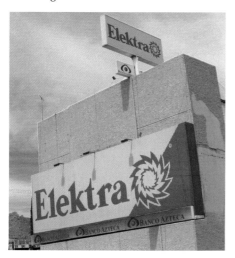 

The Channel Mixer behaves differently when working in CMYK because it is a subtractive color mode. Increasing the numeric value of cyan by dragging its slider to the right increases the density of cyan in the Cyan channel. Decreasing the numeric value or dragging the slider to the left decreases the density of cyan from the channel. Adjusting the color slider of any other color, such as magenta, while the Cyan channel is targeted alters the amount of the cyan based on the relationship between the brightness values of magenta and cyan. It is entirely possible that adding magenta, (increasing its value by dragging the slider to the right) could actually reduce the amount of magenta in the image.

The Constant slider is like having an independent Black or White channel, with an Opacity slider added to the targeted color channel to increase or decrease the channel's overall brightness values. Negative values act as a Black channel, decreasing the brightness of the target channel. Positive values act as a White channel, increasing the overall brightness of a channel.

Increasing the brightness of a color channel does not necessarily mean that the image will become lighter. It actually adds more of the target channel's color to the image. You can demonstrate this by targeting the Blue channel, for example, and moving the Constant slider to the right. Any image will become bluer. Drag it to the left, and it becomes more yellow, the complement of blue on the color wheel.

CROSS-REF The Channel Mixer's other primary function is to make perfect grayscales from RGB or CMYK images. You can find out more about this and other color-to-black-and-white techniques in Chapter 8.

Blending Channels

There are several ways to combine channels other than cutting and pasting or mixing them together with the Channels Mixer. The Apply Image command lets you blend channels from one document to another or within the same document while at the same time applying a blending mode to the mix.

Using the Apply Image command

The Apply Image command applies a source image to a target image. You can also use it to apply channel information to a layer within the same document. Because it has so many variables, you can use it to produce many effects.

CROSS-REF You can find out about several more Apply Image techniques in Chapter 22.

If you are using Apply Image to combine two images, both have to be open on the desktop. The images must be exactly the same physical size and resolution. But if you are blending two layers all you have to worry about is which layer is targeted and is going to be affected. The Apply Image dialog box (see Figure 7.3) is accessed by choosing Image ⇨ Apply Image.

FIGURE 7.3

You can use the Apply Image dialog box for channel-based compositing.

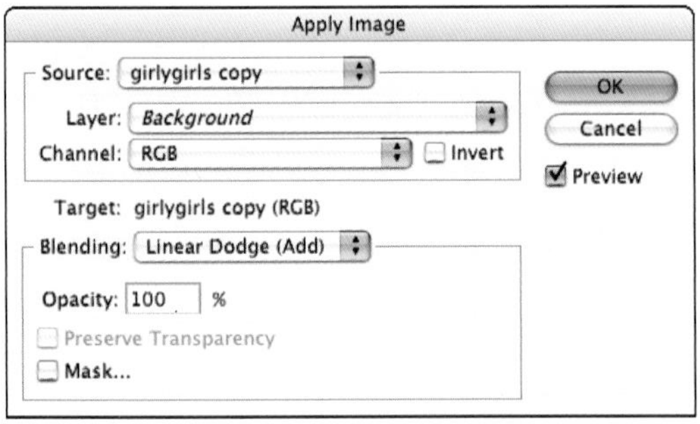

There are several variables to choose from and this is what they do:

- **Source:** The image that is applied, or overlaid over the Target image. The Source pop-up list displays all open images on the desktop that are the same size and resolution as the target image.

- **Layer:** This pop-up list shows all the layers and the background in the source image. You can overlay any one of the layers or all the layers if you choose Merged.

- **Channel:** The pop-up list displays the channels in the source image that you can apply to the target image or layer. If you choose the Composite channel (RGB, CMYK, and so on.), the contents of all the color channels will be mixed.

- **Invert:** Select the check box to invert the contents of the selected channel. Pixels that are black will be applied as if they are white and pixels that are white will be applied as if they are black.

- **Target:** This is the image that is affected. The target lists the current channel(s) and layers that are currently targeted in the Layers and Channels palette and will be affected by the operation.

- **Blending:** The pop-up list displays the blending modes in which the color will be applied.

- **Opacity:** Type a percentage value to control the opacity of the effect.

- **Preserve Transparency:** Select this check box to leave transparent areas on a layer unaffected.

- **Mask:** When you choose Mask, the Apply Image dialog box expands. From the menus, choose an image and the layer that will be used as a mask. Choose a color channel, an alpha channel, or an active selection on the source image to isolate the application of the affect.

- **Scale and Offset:** If you choose either the Add or Subtract blending modes, you can enter values for scale and offset. These values are used in the calculation to determine the brightness values of the superimposed pixels.

Reducing glare

Sometimes the highlights in an image can be too hot and the lighting needs to be evened out. Combining channel information can be the solution to correct these problems. This technique is subtle, but it can improve the look of an image that is overburdened with harsh highlights. This technique uses several operations to achieve results. The Apply Image command combines the color values from one color channel to another through the use of a blending mode to reduce glare and even out highlights. A filter is applied to defuse the contents of an alpha channel so that the application of the color values is softer. A blending mode in the Layers palette and Advanced Blending controls further balance the effect. Combine these powerful techniques and you have an industrial strength method of blending color channels.

NOTE This technique does not restore specular highlights — areas whose pixels are pure white. There must be some color variations in the highlights.

1. Open an image whose highlights are too harsh, as the image in Figure 7.4.

2. Click the Background Layer to target it and then press ⌘/Ctrl–J to duplicate it.

3. Click the Channels tab in the Layers Channels Paths palette cluster or choose Window ➪ Channels to display the Channels palette.

4. Click the visibility icon to display each channel individually. You can see each channel's contents in the Image window. Find the channel with the most contrast and click it to target it. In this case it's the Red channel.

5. Drag the channel to the new channel icon to create a duplicate channel as an alpha channel, as in Figure 7.5.

FIGURE 7.4

The highlights in this portrait are too harsh and need to be softened.

FIGURE 7.5

Duplicate the channel with the most contrast. In this case it's the Red channel.

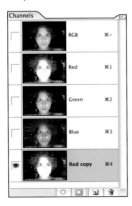

6. Press ⌘/Ctrl-4 to see the alpha channel. Choose Filter ⇨ Blur ⇨ Gaussian Blur. If the image is 72 ppi, blur it 12 pixels. If the image is 300 ppi, blur it 36 pixels (see Figure 7.6).

FIGURE 7.6

Blur the duplicate Red channel.

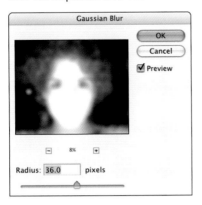

7. The channel needs to be inverted so that the black areas become white and the white areas become black. Choose Image ⇨ Adjustments ⇨ Invert as in Figure 7.7.

FIGURE 7.7

Invert the alpha channel.

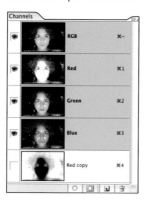

8. Click the visibility icon next to the composite channel. Choose Image ⇨ Apply Image (see Figure 7.8). The target channel, Green copy will appear in the Channel menu.

9. Change the blending mode to Overlay and click OK.

FIGURE: 7.8

The Apply Image dialog box.

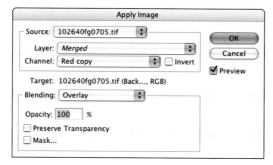

10. In the Layers palette, change the blending mode to Darken.

11. The image may have taken on a color-cast. Double-click the layer to display the Layer Style dialog box (see Figure 7.9). Set the Blend If channel to Green. Drag the black Underlying Layer slider to the left until the fleshtones normalize. Then Option/Alt-click and drag the right half of the Black Underlying Layer slider to the right to soften the transitions.

FIGURE 7.9

The Layer Style dialog box with the Blend If sliders adjusted to eliminate the color cast.

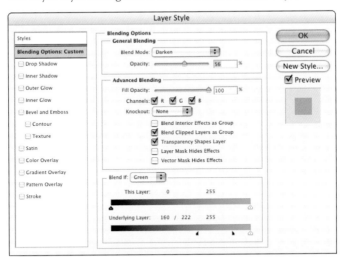

Excluding Color

The previous step-by-step list demonstrated that you can use the Layer Style dialog box to exclude colors from one layer to another. Blending Options can exclude color information on a specific channel. Selecting the channel's check boxes controls what color information will be visible or suppressed. The Blend If sliders are designed to enhance certain color ranges and suppress others. By dragging them, you can precisely control the visibility of colors within a specific brightness range.

The channel blending features of the Blending Options in the Layer Style dialog box are as follows:

- **Channels:** Select or deselect the color channel boxes in the Advanced Blending field to include or exclude the information of a color channel when blending layers.

- **Blend If:** These controls can be tricky. The two sliders in this field control the visibility of pixels from the target layer and the underlying layer.

  - **Pop-Up menu:** Gray specifies a blending range for all channels. The individual color channels specify blending for a specific color channel.

  - **This Layer:** These sliders determine the range of pixels on the target layer to blend. For example, if you drag the white slider to 228, pixels with higher brightness values are unblended and do not appear on the image.

  - **Use the Underlying Layer:** These sliders determine the range of pixels in all underlying visible layers that will be visible. Underlying pixels are blended with pixels in the target layer. Pixel values in the unblended ranges show through overlying areas of the target layer. Click and drag the black slider to set the shadow value of the range. For example, if you drag the black slider to 40, pixels with brightness values lower than 40 will be visible on the target layer.

Sometimes omitting pixels of a specific brightness range produces harsh color transitions and jagged edges. These transitions can be softened by adjusting the Fuzziness setting. Option/Alt-click and drag the *left half* of the white slider to the left or the right half of the black slider to the right to determine a range.

CROSS-REF Advanced Blending gives you precise control over the visibility of color information as you can see in the following numbered step list. If you want a detailed description of all Blending Options in the Layer Style dialog box, and a little bit of practice on some of the of the cool things you can do with them, take a look at Chapter 21.

The following list illustrates the power of the Blending Options. Figure 7.10 shows a landscape. To achieve a shot such as this, set up your camera on a tripod. For your first shot, set the exposure for the sky which darkens the ground. Name this image Sky. With your second shot, expose for the ground which lightens the sky. Name this image Ground. Use the Blending Options in the Layer Style dialog box to combine the best parts of these two exposures into a perfect picture.

1. Open both images and place them side by side on the desktop. Click the ground image.

FIGURE 7.10

The two original exposures.

2. Select the Move tool. Press the Shift key and click and drag the ground image onto the Sky image. (Using the Shift key assures that the images are perfectly aligned.)

3. Click the Channels tab in the Layers, Channels Paths palette cluster. Examine the Channels palette. Look at each color channel in the Image window to determine which one has the most contrast between the sky and the ground. In this case it's the Green channel (see Figure 7.11).

FIGURE 7.11

The Green channel has the most contrast.

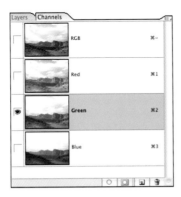

4. Click the Layers tab in the Layers, Channels Paths palette cluster. Double-click the top-most layer to display the Layer Style dialog box or click the Layer Styles menu at the bottom of the palette and choose Blending Options.

5. In the Blend If field, choose Green from the pop-up menu.

6. Click and drag the white slider on the This Layer ramp to the left until you see the sky from the Sky layer emerge into the image (see Figure 7.12). The Sky is greatly improved but there is some pixelization and darkening in the ground.

FIGURE 7.12

The Blend If sliders control the visibility of specific channel content on each layer.

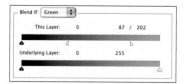

7. To correct this problem, Opt/Alt-click the right half of the black slider and drag it to the right. Repeat the process on the left half of the white slider and drag it to the left to adjust the fuzziness and soften the transitions.

8. When satisfied with the sky and ground, click OK (see Figure 7.13).

FIGURE 7.13

The completed blended image.

Offsetting Color Channels

Moving the contents of a color channel up or down, or to the left or right misregisters the channel and, depending on the mode, can produce rather weird results in the appearance of the image. In Figure 7.14 the Red, Green, and Blue channels have been moved a few pixels to the right and left to produce this image. Granted, it looks odd but that doesn't mean it's not interesting if not even beautiful in a peculiar sort of way, and if you are looking to create a piece of avant guarde art, you might try this approach varying the degree of offset in each channel.

FIGURE 7.14

The result of offsetting color channels.

If you're not particularly interested in this form of experimentation, you can produce a rather startling effect with the controlled offsetting of color channels. 3D images, the kind that require red and blue 3D glasses to see, can be created by offsetting color channels in varying degrees. To control the effect, you use the Offset filter and some History palette acrobatics. You can perform the effect on full-color RGB images and grayscale images that have been converted to RGB color mode. It works best on images that do not contain areas of solid red, green, or blue, (such as solid-colored type, for example) because when those areas are offset the absence of the other colors in the color channels produces little or no effect.

To see this effect, you need to look through a pair of anaglyphic red and cyan or red and blue 3D glasses. You can get a free pair at the Rainbow Symphony Web site: www.rainbowsymphony.com/freestuff.html.

Creating two-level 3D images

Choose an image with natural perspective to enhance the effect. In the first example you create two levels of depth on a black and white image. In the second example, I demonstrate how you can create more than two levels of depth on a full-color image.

To create a 3D image with two levels of depth follow these steps:

1. Open an image that has natural perspective, such as Figure 7.15.

2. Make any tonal, size, or content adjustments that are necessary.

3. If the image is a grayscale, as this picture is, choose Image ➪ Mode ➪ RGB Color to convert the grayscale to RGB mode.

4. Choose Image ➪ Duplicate to make a copy of the image. Name the new image.

5. If the image is layered, choose Layer ➪ Flatten Image.

6. Click the Create New Snapshot icon (the little camera at the bottom of the History palette) in the History palette. A new Snapshot labeled Snapshot 1 appears in the History palette (see Figure 7.16).

FIGURE 7.15

The original image.

FIGURE 7.16

Make a snapshot of the RGB image in the History palette.

7. Click the Channels tab in the Layers,/Channels/Paths palette cluster to display the Channels palette.

8. Click the Red channel to target it (see Figure 7.17).

FIGURE 7.17

Target the Red channel.

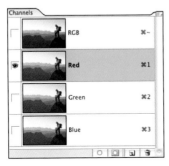

9. Choose Filter ⇨ Other ⇨ Offset to display the Offset Filter dialog box (see Figure 7.18). Drag the Horizontal slider to the left to specify a negative value. The value you enter will depend on the image's resolution. For low resolution images (72 ppi) enter a value of -6. For high resolution images (300 ppi) enter a value of 24. The higher the value the further back in the picture plane the image will appear. Click the Repeat Edge Pixels radio button.

FIGURE 7.18

Offset the Red channel horizontally using a negative amount.

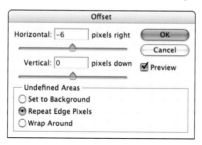

10. Look through the 3D glasses and notice that the image appears to have moved back into the picture plane.

11. In the History palette, click the source column to the left of Snapshot 1. Choose the History brush. Click and drag the brush over the areas of the image that you want to restore to the picture plane. The image in Figure 7.19 now has two levels of depth.

FIGURE 7.19

The image with two levels of depth.

Creating 3D images with continuous depth

This effect creates a 3D image that deepens continuously as it recedes in the picture plane. It uses a gradient alpha channel to control the application of the Offset Filter.

To create 3D images with continuous depth, follow these steps:

1. Open an image.

2. Follow Steps 1 through 6 in the previous 3D numbered step list.

3. In the Channels palette, click the Create New Channel icon. A new empty alpha channel appears in the stack named Alpha 1. Click it to target it (see Figure 7.20).

FIGURE 7.20

Make a new empty channel.

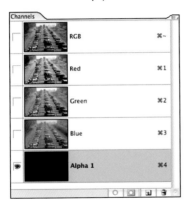

4. Press the D key to set the foreground and background color, so they default black and white.

5. Choose the Gradient tool from the Tools palette. Click the bottom of the Image window, press the Shift key, and drag upward to the top to apply a black and white gradient to the alpha channel. The black should start on the part of the image that will be closest to the viewer (see Figure 7.21).

6. Click and drag the alpha channel to the load selection icon. A selection marquee now covers approximately half of the image.

FIGURE 7.21

With the alpha channel highlighted, drag a black to white gradient.

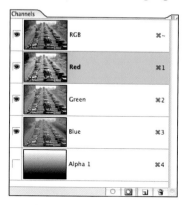

FIGURE 7.22

The selection appears to cover only half of the image but the areas below the selection are less than 50% selected and therefore don't display a marquee.

7. Choose Filter ➪ Other ➪ Offset to display the Offset dialog box, as in Figure 7.23. Drag the Horizontal slider to the left to specify a negative value. Click the RepeatEdge Pixels radio button, and click OK. The image now appears to gradually recede into the picture plane, as shown in Figure 7.23.

FIGURE 7.23

Apply a negative horizontal offset to the selection. The image appears to gradually recede into the picture plane.

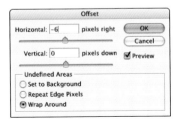

Summary

In this chapter, you found out how to create interesting color relationships using the Channel Mixer. I also discussed how to reduce glare in your images.

You found out how to do the following:

■ Swap color information

■ Blend channels

■ Exclude color

■ Offset color channels

In Chapter 8, you discover how to create the perfect monochrome image.

Chapter 8

Creating the Perfect Monochrome

When you convert an image from color to black and white, you discard its color information. Simply changing modes doesn't always produce the best results even though the image may look spectacular in color. Sometimes the image's tonality becomes flat and really disappointing.

There are several methods for creating a better grayscale using the source channels; each method has its own particular advantages. If one technique doesn't produce brilliant results you can always try another. All offer more control and produce results that you don't get using direct grayscale conversion. This chapter walks you through these methods.

Choosing the Best Channel

This technique is quite easy because it involves looking at the color information in each channel and determining which one looks the best. Then there's a little bit of layer finagling that makes the image pop.

1. Open a full-color RGB image (see Figure 8.1). Choose Image ➪ Duplicate to display the Duplicate Image dialog box. Name the image and click OK.

2. Click the duplicate image. Choose Window ➪ Channel to display the Channels palette or click the Channels tab in the Layers, Channels, Paths palette cluster.

FIGURE 8.1

The RGB image.

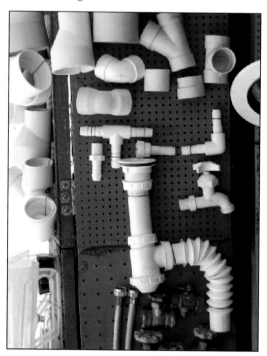

3. Press ⌘/Ctrl+1 to observe the Red channel. It should appear as a grayscale. If it doesn't, choose Photoshop (Mac) or Edit (Win) ➪ Preferences ➪ Display & Cursors and uncheck the Show Color Channels in the Color checkbox.

4. Press ⌘/Ctrl+2 to see the Green channel and ⌘/Ctrl+3 to see the Blue channel. Compare the three color channels and target the one that looks the best. (In this case it's the Red channel, as shown in Figure 8.2.)

NOTE You'll find throughout the book that observing individual channel information is a technique that is frequently used. Most often it is used to find the best looking grayscale but it can be used to determine which channel will create the best blend between layers, which channel has the most contrast and which channel, if copied can best serve as an alpha channel.

5. In the Channel Palette Options menu, choose Duplicate Channel to display the Duplicate Channel dialog box, shown in Figure 8.3. In the Document pop-up menu, choose New to save the channel as a separate document.

FIGURE 8.2

Compare the three channels by clicking their visibility icons in the Channels palette.

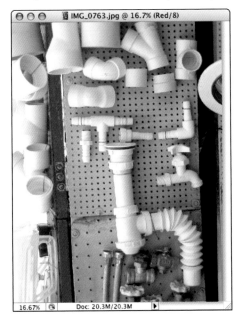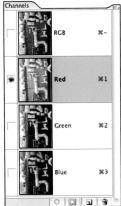

FIGURE 8.3

The Duplicate Channel dialog box.

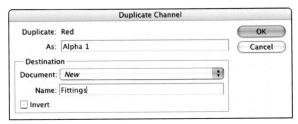

6. When you make a new document from a color channel the new document is automatically configured in Multichannel mode, which does not support layers. You'll need to convert the document into grayscale. With the new document active choose Image ⇨ Mode ⇨ Grayscale.

7. A Caution appears asking you to discard other channels. Click OK.

8. Click the Layers tab to display the Layers palette. Drag the background layer to the New Layer icon to create a new duplicate layer.

9. From the Blending Mode menu, choose the Soft Light option to enhance the contrast of the image, shown in Figure 8.4.

FIGURE 8.4

The Soft Light blending mode applied to the duplicate layer enhances the grayscale image.

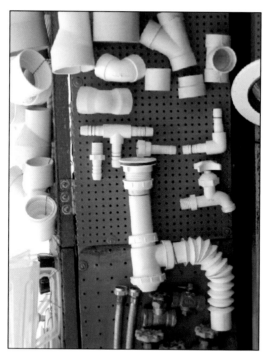

Using the Channel Mixer to Create a Monochrome

This variation of the color to black and white technique uses the Channel Mixer on an adjustment layer to combine values of all the channels into a an image with a wide tonal range. The advantage of using the Channel Mixer technique is the flexibility of the process in that all the controls are in one interactive dialog box. This technique also employs a layer mask for more precision and control.

1. Open a color photograph (see Figure 8.5).

2. Choose Layer ⇨ New Adjustment Layer. Choose Channel Mixer from the pop-up menu to display the Channel Mixer dialog box.

3. Select the Monochrome checkbox. The image now appears black and white and the Red and Green sliders read 40% and the Blue slider reads 20%. This produces a rather disappointing monochrome. You have to adjust the sliders to get more punch and pop out of your image (see Figure 8.6).

FIGURE 8.5

The original color photograph.

The default Channel Mixer dialog box with the monochrome settings produce a disappointing monochrome.

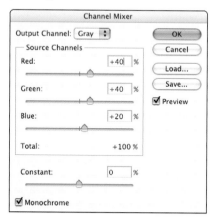

4. Drag the Red slider to the right to 75%, and then drag the Green and Blue sliders to the left until the image shows a good contrast (see Figure 8.7). Drag the constant slider to -12 to darken the image slightly. Click OK.

FIGURE 8.7

A little fanagaling with the sliders produce more contrast.

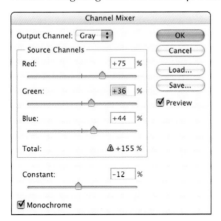

> **TIP** You can determine if the contrast is good by observing the lightest and darkest areas of the image. The lights should be bright. The darks should be to dark maintain detail.

5. Click the background layer. Choose ⇨ Image Adjustments ⇨ Desaturate (⌘/Ctrl-Shift+U) to eliminate color from the image.

6. Click the adjustment layer's layer mask to target it. Choose the Brush tool and a medium soft brush from the Options bar brush menu. Press the D key to set the foreground and background color to the default white and black. Click and drag over the image to paint the highlights back in as shown in Figure 8.8.

7. Don't forget that even though the image appears as black and white, it was captured in RGB mode. To convert it to grayscale, you must first flatten it (Layer ➪ Flatten Image) and then choose Image ➪ Mode ➪ Grayscale.

FIGURE 8.8

The image converted with the Channel Mixer and worked with the layer mask has optimal tonality.

Creating a Monochrome in Lab Mode

When an image has been converted to Lab mode, the color information is separated from brightness information. Having the brightness information on a separate channel gives you the ability to control it independently and, therefore, you can use it as the foundation of your monochrome. This technique also uses blending modes and a layer mask for further control.

1. Open a full-color RGB image (see Figure 8.9).

2. Choose Image ⇨ Mode ⇨ Lab Color. Look at the Channels palette to see how the color is configured. There are two color channels and the Lightness channel, as shown in Figure 8.10.

3. Press ⌘/Ctrl+1 to display the contents of the Lightness channel in the Image window.

FIGURE 8.9

The full-color image.

FIGURE 8.10

Click the Lightness channel in the Channels palette to display it in the Image window.

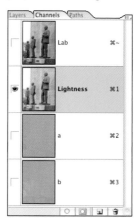

4. Choose Image Mode ➪ Grayscale. A caution box appears that asks if you want to discard other channels. Click OK.

5. The Lightness channel may be okay as is but if not, display the Layers palette. Drag the background layer to the Create New Layer icon to duplicate it.

6. Choose the Overlay blending mode for the layer. Adjust the Opacity slider until you get the image you want, as shown in Figure 8.11.

CROSS-REF Blending modes can perform miracles on color images. The Overlay blending mode and all of its siblings are covered in Chapter 21.

FIGURE 8.11

The new grayscale image and the Layers palette with the blending mode set to overlay and the opacity reduced.

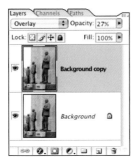

TIP If you want even more control over specific areas, Choose Layer ⇨ Add Layer Mask ⇨ Reveal All. Press D to make black the foreground color. With the brush tool, paint out areas on the layer mask that you want to restore back to the original image. Adjust the opacity of the brush in the Options bar and paint on the layer mask with gray to partially restore the areas.

Desaturating Color with Calculations

The Calculations command is a formidable dialog box, and at first glance it appears quite complicated because its elements remain undefined. But after you know what its pop-up menus actually do, you can see that it's really quite simple. The Calculations command combines channels from two sources into one channel and throws a choice of blending mode into the mixture for incredible variations.

You can make good monochromes from a colored image with the Calculations command because after all, color channels are actually grayscales.

CROSS-REF **Calculations intimidate the beginner because the dialog box is big and full of cryptic pop-up menus. But after you understand it, it's really simple and quite useful. See Chapter 22 for more information about calculations.**

1. Open an RGB image. See Figure 8.12.

2. The first step is to look carefully at the color channels in the RGB image. Click each one and observe it in the Image window. Determine which two channels look the best. Look for detail and good shadow in one of the channels and look for good highlights in the other. In this case, I've chosen the Red and Green channels (see Figure 8.13).

3. Click the RGB composite channel to be sure it's displayed in the Image window. Choose Image ⇨ Calculations (see Figure 8.14).

FIGURE 8.12

Open an RGB image.

FIGURE 8.13

The Channels palette showing the channels.

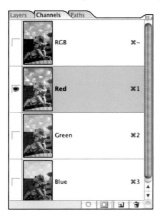

FIGURE 8.14

The Calculations dialog box with the settings for the monochrome.

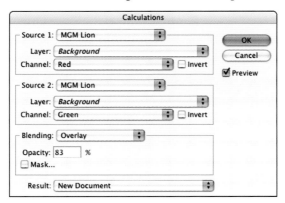

4. For the Source 1 channel, I chose the Red channel. For the Source 2 Channel, I chose the Green channel.

5. In the Blending pop-up list, start with Soft Light and see how the image looks. Then try Hard Light and Overlay and all the other blending modes to see which one works the best. Some will produce terrible results. In the pop-up list, choose New Document and click OK (see Figure 8.15).

FIGURE 8.15

The image converted using the Calculations technique to combine the two channels.

6. When you make a new document from a color channel the document is automatically created in Multichannel mode. You need to convert the document into grayscale. With the new document active, choose Image ➪ Mode ➪ Grayscale.

Working with Sepia Tones

A sepia tone is a tinted monochromatic image. In the darkroom, photographic papers can produce a variety of blacks from icy cold blue blacks to warm earth tone blacks. Sepia tones produce the warmer off-white to dark brown shades and can give the image an antique or even dream-like appearance. Traditionally, sepia tones were produced by adding a reddish pigment made from the

Sepia Cuttlefish to the positive print of a photograph. They were originally created as a preservation method because the chemical process changes the metallic silver in a photograph to a sulphide that resists deterioration over time. Many antique photos survive today because they were printed as sepia tones. There are several methods of emulating sepia tones in Photoshop. You can use filters, blending modes, and adjustments.

CROSS-REF Presented here are three tried-and-true methods for creating sepia tones. See Chapter 9 for another method using duotones.

Using a photo filter

Perhaps the easiest method to achieving the sepia look is to simply apply the photo filter to a grayscale image.

1. Open a full-color RGB image (see Figure 8.16).
2. Choose Image ➪ Adjustments ➪ Desaturate to convert the colors to a black and white version while maintaining the image in RGB mode (see Figure 8.17).

FIGURE 8.16

The full-color RGB image.

FIGURE 8.17

Desaturate the image to eliminate its color and maintain its color mode.

3. Choose Layer ➪ New Adjustment Layer ➪ Photo Filter. In the New Layer dialog box, keep the default settings. Click OK to display the Photo Filter dialog box (see Figure 8.18).

FIGURE 8.18

Enter settings in the Photo Filter dialog box.

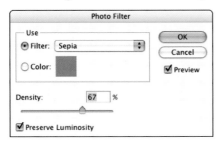

4. Enter the following settings:

   ■ **Filter:** Sepia

   ■ **Density:** 67%

   ■ **Preserve Luminosity:** Checked

5. Click OK. Of course you can experiment with any of the settings of this filter to produce other variations. Figure 8.19 shows the sepia-toned image.

TIP
Another method to desaturtate is to choose Image ⇨ Adjustments ⇨ Hue Saturation and drag the Saturation slider to the far right.

FIGURE 8.19

The Photo Filter dialog box can change a black and white image into a warm sepia tone.

Channel curve technique

In this technique you manipulate channel information with Photoshop's most powerful adjustment feature — Curves. The advantage of this method is you have more control over the color combinations and the contrast of the image.

Follow these steps to make an adjustment using Curves.

1. Open a full-color RGB image (see Figure 8.20).

FIGURE 8.20

The original image is in full color.

2. Choose Image ➪ Adjustments ➪ Desaturate to convert the colors to a black and white version while maintaining the image in RGB mode as in Figure 8.21.

3. Choose Layer ➪ New Adjustment Layer ➪ Curves. In the New Layer dialog box that appears keep the default settings and click OK.

4. In the Curves dialog box that appears, adjust the Red and Blue channels as shown in Figure 8.22. Press the Opt/Alt key and click on the grid to display the 100 cell grid. Choose Red from the Channels pop-up menu. Click and drag the center of the Red curve upward until the Output box reads 150.5.

CROSS-REF The Curves dialog box is Photoshop's most powerful color adjustment feature. You can read more about it in Chapter 5.

FIGURE 8.21

The desaturated image.

FIGURE 8.22

Adjust the curve on the Red and Blue channels to alter the color.

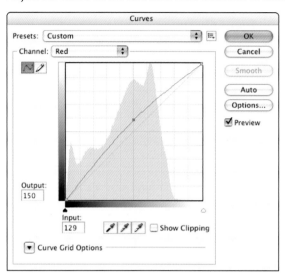

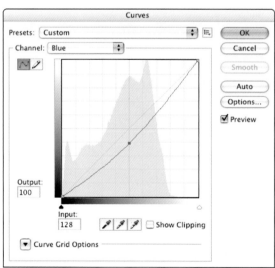

5. Choose Blue from the Channels pop-up menu. Click and drag the center of the Blue curve downward until the Output box reads 100. Click OK. Figure 8.23 shows the result.

FIGURE 8.23

The sepia-toned image created with curves.

Using Black and White

The new Black and White feature in Photoshop CS3 enables you to control all the characteristics of your color to black and white conversions in one concise interface. The command is similar to the Channel Mixer in that it lets you target specific ranges of the color in the original image. Choose Image ➪ Adjustments ➪ Black and White to display the dialog box. The individual sliders adjust the brightness percentage of each range. Drag the slider to the right to lighten and to the left to darken the black and white within the range.

You can apply preconfigured brightness and contrast values to your black and white images by choosing one from the Preset pop-up menu at the top of the palette. These values simulate photographic filters or specific photo effects. Click the Tint checkbox to apply a color tint to the image. Drag the Hue and Saturation sliders to modify the black and white image into a sepia tone or other monochromatic colored image.

> **NOTE** The Black and White command works only in RGB mode. When you apply the command the image is not automatically converted to grayscale although it appears as a black and white image. It remains in RGB mode until you convert it by choosing Image ⇨ Mode ⇨ Grayscale.

Summary

After reading this chapter, you should be able to create the perfect grayscale image. I covered many helpful techniques such as

- Choosing the best channel
- Using the Channel Mixer
- Desaturating color
- Working with sepia tones
- Using the Black and White feature

Now read Chapter 9 to find the ins and outs of printing black and white photographs.

Chapter 9

Specifying Duotones

If you produce a lot of black and white photographs, you may find that printing them to a single color on a printing press leaves plenty to be desired. They may look much flatter than they do on-screen or even when printed as a proof on your inkjet printer because they don't have sufficient tonal depth.

Or the occasion may arise when you need to create images using a custom color ink system, either for a specific look or for reasons of economy.

Duotones are the answer to better looking black and white, sepia, tinted, or custom-colored images. In this chapter, I go over all you need to know about duotones, tritones, and quadtones.

IN THIS CHAPTER

Examining duotones, tritones, and quadtones

Choosing duotone colors

Adjusting duotone curves

Exploring at Duotones, Tritones, and Quadtones

Duotone is the general term to describe images printed with multiple custom inks. Within this category are *duotones*, which use two colors, *tritones,* which use three colors, and *quadtones,* which use four colors. Usually the inks are colored, but you may also see a duotone created using multiple black plates. The two blacks can attain a tonal richness and depth that is out of reach of the simple one-color halftone which ultimately means a better-looking image.

Duotones differ from process color. Process color produces a complete color spectrum and tonal range by mixing cyan, magenta, yellow, and black ink together in varying densities. Duotones produce color and tone using specific premixed ink.

When a grayscale digital image is printed as a halftone with black ink on paper, the 256 shades of gray that you create on your computer are represented by the size and concentration of dots. The halftone is limited to the 100 percentage values that it can represent. It can't fully represent 256 shades of gray of the grayscale.

Duotones can produce a wider tonal range by using more than one shade of ink. You can enhance the detail and texture in an image. If you're printing a two-color book with halftones, adding the second color to the halftones can add an elegant touch. You can use two or more colors of ink to create a sepia tone. Duotones using a dark, metallic ink can impart an opaque, antique quality, while lighter pastel shades might approximate a hand-tinted look or other variations. These effects can be seen the images in Figure 9.1, but be aware that these images were produced as duotones and later converted to CMYK for the printing of this book.

FIGURE 9.1

A variety of duotone effects: a sepia-toned image mixing dark and light shades of brown (a); a medium green ink mixed with a cool dark gray (b); a black ink mixed with dark gray (c).

One potential problem you may encounter when creating a duotone may be ink overfill. Because the inks are printed on or next to each other, it is possible to generate too much ink. If the distribution of ink is not dealt with properly, it could saturate the paper and fill in the spaces between the fine halftone dots. Photoshop deals with this problem by providing a Curves feature that lets you individually adjust the density of each ink.

Another problem, or should I say inconvenience, is that you can't accurately proof a duotone. Because proofers are CMYK devices, the duotone is converted first to RGB and then to CMYK by the printer's raster image processor — it only shows you a CMYK simulation of duotone inks. Photoshop deals with this problem by displaying a fairly decent, though RGB, soft proof.

Choosing Duotone Colors

The beauty of duotones of course is that you can change the tonal depth of monochromatic images that would otherwise appear flat. You also have the ability to create tinted images using a variety of special solid ink colors.

Start with an image scanned in RGB mode. Go to the Image ⇨ Mode submenu. Duotone mode is grayed out, unavailable as an option. To make this option available, first you have to convert the image to Grayscale mode. Wait! Prior to discarding color information and reducing the image to a single channel, it's best to correct tonal and color values first by using the tonal adjustment features described in Chapter 5, or better yet, create the perfect monochrome with the features described in Chapter 8. After you're satisfied with the image, choose Image ⇨ Mode ⇨ Grayscale. If you want to do any further tweaking, do it while you're in Grayscale mode. Now you can proceed with the following steps:

1. Choose Image ⇨ Duotone. The Duotone Options dialog box appears, shown in Figure 9.2.

   When you open the dialog box, *Monotone* is the default color type. The designated Ink 1 color is Black and Ink 2, 3, and 4 are grayed out.

FIGURE 9.2

The default Duotone Options dialog box. You can configure ink colors and densities for monotones, duotones, tritones, and quadtones.

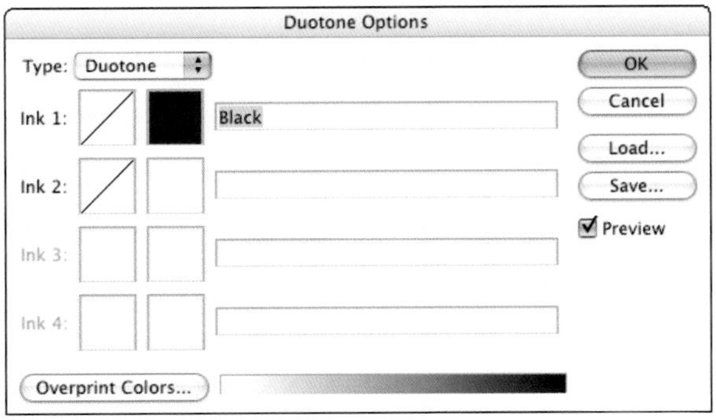

2. From the Duotone Options dialog box choose a Type from the pop-up menu: Monotone, Duotone, Tritone, or Quadtone.

3. To choose a color individually, for each ink click a color swatch to display the Color Picker.

4. Click the Color Libraries radio button to display the dialog box as shown in Figure 9.3. Choose from a variety of ink swatch books in the Books: pop up menu, such as Pantone and its numerous variations, ANPA or Focaltone, among others. The default book is PANTONE solid coated.

FIGURE 9.3

Choose an ink color from the Color Libraries dialog box.

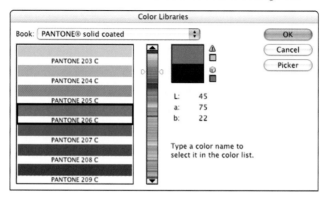

5. To choose a color, drag the color slider on the color ramp to the range of color that you want and then click a swatch. Or you can type a color's number if you know it. When you choose a color two things happen: the swatch in the Duotone dialog box changes to reflect your choice and the image in the Image window also displays the color choice as live preview. Click OK.

CAUTION If you plan to import the duotone into a page layout program make a note of the names of your inks. Make sure that the duotone ink has exactly the same name as the other application's color dialog box. If necessary, reopen the Duotone Options dialog box and rename the ink so that the page layout program can recognize it.

6. To choose a second ink, click the Ink 2 swatch to again display the Color Libraries dialog box (to add a second color Duotone must be the current Type). Choose an ink color from the list, and click OK. Define additional inks in the same way for tritones and quadtones. The color bar at the bottom of the dialog box displays the tonal range, from light to dark, of the ink mix you've specified. The Image window displays a live preview. In most cases Ink 1 should be the darkest ink and each additional ink should be progressively lighter to produce the most accurate preview.

Adjusting Duotone Curves

Duotone curves control the density of each ink. Click the curve thumbnail for any ink to display the corresponding Duotone Curve dialog box as shown in Figure 9.4. Curves define ink coverage for the highlight, midtone, and shadow ranges of each color.

The curves are straight by default. If left unadjusted, the ink is consistently distributed across the entire tonal range of the image and you can potentially end up with a dark, muddy mess. Generally you bend the curves of each ink so that the darkest ink is most dense the shadows, medium tone inks are most dense in the midtones, and light inks enhance the highlights.

FIGURE 9.4

The Duotone Curve dialog box presents a curve that controls ink densities.

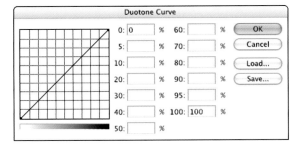

Bending the curve

You can either type numeric settings for ink percentages in the percentage text boxes, or drag the curve's grid to bend the curve. The grid's horizontal axis represents the gradations in the image from white (highlights) on the left to black (shadows) on the right. The vertical axis maps ink density, increasing as you go up. Click anywhere on the line and drag up or down to add or subtract ink in that part of the curve. As you drag the curve, the numbers change accordingly in the percentage boxes to reflect the adjustment. Likewise, when you type numbers in the percentage boxes, the curve adjusts itself to match. The first curve shown in the Duotone Options dialog box in Figure 9.5 is most dense in the shadow areas, and leaner in the highlights. The second curve concentrates its ink in the midtones, and the third emphasizes the highlights only.

Saving and loading curves

Click the Save button in the Duotone Options dialog box to save or load a complete set of inks and curves. Choose a folder and click OK. To load a set, click the Load button and find the curve you want in the directory. Photoshop provides several ink and curve sets in its Presets folder for duotones, tritones, and quadtones that you can use as a starting point.

FIGURE 9.5

Tritone curves for the shadow, midtone, and highlight inks. And the image as it appears after the adjustment.

Separating color

A duotone is represented by one channel in the Channels palette, labeled Monotone (Duotone, Tritone, or Quadtone). Photoshop creates duotones by applying the various curves you've defined to a single channel. You can print color separations directly from Duotone mode. To do so follow these steps:

1. Choose File ➪ Print.

2. Scale and position the image using the features in the dialog box.

3. In the pop-up menu, choose Color Management (the default). From the Color Handling pop-up menu choose Separations (see Figure 9.6).

4. In the pop-up menu, choose Output. Click the Calibration Bars, Corner, and Center Crop Marks, Registration Marks, Labels, and Negative checkboxes.

5. Click the Print button.

FIGURE 9.6

The Print dialog box.

Multichannel mode

Although you can print separations from duotones, to view the channels independently, you have to convert the image to Multichannel mode. Choose Image ➪ Mode ➪ Multichannel. Figure 9.7 shows the Channels palette with a Tritone channel. Next to it, the image has been split into three independent channels, listed separately, and labeled with the ink color names. After you've converted to Multichannel mode you cannot reconvert to Duotone mode so duplicate the image first. (Of course you can always return to a former state in the History palette.)

FIGURE 9.7

The Channels palette of the same tritone image, in Duotone mode (a) and Multichannel mode (b).

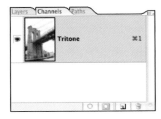
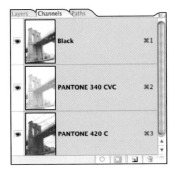

You can print directly from Multichannel; if you do, you will get two, three, or four separated prints called color separations, one for each color. The advantage of using Multichannel is that the three channels can be edited independently.

Overprint colors

The Overprint Colors dialog box (see Figure 9.8) displays a chart that shows how different pairs of colors (or groups of three or four) will blend when printed. If you click any of the color swatches, the Color Picker comes up and allows you to replace the color. The overprinted colors are applied to the image but only affect how the image appears on-screen. These settings do not affect how the image prints but provide a comparison chart to help you predict how colors will look when printed. When you look at the Overprint Colors dialog box be sure your monitor is calibrated.

FIGURE 9.8

The Overprint Colors dialog box.

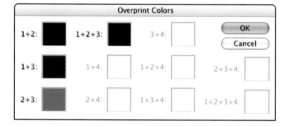

Summary

This chapter provided you with the information you need to create black and white images with proper tonal depth.

Specifically, I covered:

- Duotones, Tritones, and Quadtones
- Choosing duotone colors
- Adjusting duotone colors

Chapter 10 details the fun you can have when applying spot color. Learn fun techniques, such as creating knockouts and traps.

Chapter 10

Applying Spot Color

L et's say that your job is to produce 1,000 Christmas brochures printed in red and green ink. To print this job on an inkjet printer is inefficient because of the cost of ink cartridges that mix CMYK process colors to produce the red and green on the brochure. Two color jobs printed in any substantial quantity are most often printed on offset printing presses that impress *spot colors* onto paper.

As with duotones, spot colors use premixed inks. Spot colors are used for printing one, two, and three color jobs where full color is not required or not affordable. Spot colors are also used when a very specific color is required or the color is outside the range of the CMYK gamut because spot color can extend the range CMYK to bump a particular color or to build a vibrant solid color. In Photoshop, spot colors are channel-based. Because they are often applied as solid colors they need to be overlapped or *trapped* when two or more spot colors butt up against each other. This chapter covers all you need know to work with spot colors: how to choose them, how to view them, and how to prepare them for printing.

Working with Spot Color Channels

Spot colors are supported by all the color modes except Bitmap, yet they are independent and do not appear as part of the composite channel. Spot Color channels exist only in the Channels palette. They are also independent of layers. By default, they print separately from the color channels when printed to separations.

In the Channels palette, the Spot Color channels appear just below the color channels. In a grayscale image, the first Spot Color channel is under the gray channel. In an RGB image, it's below the Blue channel. Spot Color channels cannot be repositioned above the color channels unless the image is converted to Multichannel mode. Likewise, alpha channels are under the Spot Color channels in the stacking order. As with Duotone mode, Spot Color channels print in the order in which they're listed in the Channels palette.

CROSS-REF   To learn more about the various color modes and models that Photoshop supports, see Chapter 3.

There a few alternatives for applying spot colors. You can overlay them on top of an image so that they mix with the underlying color or you can apply them to a *knocked out* area of an image. Spot Color channels can either be applied as a solid color, a tint, or a tonal image.

The following step-by-step list demonstrates how a spot color can be overlaid on an image.

1. **Open an image.** In this example, the image I am using is a grayscale image, but you can also use an image in RGB, CMYK, Duotone, Indexed, or LAB mode.
2. **Choose Window ➪ Channels** to display the Channels palette.
3. **Make a selection** with any of the selection tools (see Figure 10.1).
4. **Click the Channels Palette Options menu** in the upper right corner of the Channels palette. Choose New Spot Channel. The New Spot Channel dialog box, shown in Figure 10.2 appears, and your selection fills with red, the default spot color.

FIGURE 10.1

Make a selection of the area where you want to apply spot color and display the Channels palette.

FIGURE 10.2

The New Spot Channel dialog box.

5. Click the color swatch to display the Color Picker. Click the Color Libraries button and choose a premixed ink, such as PANTONE color (see Figure 10.3). The Spot Color channel is named with the name of the selected Ink and appears as a colored area overlayed on top of the image (see Figure 10.4).

FIGURE 10.3

The Color Libraries dialog box.

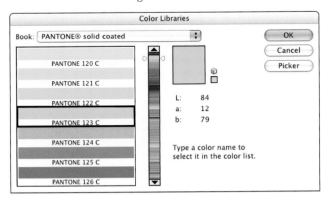

6. Choose a Solidity percentage and Click OK.

FIGURE 10.4

The new spot channel named with the color will appear in the Channels palette (left) and the image will display the spot color overlay (right).

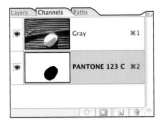 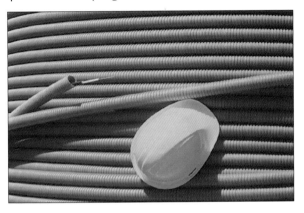

Differentiating between Solidity and Opacity

The Solidity control in the dialog box is a visual reference. Its purpose is to help you visualize what an ink might look like when printed. You can specify a tint value from 0% to 100%. The Solidity box lets you view the color density of the Spot Color channel but it does not affect the image.

Don't confuse solidity with opacity. Opacity affects the amount of color applied to an image with the paint tools, or the transparency of an image on a layer. Solidity is a visual reference that does not affect the channel itself (see Figure 10.4). If, however, you merge the spot colors with the other color channels by choosing Merge Spot Channels from the Channel Palette Options menu, the tint value of the color is applied to the image. The color is integrated into the composite channel and loses its status as a spot color.

If you want the spot color ink to print as a tint, you have to configure the spot color as a gray instead of a black value. Spot color inks always print full intensity unless your selection mask in the Spot Color channel itself contains a gradation or tint.

Here is how to create a tint value for your spot color:

1. Open an image or create a new document where you want to apply the spot color.
2. Choose Window ➪ Channels to display the Channels palette.
3. Select an area of the image as shown in Figure 10.5. From the Channels Palette Options menu choose New Spot Color channel.

FIGURE 10.5

Select the area you want to tint.

4. From the Channels palette pull-down menu, choose New Spot Channel. The New Spot Channel dialog box appears and your selection fills with red, the default spot color.

5. Click the color swatch to display the Color Picker. Click the Color Libraries button and choose a premixed ink, such as PANTONE and click OK. The color appears in the Spot Color Channel dialog box (see Figure 10.6).

When the spot color is selected, the swatch displays it. You can enter a solidity value to see the effect prior to clicking OK.

6. Choose a Solidity percentage to view the color as it will appear when printed as in Figure 10.7. Click OK. The area displays the tint value of the color, but prints with 100% of the color.

7. Press your D key to restore the foreground and background colors to the default black and white and click the foreground color to display the Color Picker. Enter a percentage value in the brightness textbox. Click OK.

Click OK and the area has the appearance of the tint value of the color.

221

8. Click the spot channel. Drag it to the New Selection to load it as a selection. Press Opt/Alt + Delete/Backspace to fill the selection on the spot channel with the gray value specified in the Color Picker. The color on the image becomes lighter as the tint value is applied.

Viewing Spot Colors

To view or conceal the spot color on the image, click the Visibility icon in the Channels palette. If you're viewing the composite image, and your spot channel is targeted in the Channels palette, the foreground color becomes black, white, or gray depending on the tint value of the spot color and the background color becomes white. You can edit a Spot Color channel exactly as you do an alpha channel by using the painting tools, selection tools, filters, type, or any other Photoshop operation placed artwork, to impose the image you want to print.

Special rules apply to type in Spot Color channels. Type behaves in spot channels as it does with the Type Mask tool. In other words, when you apply type to a Spot Color channel, the text shows up as a selection outline on the channel (see Chapter 19 for more on type masks).

Creating Knockouts and Traps

If you don't want your spot color to overprint over a part of the underlying image, you can create a *knockout*. A knockout removes part of the image so the spot color can print directly on the white paper. The color can then appear at full intensity. If you do decide to knock out the image you'll need to create a *trap*. Traps are created by slightly reducing or enlarging the selection outline to allow a small outline of both inks to overprint. Trapping prevents white space between two colors due to the printing press wobbling during printing.

Knocking out and trapping solid colors

Lighter-colored inks are usually *spread*, meaning that the knockout hole stays the same size, while the original spot color shape that prints over the hole is expanded slightly. Darker inks *choke*, meaning that the spot color shape stays the same size, while the knockout hole is contracted slightly to form the trap. Here's how to do it:

1. Select an area on an image. Make a Spot Color channel as shown in Figure 10.8.
2. In the Channels palette, click the Spot Color channel. Drag the Spot Color channel to the Load Selection icon in the Channels palette to select it.

FIGURE 10.8

Select an area on the image and make a Spot Color channel.

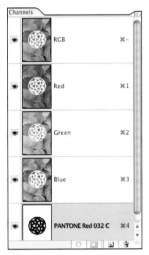

3. Choose Select ➪ Modify ➪ Contract to adjust the fit of the knockout. Enter a value of 1px in the Contract dialog box and click OK (see Figure 10.9).

4. Target the Composite channel. Target the background layer in the Layers palette.

CAUTION If the image is layered, target the layer with the portion of the image that you want to knock out. If the layer's content is overlayed on content on the background layer you need to knock out both the target layer and the background.

5. Press the D key to set the foreground and background colors to black and white.

6. Press your Delete key to eliminate the image content on the background (see Figure 10.10). The Spot Color channel overlaps the edge of the image content on the background layer as shown in Figure 10.10.

FIGURE 10.9

The Contract Selection dialog box.

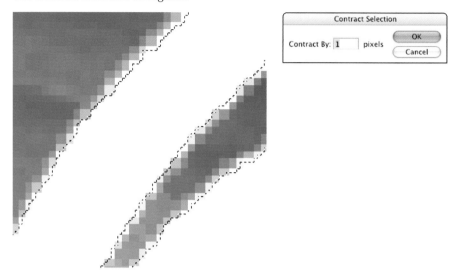

FIGURE 10.10

The Spot Color channel superimposed over the knockout (left). A close-up of the trap. The two colors overlap by one pixel (right).

 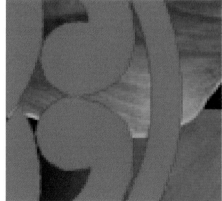

Creating tonal Spot Color channels

You can select a portion of the image, copy it and then make it into a spot color using its tonal qualities. To create a spot color from a tonal area on the image, follow these steps:

1. Open an image.

2. Choose the Magic Wand tool. In the Options bar, deselect the Contiguous checkbox. Click areas outside the element to select the surrounding area. Choose Select ➪ Inverse to inverse the selection, as shown in Figure 10.11.

3. Choose Edit ➪ Copy or press ⌘/Ctrl+C to copy the content of the selection to the clipboard.

FIGURE 10.11

The original image is selected and copied to the Clipboard.

4. From the Channels Palette Options menu, choose New Spot Channel. In the dialog box, click the swatch and choose Pantone color from the Color Libraries. Click OK twice and a new Spot Color channel is created. The Pantone color is overlaid onto the image as in Figure 10.12.

5. In the Channels palette, drag the Spot Color channel to the Load Channel icon to select it.

6. Make sure that the Spot Color channel is the target channel. Choose Edit ➪ Paste Into to paste the contents of the Clipboard into the selection. The solid area is now filled with the tonal area of the image, and the Spot Color channel is tonal rather than solid as shown in Figure 10.13.

FIGURE 10.12

The Spot Color channel (left) overlays the Pantone color on top of the image (right).

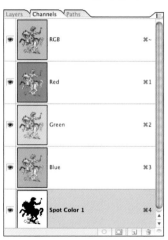

FIGURE 10.13

The Spot Color channel has become tonal (left). The area that was a solid Pantone color is now filled with a tonal image (right).

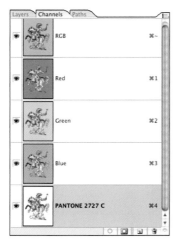

7. Now you can create the trap and the knockout. Click the composite RGB channel.

8. Drag the Spot channel to load it as a selection, as shown in Figure 10.14.

9. Choose Select ➪ Modify ➪ Contract. In the Contract dialog box, enter a value of 1 pixel.

10. Press D to set the default black and white for the foreground and background colors. Press your Delete key to create the knockout. Deselect. The tonal spot color is superimposed over the knocked out area with the edges trapped (see Figure 10.15).

FIGURE 10.14

The Spot Color channel loaded as a selection.

FIGURE 10.15

The final spot colored and trapped image appears in a solid Pantone color.

Printing Spot Colors

As with printing duotones, spot colors present their own set of problems. Here are a few things to consider when using spot colors:

- Many of the colors in the Color Libraries are often not accurately displayed on the monitor, so you should purchase a color book (such as a PANTONE book) with the actual ink colors printed on paper stock to be able to see the color as it is printed.

- You can save spot colors in PSD, TIF, EPS, PDF, or DCS2 formats. If you plan on importing an image with Spot Color channels into a layout or illustration program, you must save it in Photoshop's DCS 2.0 format. This is the only format that allows other applications to recognize the individual Spot Color channels.

- Spot color jobs are difficult to proof. Most color proofers convert images to CMYK when printing; PANTONE ink colors are converted to CMYK equivalents. When you print a job with spot colors on your inkjet or color laser printer, a composite is printed. When you print to separations the Spot Color channel is printed out separately along with the other ink colors.

- If you want a composite CMYK proof of the spot color image, always duplicate the file first. Print the duplicate image to your inkjet or other proofing device and print the separations to an imagesetter or laser printer from the spot color original.

Summary

Using spot color may be a good option for you; it's usually more affordable and often a good choice for many projects. In this chapter I covered:

- Working with spot color
- Viewing spot colors
- Creating knockouts and traps
- Printing spot colors

Now that you have an understanding of basic color techniques, you can move on to Part III in which I cover more advanced color techniques.

Part IV

Color Channel Pyrotechnics

Chapter 11

Working with Lab Color

An image's color mode ultimately affects its appearance. In Photoshop, you can choose a specific color system or mode that organizes the color information. RGB Color Color, CMYK Color, Lab Color, and Grayscale are common choices and are used to achieve specific output results. Each mode has a system of color channels with specific characteristics. An image that has been converted to Lab Color is unique in that it provides access to color information that is unavailable in the other modes.

You may have avoided this color system simply because it seems mysterious with its three channels, cryptically named with letters and its peculiar system of positive and negative numbers. In this chapter, I attempt to demystify Photoshop's most powerful color mode.

Understanding Lab Color

Lab Color is *device independent* — sort of. It is independent of the kind of information that peripheral devices, such as monitors, scanners, and digital cameras use to describe color. But in fact, it is directly related to the most perfect optical device of all — the human eye. Lab Color is used to describe the complete range of colors that humans can see.

The three color channels in Lab images divide the information into an L channel, which contains brightness information and two color channels — *a* and *b* (see Figure 11.1).

- The L channel has 100 possible values from 0, which indicates, black to 100, which equals white.

- The *a* channel is composed of magenta and green. Negative values which range from 128 to -1 indicate green and positive values between 0 and 127 indicate magenta.

- The *b* channel is composed of yellow and blue. Negative values between -128 and -1 indicate blue and positive values between 0 and 127 indicate yellow.

CROSS-REF **Chapter 3 explains the characteristics of all the color modes including Lab Color.**

Having access to the lightness information separate from the color information enables you to control each independently. With the creative use of these channels, you can take your images to a whole new level.

FIGURE 11.1

The channels of a Lab image consist of a Lightness channel, two color channels, and the Composite channel.

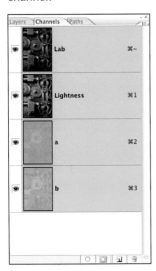

Sharpening Images with Lab

You know the importance of sharpening images before you print them. Sharpening can enhance the illusion of focus by increasing edge contrast. But sometimes sharpening at the necessary levels to make the image pop can produce auras around the edges and even worse, severely shift colors especially when applied to an RGB image. If you sharpen in Lab mode you can achieve better results and avoid color shifts because you target the contrast in only the brightness values and leave the color information untouched.

> **NOTE** Sharpening images can really improve their appearance. You can sharpen images in Lab mode as described here, but you can also sharpen images in RGB or other color modes. Chapter 12 offers a thorough explanation of sharpening.

High radius Lab sharpening

As with RGB mode, Lab mode separates the image data into three channels. In RGB, however, the Red, Green, and Blue channels each contain 256 brightness levels. In Lab mode, there are 100 brightness levels all contained in the L channel. Targeting the L channel focuses the sharpening where it does the most good, in the brightness information leaving the colors untouched and the image unchanged by color shifts and halos.

You can experiment with a sharpening technique called *hiraloam,* which works particularly well on Lab images. This technique applies high radius, low amount values.

A common mistake when sharpening is to view the image larger than actual size on-screen and therefore misjudge the amount of sharpening required. For best results choose Actual Pixels from the View menu to see the on-screen image at 100%. Because sharpening can drastically affect the images quality, make a copy of it first.

To sharpen an image, follow these steps:

1. Choose Image ⇨ Duplicate to make a copy of your image.
2. Choose Layer ⇨ Flatten Image.
3. Choose Image ⇨ Mode ⇨ Lab Color to convert the image to Lab mode.

> **NOTE** There is no appreciable loss of color information in this conversion as there is when you convert from RGB to CMYK.

4. Choose Window ⇨ Channels. Click on the Lightness channel to target it.
5. Click the visibility icon next to the composite Lab channel in the Channels palette so that the full-color image is visible in the Image window (see Figure 11.2).
6. Choose Filter ⇨ Sharpen ⇨ Unsharp Mask.
7. Drag the Amount slider to less than 100%.
8. Drag the Radius slider until the image begins to look a little too sharp.
9. Drag the Threshold slider enough to reduce artifacts and noise but not too much to cancel the affect of Amount and Radius (see Figure 11.3).
10. Click OK. Figure 11.4 shows the results.

FIGURE 11.2

The Channels palette with the Lightness channel targeted and the composite channel visible.

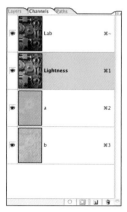

FIGURE 11.3

The Unsharp Mask dialog box with the hiraloam settings.

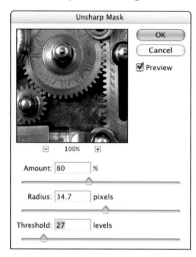

FIGURE 11.4

Sharpening the Lightness channel avoids color shifts.

Two pass Lab sharpening

As in the hiraloam technique, you apply the sharpening to the luminance only. But with this technique you're going to focus the sharpening on the edges only by making a *luminance mask*, and then applying a sharpening filter twice. This technique works best on high-resolution images that are 300 ppi or greater. The Amount and Radius settings will vary depending on the specific resolution of the image.

1. Open an image that you want to sharpen (see Figure 11.5).

2. Convert the Image to Lab mode by choosing Image ⇨ Mode ⇨ Lab Color.

3. Drag the Lightness channel to the Load Selection icon in the Channels palette to create the luminance mask, as shown in Figure 11.6.

4. Choose Select ⇨ Inverse to inverse the selection or press Shift-⌘/Ctrl-I.

5. Press ⌘/Ctrl+H to conceal the selection edges to better observe the effect.

6. In the Channels palette, target the Lightness channel. Sharpening the Lightness channel will avoid color shifts.

FIGURE 11.5

The image converted to Lab Color mode.

FIGURE 11.6

Load the Lightness channel and inverse it to create a luminance mask.

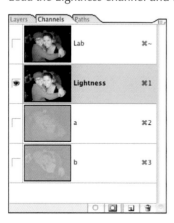 

7. Choose Image ➪ Sharpen ➪ Unsharp Mask. Type 500% for the amount and 1 pixel for the radius. Set the Threshold to 2 Levels. Click OK.

8. Reopen the Unsharp Mask filter. For the second pass, leave the amount at 500%. Drag the Radius slider all the way to the left and then slowly drag to the right until the shapes of the image become well defined. Drag the slider somewhere between 15 and 30 pixels.

FIGURE 11.7

The Unsharp Mask dialog box with the settings for the first pass.

9. Drag the Amount slider to between 50% and 60% whichever looks best. Then click OK.
10. In the Channels palette, click the Lab channel to see the results (see Figure 11.8).

FIGURE 11.8

The two pass sharpened image.

Making Colors Pop

Because color channels are separate from the Lightness channel, they can be targeted. Their colors can be strengthened and contrast can be enhanced without blowing out highlights or filling shadows. Color enhancement techniques are the stock and trade of Lab Color and are easy to perform without a great deal of experience even though they use Photoshop's three most enigmatic color enhancement features—Apply Image, Blending Options, and Curves. You can achieve astounding results in augmenting detail and creating vibrant color relationships that are difficult to attain in RGB or CMYK color modes.

Using the Apply Image technique

This technique is often used to enhance detail and definition on landscapes that are flat and whose color is lackluster, although you can try it on any color photograph. It involves applying color information to the Lightness channel with a blending mode and then modifying the image with Blending Options. You can use key commands to toggle form one channel to another as you apply the technique.

Follow these steps to use the Apply Image technique:

1. Open an image. Choose Image ⇨ Mode ⇨ Lab Color to the convert it to Lab Color mode (see Figure 11.9).

FIGURE 11.9

The original image converted to Lab mode.

2. Press ⌘/Ctrl+j to duplicate the background layer.

3. Press ⌘/Ctrl+1 to target the Lightness channel. Click on the eye next to the Lab channel so that the color image appears in the Image window (see Figure 11.10).

FIGURE 11.10

Click on the Lightness channel to target it. Display the Lab channel in the Image window.

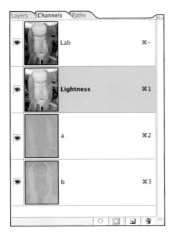

4. To enhance the contrast, Choose Image ➪ Apply Image. In the dialog box in the Channels pop-up menu, choose the *a* channel. Change the blending mode to Overlay and click OK (see Figure 11.11).

FIGURE 11.11

The *a* channel applied to the Lightness channel with the Overlay Blending mode.

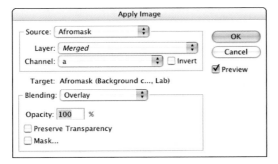

5. In the Channels palette, click the *a* channel to target it (see Figure 11.12). Choose Apply Image again. The *a* channel is automatically selected. Keep Overlay as the blending mode and click OK.

FIGURE 11.12

Target the a channel.

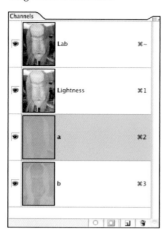

---

6. Click on the *b* channel. Choose Apply Image one more time. The *b* channel is automatically selected. Keep Overlay as the blending mode and click OK (see Figure 11.13).

FIGURE 11.13

The *b* channel applied with the Overlay Blending mode.

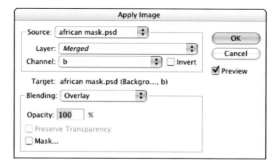

---

7. The colors really pop and the detail and contrast have been improved but they might be a little too strong, as in Figure 11.14. You can ease them off a bit with the Blend If feature.

FIGURE 11.14

The image's colors are richer and more interesting.

8. In the Channels palette, click the Lab channel. In the Layers palette Layer 1 should still be targeted. Double-click Layer 1 to display the Layer Styles dialog box. In the Blend If pop-up menu choose the *a* channel. Drag the This Layer (white) slider to the left to blend the magenta hues on the Background layer with the colors on Layer 1. When you get close to the center point release the mouse. Press Opt/Alt and drag the right half of the slider to the right to create smoother the transitions and then click OK. The result is shown in Figure 11.15.

FIGURE 11.15

The Blend If feature in the Layer Styles dialog box blend the colors of two consecutive layers resulting in a well-balanced image with colors that "pop."

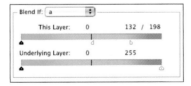

NOTE The Blend If sliders applied to the *a* channel blend green if you drag them to the left and magenta if you drag them to the right. The Blend if sliders applied to the b channel blend blue (left) and yellow (right).The Blend If sliders applied to the Lightness channel blend shadows (left) and highlights (right). If you Option/Alt drag a slider in any direction the layers blend with smoother transitions.

Applying the Curves technique

This technique involves steepening the curves on the *a* and *b* channels. It is a simple technique and even if you are new to curves you should have no trouble producing excellent results.

1. Open an RGB image whose colors seem a bit lackluster (see Figure 11.16).

FIGURE 11.16

The original uncorrected image looks a bit lackluster.

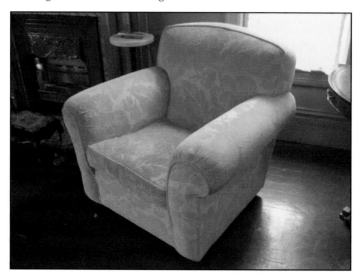

2. Choose Image ➪ Mode ➪ Lab Color to convert the image to Lab mode.
3. Choose Image ➪ Adjustments ➪ Curves.
4. Press the Option/Alt key and click on the grid to display a 100 cell grid.
5. In the Channels pop-up menu choose the *a* channel.
6. Click the top-right corner point and drag it two cells to the left (see Figure 11.17). This produces a cyan cast on the image.
7. Click the bottom-left corner point and drag it two cells to the right. The colors should start to look more vibrant.

FIGURE 11.17

Steepen the curves by dragging their end points inward two cells.

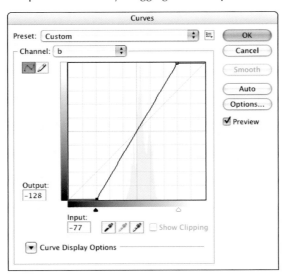

8. Choose the *b* channel from the pop-up menu and repeat Steps 8 and 9. The colors in the image will "pop" and produce an image that is richer and more vibrant without looking unnatural (see Figure 11.18).

FIGURE 11.18

The corrected image's color is more vibrant.

Adding Noise to Lab Color Images

You can create some very nice impressionist effects with Lab Color. With this technique you convert the Lightness channel into what looks like an ink drawing and add noise to it. The image is partially restored by pasting through a semitransparent mask. You can control the effect to a degree by varying the amount of noise. The effect changes the color relationships to produce a grainy pastel such as image that has a lot of graphic appeal.

Follow these steps to add noise:

1. Open an RGB image. Choose Image ➪ Mode ➪ Lab Color to convert the image to Lab mode (see Figure 11.19).

FIGURE 11.19

The original image is converted to Lab mode.

2. Press ⌘/Ctrl+A to select the image and then Cmnd/Cntrl-C to copy it to the Clipboard.
3. In the Channels palette, click on the Lightness channel and drag it to the New Channel icon to make a copy of it (see Figure 11.20).
4. With the copy of the Lightness channel active choose Image ➪ Adjustments ➪ Brightness and Contrast. Click and drag the Contrast slider to the left to -50 to decrease the contrast.
5. Click the Lightness channel. Choose Filter ➪ Stylize ➪ Find Edges to make the edges of the channel distinct as in Figure 11.21.

FIGURE 11.20

Make a copy of the Lightness channel

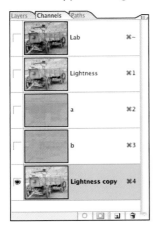

FIGURE 11.21

Apply the Find Edges filter to the Lightness channel.

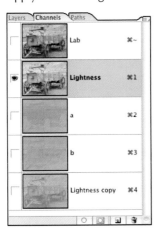

6. Choose Filter ➪ Noise ➪ Add Noise. Enter an amount. The higher the resolution the more noise will be needed. For distribution click the Uniform radio button (see Figure 11.22).

7. Choose Image ➪ Adjustments ➪ Invert, or press ⌘/Ctrl+I to invert the image.

8. Press ⌘/Ctrl+F to apply the noise filter again.

FIGURE 11.22

Add Noise to the Lightness channel. Invert it and add noise again and then reinvert it.

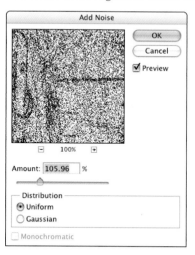

9. Press ⌘/Ctrl+I again to reinvert the Lightness channel.

10. In the Channels palette click the Lab channel. Drag the Lightness copy to the Load Channel as Selection icon to activate the channel as a selection as shown in Figure 11.23.

11. Choose Edit ⇨ Paste Into to partially restore the original image (see Figure 11.24).

FIGURE 11.23

Load the Lightness channel copy to make a selection.

FIGURE 11.24

Paste the contents of the Clipboard through the selection to partially restore the image.

Reducing Noise

Lab Color techniques can achieve amazing results when reducing noise. Of course, some noise can be beneficial in softening gradients and smoothing hard edges. Excessive noise, however, can make the image look grainy, jagged, or distressed. Excessive noise frequently appears in under-exposed images taken in low light. It can be present in sports photographs that have been snapped at a fast shutter speed. It is ever present in scanned prescreened photographs such as images scanned from magazines and it can appear in older photographs whose emulsion has deteriorated.

Noise reduction should be performed early in the editing process, just as sharpening should be applied as a final step. Depending on the image, noise reduction is usually performed with one of the blur filters. Converting the image to Lab Color first and targeting the a and b channels can achieve surprisingly good results. Again, the image should be viewed in actual pixels when reducing noise.

To reduce noise, follow these steps:

1. This image was shot in very low light and there is considerable noise (see Figure 11.25).
2. Choose Image ➪ Adjustments Levels. Drag the white slider to the left to increase the brightness of the image. This operation also makes the noise more visible as in Figure 11.26.
3. Choose Image ➪ Mode ➪ Lab Color to it convert to Lab mode.
4. Click the visibility icon next to the composite Lab channel in the Channels palette so that the full-color image is visible in the Image window.

249

FIGURE 11.25

The original uncorrected image is dark and has considerable noise.

FIGURE 11.26

The image is brightened with a Levels adjustment which increases the visibility of the noise.

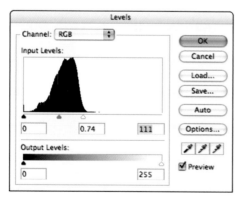

5. Choose Filter ⇨ Noise ⇨ Reduce Noise. Click the Advanced radio button. Click on the Per Channel tab. The b channel is composed of blue and yellow and that's where most of the noise usually is. Choose the b channel from the channels pop-up menu (see Figure 11.27).

FIGURE 11.27

FIGURE 11.27

The Reduce Noise filter dialog box and the resulting image.

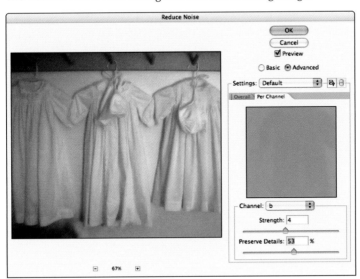

6. Observe the preview window. Adjust the Strength until the noise disappears. Adjust the Preserve Details slider until any lost detail is restored.

7. If necessary, repeat the process with the *a* channel targeted.

8. You can also apply the filter in moderation to the L channel but be careful not to blur the details. Although this process rarely filters out all noise, it certainly produces a vast improvement over hard to fix images such as this one.

Black and White to Color in Lab

This technique is an unusual approach to coloring a black and white image, to say the least. It requires the Channels palette and three tools from the same flyout: the Dodge, Burn, and Saturate tools. It is a good exercise in how Lab Color can vary on each channel. Painting with the Dodge and Burn tools directly on the a channel, which contains magenta and green and the b channel which, contains cyan and yellow can produce all the hues. Working the L channel with the dodge and burn tools will control the darkness or lightness of all the colors. And applying the Sponge tool to the Composite channel will saturate or desaturate the colors. Modifying the exposure of the Dodge and Burn tools or the Flow of the Sponge tool precisely controls the intensity of the effect.

Table 11.1 lists the affect these tools have on the various channels.

TABLE 11.1

Effect of Dodge Burn and Sponge Tool on Lab Channels

Tool	Channel	Result
Dodge	a	Changes colors towards magenta
Dodge	b	Changes colors towards yellow
Dodge	L	Lightens values
Dodge	Lab	Lightens values
Burn	a	Changes colors towards green
Burn	b	Changes colors towards blue
Burn	L	Darkens values
Burn	Lab	Darkens values
Sponge	a	No effect
Sponge	a	No effect
Sponge	a	No effect
Sponge	b	No effect
Sponge	L	No effect
Sponge	Lab	Saturates/Desaturates

The advantage of this technique is its directness. You work directly on the image with manual tools to produce colorful if not slightly unnatural results. This example shows how the technique works on a portrait. I recommend that you set the exposure (in the Dodge and Burn Options bar) or Sponge tool flow to relatively low values and make multiple passes for more control.

To convert an image, follow these steps:

1. Start by opening a grayscale image (see Figure 11.28).

2. Convert the image to Lab mode. The a and b channels will be consistently 50% gray or have Lab values of 0.

3. Click on the "a" channel in the Channels palette to target it. Click on the visibility icon of the Composite channel to display the image in the Image window (see Figure 11.29).

4. Choose the Dodge tool from the Tools palette. In the Options bar set the Exposure to 15% and the Range to Midtones.

NOTE   When using the Dodge, Burn, or Sponge tools, tools set the range to Highlights if you are working on light areas, Midtones for medium areas, or Shadows for dark areas.

FIGURE 11.28

The original grayscale image.

FIGURE 11.29

Target the a channel and click the visibility icon next to the Lab channel.

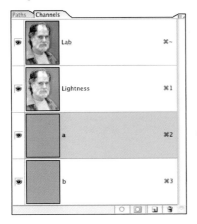

5. Choose a soft brush from the Brushes palette. Click and drag over the face with the brush. You can see the gray shift toward magenta as in Figure 11.30.

FIGURE 11.30

Dodging on the a channel with the Dodge tool produces magenta.

6. Click on the b channel to paint over the face again. As you add yellow to the face the flesh tones start to emerge (see Figure 11.31).

FIGURE 11.31

Painting on the b channel with the Dodge tool adds yellow to magenta to produce a flesh tone.

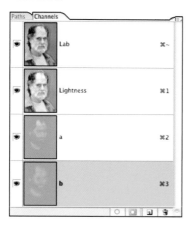

7. To paint blue click on the b channel. Choose the Burn tool from the Tools palette. Set the Exposure to 15% and drag on the image. Make multiple passes until you achieve the hue you want. If there is an area you want to paint green, choose the Burn tool and paint on the a channel. If the color becomes too bright, dilute it by painting on the area with the Dodge tool as in Figure 11.32.

FIGURE 11.32

Burning the *b* channel produces blue, burning the *A* channel produces green.

8. Target the Lab channel. Choose the Sponge tool from the Tools palette. In the Options bar, choose Saturate and set the flow to 15%. Drag over the areas you want to intensify. Choose Desaturate to tone down areas.

9. Target the L channel. With the Dodge tool, drag over the areas you would like to lighten or with the Burn tool, drag over the areas that you would like to darken.

10. If you want to smooth out the colors, click the *a* channel to target it and display the composite in the Image window. Choose Filter ➪ Blur Gaussian blur. Drag the radius slider while observing the image, then click OK. Repeat the process with the b channel.

This technique produces rich if not a slightly unnatural color as in Figure 11.33.

FIGURE 11.33

The final colored image.

Summary

In this chapter, I tried to ease you in to using Lab Color mode. Although perceived as a bit more complicated, you can access color information in Lab Color mode that's not available when using other modes.

In this chapter, I covered topics including:

- Understanding Lab Color mode
- Sharpening images
- Adding noise
- Lab colorizing

Chapter 11 shows you how to enhance even the smallest details. You'll find out some great techniques for working with flesh tones.

Chapter 12

Enhancing Details with Channels

Pay attention to the details and everything will fall into place so says the adage. Image detail can make or break a photograph. Photoshop has the ability to enhance what the camera captured by modifying color and contrast. Areas can be sharpened to enhance edge detail and colors can be blended to produce more saturation. Sharpening techniques can refine edges and blurring can reduce noise. Details from a source channel can be superimposed on an image with great precision.

With a few simple adjustments you can also enhance flesh tones and other colors that give the image more color depth and add interest. You can also create lighting effects that can add drama to an otherwise ordinary image.

In this chapter, I discuss how to get the most detail from your images and present a few simple tricks that can make a big difference.

Enhancing Flesh Tones

You can add detail and contrast to portraits with color channel manipulations. This technique focuses on enhancing flesh tones while maintaining color balance and saturation, but you can use variations of it on any image. You use the information from the channel with the most detail to modify the other channels. Normally the Green channel is the source channel for an image with fleshtones but occasionally it might be one of the others. On images without fleshtones, the most detail can be found on any of the color channels.

1. Open a full color portrait. The portrait should be in RGB color mode.
2. Choose Window ➪ Channels to display the Channels palette (see Figure 12.1).

FIGURE 12.1

The original image could use more detail in the fleshtones.

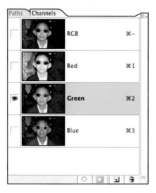

3. Click the individual channels to display each one in the Image window. Look for the channel that holds the most detail. In this case it's the Green channel (see Figure 12.2).

FIGURE 12.2

The Green channel usually contains most of the color information.

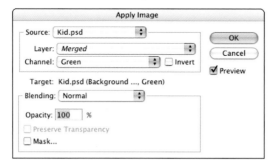

4. Display the Layers palette. Drag the Background layer to the new layer icon to duplicate it. Then open the Channels palette and click the RGB channel.
5. Choose Image ➪ Apply Image. Choose the Green channels from the Channels pop-up menu.

6. The default blending mode is Multiply, change it to Normal and click OK. The full color layer is replaced by the Green channel and it is now a black and white image (see Figure 12.3).

FIGURE 12.3

Apply Image applies the Green channel to the target layer.

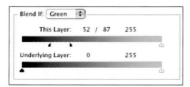

7. Choose Luminosity from the Blend options in the Layers palette to blend the detailed color information from the Green channel with the full-color background layer.

8. Sometimes this technique can adversely affect other areas of the image. If areas become too dark or if color shifts, you can correct this problem by blending the two layers. Double-click the Background copy layer to display the Layer Styles dialog box.

9. Choose Green from the Blend If pop-up menu.

10. Click and drag the This Layer black slider to the right until the original portions of the image reappear. Then press the Option/Alt key and drag the right half of the slider to the left to smooth the transitions (see Figure 12.4).

FIGURE 12.4

Blending options correct the effect in unwanted areas.

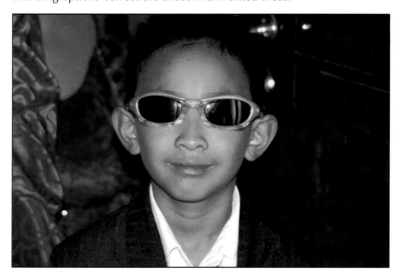

Sharpening Your Image

Sharpening can be the crucial factor that gives your picture that extra edge. We looked at sharpening Lab images in the last chapter. RGB, grayscale, and CMYK images can also be sharpened with Photoshop's extensive sharpening features.

Actually, sharpening techniques don't affect the actual focus of an image. If an image is out of focus or soft for example, there is really no way to refocus it after it is has been scanned into the computer. Instead most sharpening techniques change the adjacent edges of the areas of most contrast in the image to "fool the eye" into thinking the image is in focus. These techniques usually work if the image isn't too badly out of focus, and the focus of the content isn't critical.

The sharpening technique you choose is going to depend on a number of factors. Sharpening can improve or enhance almost any picture, from images that are blurred for camera movement, improper focal length, and poor depth of field. Photoshop offers several filters and a manual tool for sharpening: Sharpen, Sharpen Edges, Sharpen More, Unsharp Mask, and Smart Sharpen. The first three of these are fully automated — that is, the user has no control over their effect. When you click one of these, no dialog box appears. Photoshop simply applies the predefined effect of increasing contrast. Sharpening increases contrast overall; Sharpen More has a stronger effect; and Sharpen Edges focuses on the areas of highest contrast in an image.

The Sharpen tool is a manual version of these filters. Choose the tool, choose a brush, set the strength in the Options bar, and drag over the image to produce adjacent pixels of higher contrast.

Much more powerful than any of these are the Unsharp Mask and the Smart Sharpen filters letting you control the amount and quality of the effect.

Unsharpening to sharpen

Unsharp Mask gets its name from an old process photo technique of exposing an image through a blurred negative mask to increase edge contrast. This arcane bit of optical voodoo has been transformed into an incredibly useful enhancement tool by Photoshop's software designers. Its dialog box allows for minute adjustments and extraordinary control. If the three automated Sharpen filters were discarded, Photoshop users would still have all the sharpening capability you would ever need with this one filter.

The Unsharp Mask dialog box (see Figure 12.5) appears when you choose Filter ⇨ Sharpen ⇨ Unsharp Mask. These options appear for your input:

- **Amount:** Dragging this slider or entering a value from 1% to 500%, you can determine how much sharpening will be applied. The higher the value, the more the image will be sharpened. Applying only an amount, however, will not sharpen the image. To see the effect, you must also specify a radius.

- **Radius:** Defines the thickness (from 0.1 to 250 pixels) of an edge. Lower values produce crisp, sharp edges, while higher values define edges as thicker and generate greater overall contrast throughout an image.

■ **Threshold:** Entering a value from 0 to 255 allows Unsharp Mask to determine what's considered an edge. The number indicates the difference in brightness values necessary to recognize an edge. Lower numbers include lots of pixels in the effect; the higher the number, the more exclusive the value. Threshold Values that are too high will dilute the effects of Radius and Amount.

FIGURE 12.5

The Unsharp Mask dialog box.

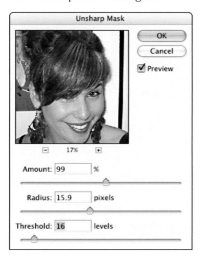

Unsharp masking techniques

The three sliders work together to do the job of heightening contrast and the illusion of focus. Experimentation and practice are necessary to discover the right combination of settings to achieve the desired effect but the following techniques can facilitate good results.

■ **Hiraloam:** Subtle effects can be produced by a low amount setting under 100% and a high radius setting. This is called the *hiraloam* technique.

■ **Repetition:** Sometimes repeated applications of a lower amount setting can produce better results than a single application at a higher setting.

■ **Threshold:** Raising the Threshold value has the effect of increasing the definition of an edge. In other words, higher values require more contrast between pixels to be recognized as an edge; lower values recognize edges between pixels with closer brightness values.

■ **Last Step:** Unsharp Masking is usually applied to a duplicate image that has been flattened as the last step to completing an image.

■ **Lightness Channel:** Application of too high settings can produce color shifts and halos in RGB images. To avoid these color aberrations apply the Unsharp Mask to the Lightness channel of a Lab image (see Chapter 11).

■ **Luminosity Layer:** To avoid color shifts on RGB images apply the Unsharp mask filter to a duplicate layer:

   1. In the Layers palette, drag the background layer to the New Layer icon to duplicate (see Figure 12.6).

   2. Choose Luminosity from the Blending Mode pop-up menu.

   3. Choose Filter ➪ Sharpen ➪ Unsharp Mask. Drag the Amount, Radius, and Threshold sliders to apply the affect and click OK.

FIGURE 12.6
_____

To avoid color shifts, assign a Luminosity Blending mode to a duplicate layer and sharpen it with the Unsharp Mask filter.

Smart sharpening

Smart sharpening presents a new level of control to image sharpening. The dialog box has a set of extensive controls that alter the amount of sharpening that affects in shadow and highlight areas in each color channel.

These are the controls you'll find in the Smart Sharpen dialog box:

■ The Amount slider controls the strength of the effect. A Higher values increases the contrast between edge pixels, creating the sharper focus.

■ The Radius slider determines the number of pixels surrounding the edge pixels that are sharpened. Larger radius values produce a thicker edge and more pronounced sharpening.

■ The Remove menu sets the type of sharpening:

   ▨ Gaussian Blur is similar to the Unsharp Mask filter.

   ▨ Lens Blur produces finer sharpening of detail and reduces halos.

   ▨ Motion Blur reduces the effects of the blur caused by camera or subject movement. Set an Angle if you choose Motion Blur to counteract the direction of the blur.

   ▨ Click the More Accurate checkbox to process the file for a more accurate blur.

To use the Smart Sharpen filter, follow these steps:

1. Open an image that is out of focus.
2. Choose Filter ➪ Sharpen ➪ Smart Sharpen.
3. Click the Preview box so that you can compare the results with the original image.
4. Click the Advanced button. You are presented with three tabs (see Figure 12.7).
5. In the Sharpen tab click and drag the Amount and Radius sliders (see Figure 12.8).

FIGURE 12.7

The Smart Sharpen dialog box showing the Sharpen tab.

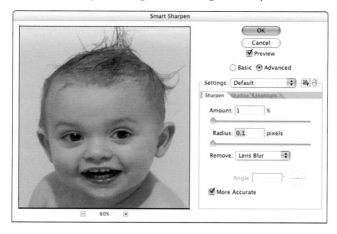

FIGURE 12.8

The Amount and Radius sliders sharpen the image.

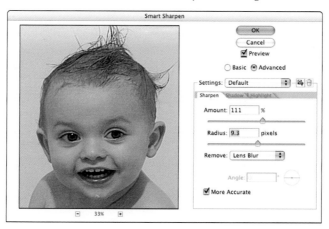

6. In the Shadow and Highlight tabs adjust the fade, tonal width, and the radius to refine and smooth the details of the sharpening and eliminate halos (see Figure 12.9).

7. Observe the effects of the filter in the preview box and when satisfied, click OK.

FIGURE 12.9

The highlight and shadow controls refine and smooth the details of the sharpening and eliminate halos.

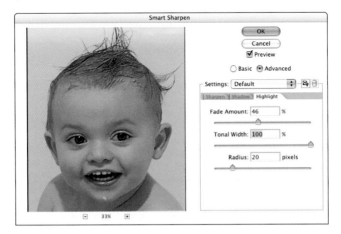

Using Lighting Effects

The Lighting Effects filter is an extensive interface with controls that can determine the source and quality of lighting. It has the amazing potential to radically transform the ambient light in an image. The Lighting Effects dialog box simulates the interplay of spotlights or floodlights over your image with a wide variety of options. Imagine that you're hanging lights in a museum, shining a flashlight into a dark cave, or driving down a wooded road at night. These and more lighting conditions can be replicated with the Lighting Effects filter.

Lighting controls

Choose Filter ➪ Render ➪ Lighting Effects. The Style menu at the top of the dialog box is preconfigured with lighting environments that can serve as a starting point for modification. The Light Type field has controls to create your own effects, which you can save to the Style list. Drag the Intensity and Focus sliders, and click on the color swatch to choose a color for the light. The properties sliders control the amount of Gloss (Matte or Shiny finish), Material (Plastic to Metallic), Exposure, and Ambience. Another color swatch lets you define the tint of the Ambience, which refers to ambient or overall lighting, separate from the spot or special lighting.

The Preview area displays an image of how the lighting variables chosen will be applied. If you choose Omni or Spotlight, you can drag the handles and change the distance and direction of the light. Clicking and dragging the Focus Spot at the end of the preview radius changes the angle of lighting. You can change the angle and distance of a Directional style but not the shape. The smaller the radius the brighter or more intense the light. As you increase the size of the radius, the light spreads out and dims accordingly. When you get an effect you like, click the Save button. Photoshop invites you to name your new lighting style, which will then appear in your Style menu.

We'll use the Lighting Effects filter to create a more dramatic environment in an image.

1. Open an RGB image (see Figure 12.10).

FIGURE 12.10

The original image.

2. Choose Filter ➪ Lighting Effects to display the dialog box (see Figure 12.11).
3. Choose a Style from the menu.
4. Choose a Light Type.
5. Click and drag the Properties sliders.
6. Click and drag the control points on the direction marquee manually to establish a light source. The preview box displays the results.
7. If you want multiple light sources, click and drag the light bulb icon onto the preview box.
8. Click OK to apply the filter to the image. The resulting image appears in Figure 12.12.

NOTE Lighting effects operate only on RGB images.

CAUTION Some of these effects require a long time to compute and render.

FIGURE 12.11

The Lighting Effects dialog box offers extensive controls to create specific lighting conditions.

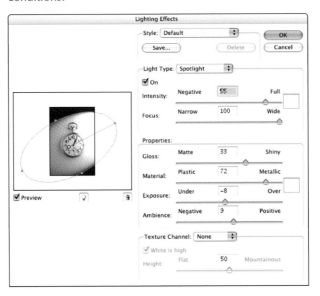

FIGURE 12.12

The original image and the image affected by the Lighting Effects filter.

Using a Texture channel

In the Texture Channel pop-up menu, you can choose a channel Red, Green, Blue, or an alpha channel that you've saved as a texture map. A texture map is a grayscale image that controls the mapping of light. The lightest areas become peaks and dark areas become valleys. To reverse the map, deselect the White Is High box. Drag the Height slider somewhere between Flat and Mountainous to control the intensity of the effect.

You can create interesting effects with type or shapes by superimposing a Texture channel to model the light.

We use the Lighting Effects filter with a Texture channel to create a three dimensional look to a shape for a Web graphic.

1. Open the image that you want to use as a graphic. The image should be divided into two layers with the graphic on the top-most layer and the background below it (see Figure 12.13).

FIGURE 12.13

The graphic is divided into two layers.

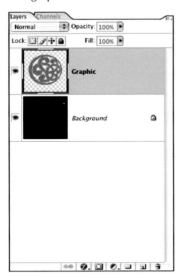

2. ⌘/Ctrl click on the Graphic Layer to select its contents.
3. In the Channels palette, click on the Save Selection as Channel icon to save it as an alpha channel (see Figure 12.14).

FIGURE 12.14

Make an alpha channel from the selection.

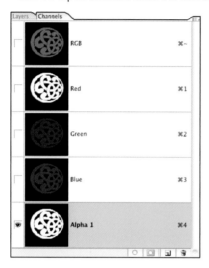

4. Click on the new channel. Press ⌘/Ctrl+I to invert it. Then Choose Filter ⇨ Blur ⇨ Gaussian Blur to blur the channel. Blur the image so that the edges are fuzzy but not enough to lose its shape. The higher the resolution the higher the value you'll need to specify (see Figure 12.15).

FIGURE 12.15

Invert and blur the alpha channel.

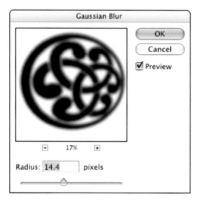

5. In the Channels palette, click the RGB channel and in the Layers palette target the Graphics layer.

6. Choose Filter ⇨ Lighting Effects to display the dialog box (see Figure 12.16).

FIGURE 12.16

Choose the Lighting Effects filter. Establish a light type and source, adjust settings, and apply the Texture channel.

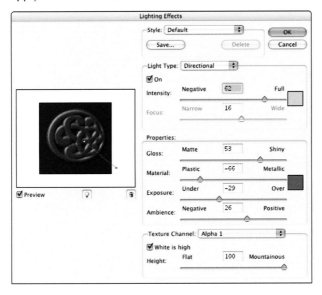

7. From the Texture channel pop-up menu, choose Alpha 1.

8. Set these specifications:

▨ Light Type: Try both Spot Light and Directional Click and drag the control points on the direction marquee manually to establish a light source. The preview box displays the results.

▨ Set the color for the light by clicking the swatch.

▨ Select the white High check box.

▨ Height: Mountainous

▨ Drag the source handle in the preview box to establish a direction for the light source.

▨ Experiment with different Properties settings.

9. Click OK to apply the filter to the image. The image appears in Figure 12.17.

FIGURE 12.17

The Texture channel produces a bold 3D effect.

Mapping Images with Channels

Similar to a Texture channel, a displacement map uses black and white on a saved channel to map topography into an image. You can make an absolutely flat image appear to conform to a three-dimensional surface while maintaining the detail of the surface. On a displacement map, black represents the valleys, white represents the peaks, and shades of gray produce variations of depth. In this step-by-step list, you map a texture to the surface of a face and with the use of channels and the Displacement Map filter you force the texture to conform perfectly to the face's contours.

1. Open a portrait. Choose the Lasso tool and outline a selection of the areas of the face as shown in Figure 12.18.

2. Choose Selection ⇨ Save Selection. When the dialog box appears, use the defaults and click OK and deselect.

3. Choose Window ⇨ Channels. Examine each color channel to determine which one has the most contrast between the subject and the background. In this case it's the Blue channel. Click the channel to display it in the Image window (see Figure 12.19).

FIGURE 12.18

Make an accurate selection of the face.

FIGURE 12.19

The Blue channel has the most contrast.

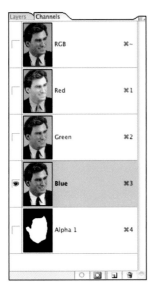

4. From the Channel Options menu choose Duplicate Channel to display the dialog box. Name the document *Displace Face*. In the Document pop-up menu choose New. This action creates an entirely new document from the channel that will be used as the displacement map (see Figure 12.20).

FIGURE 12.20

Duplicate the channel to a new document.

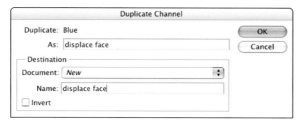

5. Click the Displace Face document. Choose Filter Gaussian Blur. To blur low-resolution documents (72 ppi) specify a 1 pixel radius. For high-resolution documents specify a 3 to 4 pixel radius (see Figure 12.21).

FIGURE 12.21

Blur the alpha channel.

6. Choose File ⇨ Save As to save the image. Save it in Photoshop (PSD) native format and close the document.

7. Click the original photo and the composite RGB channel.

8. Open the texture image that you want to map to the face. Press the V key to choose the Move tool. Drag the image and place it on the face image to create a new layer as shown in Figure 12.22.

Drag the texture image to the portrait. It will create a new layer.

9. Choose Filter ⇨ Distort ⇨ Displace. In the dialog box, leave the default settings except select Repeat Edge Pixels. Click OK. The Open dialog box appears.

10. Locate and choose the Displace Face image and click Open. The texture warps a little (see Figure 12.23).

11. Choose Select ⇨ Load Selection. From the Channels pop-up menu choose Alpha 1 and click OK.

12. Choose Select ⇨ Inverse.

13. Choose Select ⇨ Feather. For a low-resolution image feather the selection 2 pixels. for a high-resolution image feather the selection 5 or 6 pixels.

14. Press Delete/Backspace to omit all the texture outside of the facial area. Then Deselect (see Figure 12.24).

FIGURE 12.23

Apply the Displacement Filter and choose the saved document as Displacement Map.

FIGURE 12.24

Delete the areas outside the face.

15. In the Layers palette choose Multiply as the blend mode. Reduce the Opacity to 70%.

16. If you need to conceal parts of the texture such as in the areas within the eyes and teeth, choose Layer ⇨ Add Layer Mask ⇨ Reveal All. Choose an appropriate brush and black as a foreground color. Click the layer mask and paint on the image with black to conceal the texture from those areas (see Figure 12.25).

CROSS-REF Layer masks conceal, reveal, and control opacity in a specific region of the image. In-depth coverage of layer masks is found in Chapter 20.

17. To intensify the colors, drag the layer to the New Layer icon at the bottom of the Layers palette. Assign an Overlay blending mode and adjust opacity (see Figure 12.26).

FIGURE 12.25

Choose a blend mode and create a layer mask.

FIGURE 12.26

Duplicate the layer and change the blend mode to Overlay for more intense color.
Reduce Opacity if necessary.

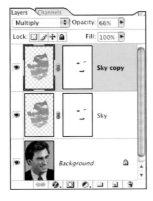

Summary

Enhance the details of your images by applying the techniques I covered in this chapter.

I discussed the following topics:

- Enhancing flesh tones
- Sharpening images
- Using lighting effects
- Mapping images

In Chapter 13, you find out how to reveal even more of your image by using light and shadows.

Chapter 13

Creating Light
and Shadows

The interplay of light and shadow is what gives images that extra dose of reality. To appear credible, composited images — images from multiple sources — frequently require that shadows be created separately. Photographs frequently need adjustment to balance light and shadow and to reveal as much detail as possible. The techniques covered in this chapter reveal how to create and manage shadow and light. There are a variety of techniques that can enhance an image by altering its dark and light extremes to impart depth and nuance. This chapter also covers methods to create realistic shadows in a variety of lighting conditions using channels and masks.

Creating Drop Shadows
with Layer Styles

Applying a Drop Shadow Layer Style is the easiest way to create a shadow from a composite image. In earlier versions of Photoshop, creating a simple drop shadow required extensive channel juggling. But the software engineers at Adobe saw fit to package this and other elaborate channel voodoo into a neat package called Layer Styles. This method works well if the shadow does not fall on multiple surfaces. It can be applied to any layer content including type layers to produce extra depth. The shadow, which is the shape of the layer content, is cast on the layer or layers below the target layer in the stack. The content of the layer must be surrounded by transparency. The Layer Styles dialog box (see Figure 13.1) controls the following features:

- **Blend Mode:** The color of the shadow will be affected by the pixels below it in the stack depending on the blending mode that you choose. Choose Normal to produce shadow that is the specified color.

- **Color:** Click the swatch to reveal the Color Picker. Choose a color for the drop shadow.

- **Opacity:** Click and drag the slider or enter a value to control the opacity of the shadow.

- **Angle:** Click and drag the indicator or enter a value for the angle of the shadow. You can also place your curser on the image and click and drag to manually establish an angle and distance for the shadow.

- **Use Global Light:** Select the check box to apply the current angle to all other layers with Layer Styles whose Global Angle box is checked.

- **Distance:** Click and drag the slider or enter a distance value between 0 and 30000 pixels. Or click and drag to manually establish a distance and angle for the shadow.

- **Spread:** The slider values between 0 and 100% increase or decrease the hardness of the shadow's edge. The lower the value the softer the edge of the shadow.

- **Size:** This slider increases the diameter of the shadow from 0, the actual size of the layer content, to 250 pixels.

- **Contour:** The contour affects the shape of the shadow and how it falls on the surface. Choose a contour preset from the list or from the Contour Preset Options menu choose New Contour to create your own in the Contour Editor (see Figure 13.2).

- **Anti-Alias:** Selecting this check box creates an anti-aliased contour.

- **Layer Knocks out Drop Shadow:** Selecting this check box changes the opacity of the shadow when the content's fill opacity is changed. If unselected, the content will become transparent but the shadow will remain at its current opacity when the Fill opacity is adjusted.

The Drop Shadow style in the Layer Styles dialog box is a convenient way to make an image element look more realistic. In the early versions of Photoshop a simple drop shadow was a labor-intensive channel juggling feat. But since the introduction of Layer styles Drop shadows are a breeze.

CAUTION   If you click on a layer style check box in the styles list in the Layer Styles dialog box, you will apply the default specifications to the layer. If you want to access the controls, click on the layer styles name, such as Drop Shadow for example, and then adjust the controls, for the desired look.

The Layer Style dialog box displaying the Drop Shadow controls.

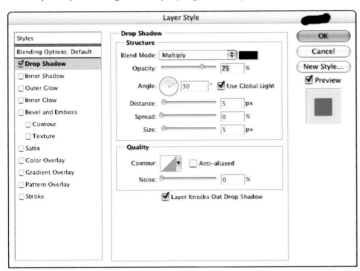

The Contour presets list.

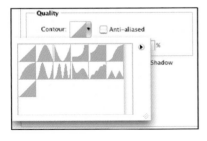

To apply a Drop shadow:

1. Target a layer in the Layers palette whose content is surrounded by transparency.

2. Choose Drop Shadow from the Add a Layer Style menu at the bottom of the Layers palette. (see Figure 13.3).

FIGURE 13.3

Choose Drop Shadow from the Add a Layer Style menu.

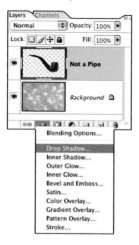

3. Set the specifications for the shadow and click OK. You can see a live preview in the Image window (see Figure 13.4).

FIGURE 13.4

Set the specifications and click OK.

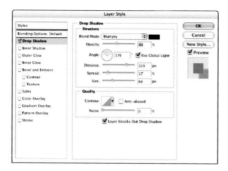
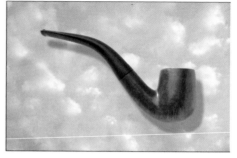

Creating Cast Shadows

Cast shadows present different problems than do drop shadows. A drop shadow is quite simply a gray, semitransparent, soft-edged duplicate of the layer content. Drop shadows can be readily applied with the Layer Styles dialog box. A cast shadow has similar qualities except that it is distorted by the direction of the light source and the terrain on which it rests. You can use the following technique to create a cast shadow.

1. Open the image that is composed a background on the bottommost layer and the content that is casting the shadow on a layer immediately above. This content should be surrounded by transparency, as shown in Figure 13.5.

FIGURE 13.5

The content of the object that is casting the shadow should be surrounded by transparency.

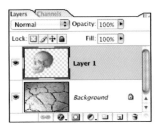

2. Drag the topmost layer to the New Layer icon to duplicate it. Double-click the new layer's name and type *Shadow*. Drag the Shadow layer so that it is between the topmost layer and the background. In the Layers palette select the Transparency lock. Press the D key to make the foreground color black. Press Option-Delete/Alt-Backspace to fill the contents of the layer with black (see Figure 13.6).

3. Deselect the Transparency lock.

4. Then Choose Edit ➪ Transform Distort. Drag the handles of the bounding box so that the contents of the shadow layer appear to lie on the ground. You may have to play with it a little to get it to look convincing. When you're satisfied, commit your transformation by pressing Return/Enter (see Figure 13.7).

FIGURE 13.6

Duplicate the layer and fill it with black.

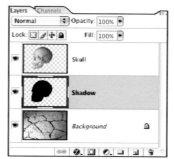

FIGURE 13.7

The shadow has been distorted into position.

5. If the shadow lies on uneven terrain, or you want to readjust it, choose Edit ➪ Transform
   Warp. Drag the handles of the warp grid to conform with the topography of the background, as shown in Figure 13.8. Commit your transformation by clicking on the check
   mark in the Options bar.

FIGURE 13.8

The shadow has been warped to conform to the terrain.

6. Choose Filter ⇨ Blur ⇨ Gaussian Blur. Click and drag the slider to the right to soften the edges of the shadow. The amount depends on the resolution of the image and how fuzzy you want to make the shadow (see Figure 13.9). Click OK.

FIGURE 13.9

Apply the Gaussian Blur filter to soften the edges of the shadow.

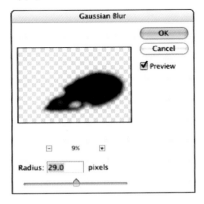

7. Click and drag the Opacity slider on the Shadow layer to 40% to make it transparent, as you can see in Figure 13.10.

FIGURE 13.10

Adjusting the Opacity slider reveals the surface of the background underneath the shadow.

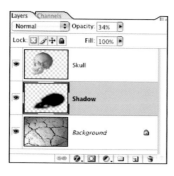 

Compositing Shadows

There is no substitute for the reality of the shadows in a photograph. Because they are transparent, compositing shadows from one image to another can be problematic . . . unless you use this technique. Ideally, you will have shot your image on a solid colored background (preferably white) with a light source similar to that of the target image.

1. Open the photograph and make a selection of the object — do not select the shadow at this time.

CROSS-REF   It is quite difficult to select an object as complex as this. The process combined several techniques. See how it's done in Chapter 15.

2. Choose Layer ➪ New ➪ Layer Via Copy to place the selected content on a new layer. Name the Layer "Object".

3. In the Layers palette, target the Background Layer.

4. In the Channels palette, drag the Composite RGB channel to the Load Selection icon or press Opt+⌘/Alt+Ctrl-~ to make a selection out of the lightness or luminosity areas of the image (see Figure 13.12).

FIGURE 13.11

The object is first selected and then copied to a new layer.

FIGURE 13.12

The Luminosity areas of the image are selected and then the selection is inversed.

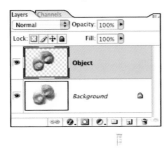

5. Choose Select ⇨ Inverse or press Shift+⌘-I/Shift-Ctrl+I to inverse the selection and select the darker or shadow areas of the image (see Figure 13.13).

FIGURE 13.13

The shadow is filled with black and appears semitransparent.

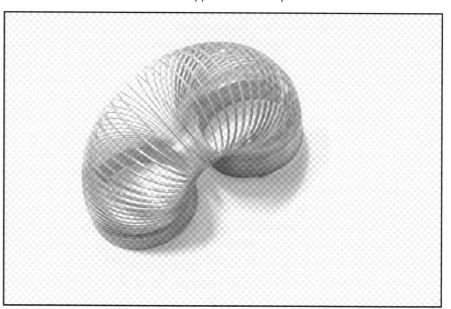

6. In the Layers palette, click the New Layer icon to create a new empty layer. Name the Layer "Shadow." Press the D key to set the default foreground and background colors to black and white. Press Opt-Delete/Alt Backspace to fill the selection on the new layer with black. The layer should look semi-transparent.

7. Click on the Background layer. Press ⌘/Ctrl+A to select all and press the Delete/Backspace key to fill the selection with white.

8. Open the image where you want the object to appear.

9. Click on the image with the object and shadow to activate it. In the Layers palette, click on the Object layer. Press the Shift key and click on the Shadow layer. Now both layers are selected.

10. Press the V key to activate the Move tool. Click and drag the two layers from the Layers palette of the object document to the Background image. When you see a rectangle appear on the destination image, release the mouse. After you've deposited it on the background image, position it into place with the Move tool.

11. If necessary click the shadow layer and adjust its opacity (see Figure 13.14).

The Object and Shadow layers composited to the destination image.

Creating a Beam of Light

Creating a beam of light is a simple way to create dramatic lighting using channels. Doing so requires that you make a selection, save it as an alpha channel, soften the edges of the channel, and then load it as a mask. You can then directly affect the image with an adjustment. Mask making is covered in detail in Part V of the book but here is a preliminary technique that uses both color alpha channels and color channels.

1. Open a photo. Press ⌘/Ctrl+J to duplicate the Background layer.
2. Press ⌘/Ctrl+L until the Polygonal Lasso tool appears in the Tools palette.

3. Draw a wedged shaped selection to define the light beam. The selection should go beyond the top and bottom edges of the image so there won't be a gap when you transform it into a light beam (see Figure 13.15).

4. Choose Window ⇨ Channels to display the Channels palette. Click the Save Selection as Channel icon to create an alpha channel from the selection as in Figure 13.16. Deselect.

5. Click on the alpha channel to display it in the Image window. Choose Filter ⇨ Blur Gaussian Blur to soften the edge of the alpha channel.

6. Load Alpha 1 by dragging it to the Load Selection icon in the Channels palette.

7. Press Shift-I to inverse the selection.

8. Choose Image ⇨ Adjustments ⇨ Levels. Drag the white Output Levels slider to the left to 150 to darken the selected area (see Figure 13.17).

FIGURE 13.15

Draw a wedged-shaped selection.

FIGURE 13.16

Save the selection as an alpha channel.

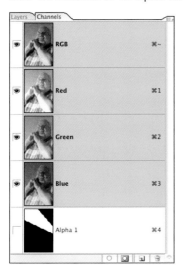

FIGURE 13.17

Levels adjustments darkens the area outside the selection.

Summary

Create depth in your images by using the techniques I covered in this chapter.

You found out how to:

- Create drop shadows
- Create cast shadows
- Composite shadows
- Create a beam of light

Chapter 14 introduces you to mask making basics.

Part V

Mask-Making Basics

Chapter 14

Exploring Masks

asks are a paradox. They consist of one entity that performs two opposite functions. Some types of masks protect areas from being affected while at the same time target other areas to be edited. Other types hide areas from view and at the same time make other regions of the image visible. Photoshop's mask-making features include a group of manual, semi-automatic, and automatic selection tools, channel-based masks that are used for creating and storing selections, layer-based masks that conceal layer content, vector masks that are composed of paths or shapes, type based masks that create selection outlines, and filter masks that reveal and conceal the effects of filters.

Photoshop's masks share similar characteristics. Most masks appear or are stored in one of the palettes, they are dynamic and they can be modified or edited with specific tools or menu items. Depending on the type of mask, they are displayed either in black and white, gray or an overlay color.

Masks are absolutely fundamental to virtually all of Photoshop's operations. They insure that a specific area is selected and ready for editing or visible in the image window.

This chapter identifies and defines the principle types of masks and how they are used.

Understanding Masks

Masking, or the process of isolating regions of an image, was at one time a manual process. In the olden days, before Photoshop, one of the most common methods of altering a photograph was to paint it with an airbrush.

Airbrushing required a person with a steady hand and an Xacto knife. A piece of clear film with a light adhesive called *frisket* was placed over the photograph. A hole was carefully and gently (so as to not damage the photograph) cut into the frisket to expose an area. Paint was sprayed with the airbrush. The frisket was then peeled back to reveal the painted shape.

Masking was also used in the photomechanical transfer process where portions of an image were masked with another type of film called *rubylith* and exposed with a process camera. The film negatives were developed, stripped, and stacked together to create optical composites that were transferred to photosensitive plates and printed on a printing press. This optical process was fundamental to the preparation of graphics for print until the computer emerged on the scene in the late 1980s.

Graphics software programs such as Adobe Photoshop replaced these low-tech practices with a plethora of virtual tools designed to quickly and accurately mask an image for editing.

Types of Masks

Each image presents a totally different set of selection and editing problems. Consequently there are numerous methods of masking that can be applied to every possible situation. Nevertheless, masking is undoubtedly the most manual and labor-intensive of all Photoshop's operations. Sometimes there are situations where one masking technique is insufficient and must be combined with other techniques to define and isolate an area.

Choosing which type of mask to use depends on the particular situation. Each type of mask presents its own set of editing requirements. For example, a layer mask can be edited with any of the painting and editing tools or the filters while a vector mask must be edited with the pen tools and the path editing tools.

NOTE Several types of masks support 256 levels of gray, just like a grayscale image, and can be edited with the same tools that you would use to modify a black and white photograph.

The following list describes the eight different types of masks available in Photoshop:

- **Selection outline:** The most basic mask types are temporary selections that define an area for instant editing. These masks are called *selection outlines*, or sometimes *marching ants* because the animated marquee looks like a column of tiny insects encircling a region on the image. A selection outline is made with one of the selection tools or the Color Range command. These outlines enable the region within their boundaries to be targeted and edited by a tool or operation. The area outside the outline remains protected from editing. Selection outlines can be altered and edited with a variety of features in the Tools palette and in the Select menu (see Figure 14.1).

FIGURE 14.1

Selection outlines are sometimes called marching ants because they look like a column of tiny insects surrounding the selected region.

■ **Alpha channel:** This grayscale mask is created by saving a selection, by painting on a empty channel, or duplicating a color channel. Alpha channels exist in the Channels palette immediately under the color channels. They can be altered with the painting and editing tools, the Stroke and Fill commands, the Filters and Transformation commands, and with many of the adjustment features. Alpha channels can contain up to 256 levels of gray. White areas on an alpha channel represent regions on the image that are selected when the channel is loaded. Black represents areas that are protected, and gray represents areas that are partially selected (see Figure 14.2).

FIGURE 14.2

Alpha channels are saved selections that reside in the Channels palette.

■ **Quick Mask:** The usual method for making a Quick Mask is to make a selection first and then click the Quick Mask mode icon in the Tools palette (or press the Q key). You are presented with a red overlay that defines the protected areas of the image. The holes in the overlay constitute the areas that the selection outline encircled. You can alter the Quick Mask with a variety of Photoshop tools and operations. Quick Masks are very similar to alpha channels in that they are grayscales that support up to 256 levels of gray and can be edited with the same features. The only real difference is that they are temporary. After you've made a Quick Mask and switched to Standard mode in the Tools palette (or press the Q key again) the Quick Mask changes to an unsaved selection outline (see Figure 14.3).

FIGURE 14.3

Quick Masks are temporary masks that can be edited with the painting and editing tools.

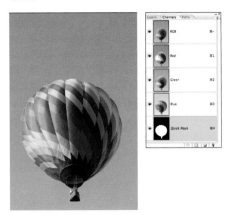

■ **Layer mask:** Layer masks reside in the Layers palette and are used to reveal or conceal pixels on a content layer. They also reveal or conceal tonal and color alterations on an adjustment layer. They support 256 levels of gray. Black areas on the mask represent areas that are hidden. White areas on the mask represent areas that are visible. Gray represents areas that are partially visible. Layer masks can be edited with the painting and editing tools, and the Stroke and Fill commands, some of the filters, and some of the adjustment features (see Figure 14.4).

FIGURE 14.4

FIGURE 14.4

Layer masks reveal and conceal image areas.

- **Clipping mask:** A clipping mask is a group of layers that conform to the shape of the bottom-most layer in the group. A clipping mask is created by placing layer content that is surrounded by transparency below one or more layers. The layers are grouped together by Opt/Alt clicking the line between them. A clipping mask can be edited by adding or removing content from the bottom layer (see Figure 14.5).

FIGURE 14.5

Clipping masks are a group of layers that conform to the shape of the bottommost layer.

■ **Vector mask:** These masks are composed of paths made with the pen or shape tools. As with layer masks they exist in the Layers palette and conceal or reveal image areas. Vector masks are editable with the Path Selection and the Direct Selection tools and the Add, Subtract, and Convert Anchor Point tools (see Figure 14.6).

FIGURE 14.6
_____

Vector masks are layer-based masks that are created with paths or shapes.

■ **Type mask:** Type masks are generated with the Type Mask tool. When you first create a type mask, it appears as a translucent red field with transparent text characters. When you commit a type mask however they transform into selection outlines in the shape of type characters. Before conversion the text characters can be edited, deleted, or re-entered as text. After being committed however, the text is no longer editable as type but can be altered with the selection tools (see Figure 14.7).

CROSS-REF   You can use the type tool to create type layers, you also can set type either vertically or horizontally. Learn more about the type tool in Chapter 20.

■ **Smart Filter mask:** Used to mask the effects of filters, this type of mask is new to Photoshop CS3. Smart Filters are attached to Smart Objects which are nondestructive layers that use data from a source document to effect an image (see Figure 14.8).

CROSS-REF   Masking is fundamental to all Photoshop work sessions. Learning how to use the different types of masks and making them quickly and accurately can streamline your workflow and produce quality images. The nuts and bolts of mask masking are found in the chapters that follow.

FIGURE 14.7

Type masks ultimately produce selection outlines that are shaped like type characters.

FIGURE 14.8

Smart Filter masks are attached to Smart Objects and mask the application of filters.

Creating and Editing Virtual Masks

Each type of mask differs in its function and the methodology used to create it. You start the mask-making process by looking at the image and asking yourself what type of mask is appropriate for your needs. Start by asking yourself the following questions:

- Will a simple selection suffice?
- Does the selection need to be refined with one of the painting tools?
- Is the selection complex?
- Do you need to save it for later use?
- Do you need to conceal part of a layer?
- Is it more appropriate to make a path than a selection?

In many cases, the physical process of mask making begins with selecting an area either with one of the selection tools or with a vector tool. If you make a selection you can save it as an alpha channel, convert it to a Quick Mask, or automatically make a layer mask. If you've drawn a path, you can make a vector mask, and if you've generated a type mask you can convert it to a selection outline.

The quality of the mask depends on the precision of the selection and there are numerous techniques that enable you to make adjustments and alterations to the mask after you've created it. In fact, alpha channels, Quick Masks, and layer masks behave exactly as grayscale images in their editing capabilities. Clipping masks are completely layer-based and are edited by affecting layer content. And of course, vector masks and type masks are edited with the vector and type tools.

Although they can be edited with Photoshop's tools and commands, selections, alpha channels, Quick Masks, and type masks are not part of the image. They are separate entities that you create and use to alter the image. Similarly layer masks and vector masks do not contain layer content. They too are tools that you make to reveal or conceal parts of the image. Clipping masks are unique in that they actually contain content and constitute a relationship between two or more consecutive layers.

Saving Masks

If you make a selection with any of the selection tools and you save the document, the selection will not be saved with it; therefore, if you want to preserve the selection for later use, save it as an alpha channel. Quick Masks are also temporary. You need to first convert the Quick Mask into a selection outline and then save it as an alpha channel. The same is true with a type masks. All other masks are saved with the Photoshop document including alpha channels, layer masks, clipping masks, vector masks, and filter masks providing you save them to a format that supports layers or channels. PSD, PSB, TIFF, and PDF formats support both layers and alpha channels. BMP, Photoshop 2.0, Photoshop Raw, PICT, PICT Resource, Pixar, and Targa formats support only alpha channels.

Summary

In this chapter, you were introduced to masking concepts. I discussed the essential information you needed to know to start using masks.

Specifically, I discussed the following:

- Understanding masks
- Types of masks
- Creating and editing masks
- Saving masks

In Chapter 15, I discuss the many selection tools available to you.

Chapter 15

Making Selections

The process of making a selection is fundamental to all Photoshop documents. A selection isolates an area of an image so that you can apply an effect to a specific region. You can select the entire image or you can precisely define any region down to a single pixel.

When an area is selected, it is encircled by an animated selection outline. You can make a selection with any one of the nine Selection tools found in the Tools palette or by the Color Range command. When you apply a Photoshop tool or operation, the area within the bounds of the selection outline is affected, and the area outside of the selection outline remains unaffected. Photoshop provides a range of methods — from the labor-intensive to the fully automatic — that enables you to select pixels for the ultimate purpose of altering their appearance. This chapter shows you how to use these features to your best advantage.

Finding Out About Selection Tools

The Selection tools range from manual to fully automatic. Each of these tools facilitates the masking process with its own unique method of making selections. The one you choose depends on the characteristics of the image. Because images vary in contrast, tonality, color, and content, Photoshop provides tools and methods that can be applied to every possible situation. When you make a selection in Photoshop, an animated marquee defines the boundaries of the selected area. This animated, dash-lined border is often called *marching ants* to reflect its resemblance to a single column of tiny insects encircling the selected area.

Using Selection tools

Three of the Selection tools are visible at the top of the Tools palette; the Rectangular Marquee, the Lasso, and the Magic Wand. If you hover your mouse over any visible tool, you can see a tool label with the name of the tool and its tools character key. Click and hold your mouse button to expand the tool's flyout menu to reveal even more tools (see Figure15.1). Drag down the flyout menu to choose the Selection tool that you want and release the mouse.

 TIP It's worth the minor investment of time to open an image and try out all the Selection tools and all their options to get a feel for their many capabilities.

FIGURE 15.1

The Selection tools in the Tools palette.

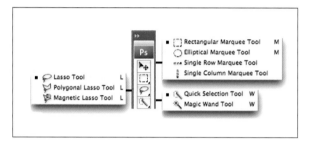

A more efficient method of choosing a Selection tool is to type the tool's character key. Press the shift and the character key to toggle through the flyout. Use the key command in the following list to easily access the Selection tools:

- **M, Shift+M**: Rectangular Marquee tool, Elliptical Marquee tool
- **L, Shift+L**: Lasso tool, Polygonal Lasso tool, Magnetic Lasso tool
- **W, Shift+W**: Magic Wand tool, Quick Selection tool

 TIP Although the Single Column and Single Row tools are in the Marquee tool flyout menu, by default they cannot be accessed with key commands. You can, however, create a key command for these tools by accessing Edit ⇨ Keyboard Shortcuts ⇨ Shortcuts for Tools. Click the Single Column or Single Row Marquee. Type a key sequence in the Text box and click OK.

Using the Options bar

The Options bar displays tool specifications of the current Selection tool. From the Options bar, you can program the tool's behavior by typing numbers in the value fields or choosing specific options (see Figure 15.2).

FIGURE 15.2

The Options bar showing the default options for the Rectangular Marquee tool.

Working with Boolean icons

When you choose a Selection tool, the icon that represents it appears on the left end of the Options bar, which is also the Tool Preset menu. The next four icons (called *Boolean icons*) determine the relationship of the tools behavior to existing selections. Click one of the buttons to influence how the tool will make a selection:

■ **New Selection:** Use this option to create a new selection with the current Selection tool. If there is an existing selection it will deselect it when it selects the new area.

■ **Add To Selection:** Click this button to add an existing selection with the chosen Selection tool. The addition can either expand an existing selection's boundaries or add an entirely new noncontiguous area. You can Shift-click and drag with the Selection tool as an alternative method of adding to the selection.

■ **Subtract from Selection:** This option excludes area from an existing selection. You can also Option/Alt-click and drag the Selection tool as an alternative method of subtracting from the selection.

■ **Intersect Selection:** After making an initial selection and choosing this option, make a second selection overlapping the first. Only that portion of the image common to both selections will remain active. You can perform the same operation by pressing Shift+Option (Mac) or Shift+Alt (Win) as you use the second Selection tool.

Feathering borders

Feathering creates a gradual transition between the inside and the outside of the selection outline. When you apply an effect to a feathered selection, the edges gradually become transparent, as shown in Figure 15.3

Editing through a soft-edged selection increases the credibility of your composites by gradually blending colored pixels into each other and eliminating any evidence of a hard edge. You can program the selection to be feathered prior to making it by typing a value in the Feather field. If you want to feather an existing selection choose Select ➪ Modify ➪ Feather to display the Feather dialog box (see Figure 15.4). Type a value in the Feather Radius field. Or you can interactively control feathering with the Refine Edges dialog box. (See the "Refine Edges" sidebar.)

The Feather Radius value extends the specified number of pixels into the selection outline (becoming increasingly more opaque) and outside the selection border (becoming increasingly more transparent). For example, if you enter a value of 5, the distance of the feather will be 10 pixels from the opaque pixels inside the selection border to absolute transparency outside the selection border.

FIGURE 15.3

The elliptical soft edge matte was made by inversing a feathered selection and filling it with black.

FIGURE 15.4

Enter a value in the Feather Selection dialog box after the selection has been made.

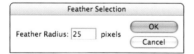

Sometimes applying a feather to an existing selection border decreases its size or changes its shape. This is because a selection border is not displayed around areas that represent 50% transparency or more. Although the areas may be selected and change when an effect is applied, you do not see an outline around them.

Refining Edges

The New Refine Edges dialog box is a nice addition to the selection menu in that it the controls many of the characteristics of your selection while you observe the results in the Image window. Either type a value in the textbox or drag the sliders to increase or decrease the effect. The dialog box contains the following controls:

- **Radius:** Improves the edge of a selection that has soft edges and fine details. If artifacts are inadvertently created, they can be removed with the contrast slider.
- **Contrast:** Sharpens the edge and removes fuzzy artifacts.
- **Smooth:** Eliminates jagged edges. If edge detail is affected it can be restored with Radius.
- **Feather:** Uniformly blurs a selection edge.
- **Contract/Expand:** Decreases or increases the size of the selection.

Control the display of the selection in the Image window by clicking one of the display icons. You can preview the selection as a standard selection border, as a Quick Mask, on black, on white, or as a mask.

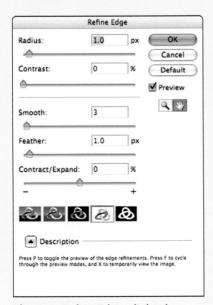

The new Refine Edges dialog box.

Anti-aliasing edges

An anti-alias is a two- or three-pixel border around an edge that blends into the adjacent color to create a small transition zone. Without the anti-alias, an image would look "aliased," or stair-stepped, without smooth transitions between colors. Anti-aliasing is different than feathering because the size of the transition of a feather can be controlled, whereas an anti-aliased edge is automatically applied when the option is chosen and is usually just a few pixels wide, depending on the resolution of the document.

Using Shape Selection tools

Shape Selection tools select rectangles, ellipses, or a single line of pixels as you apply them. The Rectangular and Elliptical Marquee tools perform in a similar way. They can be manually applied or controlled with a variety of techniques to conform to a precise size or proportion. The Single Column Marquee and Single Row Marquee select adjacent pixels either vertically or horizontally across the entire surface of the image. These tools are essential when you have specific geometric forms to select such as architectural details, as in Figure 15.5, for example.

FIGURE 15.5

The Marquee tools select rectangular and elliptical shapes.

Working with the Rectangular and Elliptical Marquee tools

The Rectangular Marquee tool and its sibling, the Elliptical Marquee tool, are used to select a rectangular, square, elliptical, or circular shape within your image. To select a rectangular or elliptical area, click in the image and drag in any direction. Press the Shift key as you drag to constrain the selection to a square or circle.

Figure 15.6 shows the Style menu in the Options bar which enables you to precisely control the size and proportion of the marquee. Choose from any of the three methods for sizing the Rectangular and Elliptical Marquees:

- **Normal:** Use this default setting for manual control of the Marquee tools. By choosing Normal, you determine the size and proportion of the marquee by dragging.

- **Fixed Aspect Ratio:** Type a value for the proportion of the marquee in the Height and Width fields. Then drag-click and drag the tool across the image. The proportions of the marquee remain constant as you change its size.

- **Fixed Size:** Type values in the Height and Width fields to determine a fixed size. If you want Photoshop to accept values in units other than pixels — inches, for example — Control-click on the Width and Height fields and drag to your preferred units. Photoshop creates a marquee to the nearest pixel that you specify.

FIGURE 15.6

The Marquee Style options in the Options bar.

Table 15.1 describes the keyboard modifiers you can use with the Rectangular and Elliptical Marquee tools that allow you to control the behavior of marquees as you draw them.

TABLE 15.1

Moving and Constraining Marquees

Goal	Technique
Constrain to a square or circle	Shift-click-drag to constrain the Rectangular Marquee selection to a square or the Elliptical Marquee to a circle.
Draw from a center point	Option-click-drag/Alt-drag.
Reposition while dragging	Spacebar-click-drag to reposition the marquee.

continued

TABLE 15.1 *(continued)*	
Goal	**Technique**
Reposition after drawing	Choose any selection tool. Click the New selection Boolean icon from the Options bar. Click inside the marquee and drag to reposition it.
Combination techniques	You can combine any of these key command techniques. For example, Shift-Option/Alt-drag to constrain the marquee to a circle or square and radiates it from its center point.

Selecting with the Single Row Marquee

The Single Row Marquee tool selects a single *horizontal* row of pixels. Click the image and a selection marquee appears around a single row of adjacent pixels that runs horizontally across the entire image.

Working with the Single Column Marquee tool

The Single Column Marquee tool selects a single *vertical* column of pixels. Click anywhere in the image, and a selection marquee appears around a single column of adjacent pixels that runs vertically across the entire image (see Figure 15.7).

FIGURE 15.7

The Single Column and Single Row marquees select vertically or horizontally across the image.

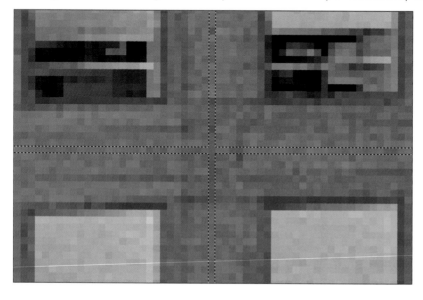

Using Free-Form Selection tools

Photoshop offers three tools for making irregularly shaped selections. The Lasso tool and its flyout siblings, the Polygonal Lasso, and the Magnetic Lasso draw selections based on your mouse movements. Cycle through these tools by pressing Shift+L.

Selecting with the Lasso tool

The Lasso tool draws free-form selections. Click and drag to select an area (surround it with marching ants). Close the marquee by placing the cursor on the starting point or release the mouse to close the selection with a straight line (see Figure 15.8).

FIGURE 15.8

The Lasso tool makes free-form selections.

Selecting with the Polygonal Lasso tool

The Polygonal Lasso tool draws straight-edged selection borders. Click and release the mouse. Then reposition the mouse to the next corner of the polygon and click and release again. You can repeat the process until you return to the point of origin and close the marquee by clicking the starting point, or by double-clicking to close the selection from the most recently established point. Shift-drag to constrain the selection segments horizontally, vertically, or to a 45-degree angle (see Figure 15.9).

FIGURE 15.9

The Polygonal Lasso tool makes selections with straight sides.

You can toggle between the Lasso and Polygonal Lasso tools as you draw. Do the following:

1. Choose the Lasso tool and click-drag a line.
2. Press and hold the Option/Alt key and release the mouse. The cursor changes to the Polygonal Lasso.
3. Reposition the cursor to draw a straight segment. Reposition and click to draw additional straight segments.
4. Press and hold the mouse button again and release the Option/Alt key and resume dragging the Lasso.

Selecting with the Magnetic Lasso tool

As you click and drag, the Magnetic Lasso automatically deposits a path between pixels of the greatest contrast. Release the mouse and the path becomes a selection (see Figure 15.10).

The Magnetic Lasso tool rarely makes perfect selections; inevitably you have to clean up most selections with another Selection tool. Using it can work to your advantage, however. You can make fast selections with relative accuracy.

> **TIP** The Magnetic Lasso Selection tool takes awhile to get used to. If you find that you've lost control over the path, double-click the mouse to complete the selection and then deselect (using Select ⇨ Deselect or ⌘/Ctrl+D), and begin again.

FIGURE 15.10

The Magnetic Lasso intuitively selects areas whose edges contrast.

The Magnetic Lasso tool's Options bar has four settings:

- **Width:** This setting determines the distance of pixels from the path of the mouse that are measured for contrast.

- **Edge Contrast:** This percentage determines the minimum percentage of pixel contrast that the tool will be attracted to. The higher the number, the smaller the range of contrast, and the more selective the tool will be.

- **Frequency:** This setting determines how often points are automatically deposited. The points create segments along the path that fix the previous segments and better control the position of the path.

> **TIP** Deposit extra points manually along the path for more control. Click your mouse at key points as you drag. These manual anchors can help guide the Magnetic Lasso tool when making a selection in an area of less contrast.

- **Pen Pressure:** Select this check box to increase the width of the tool with stylus pressure when using a tablet.

Using Auto Select tools

You use the Magic Wand tool and the new Quick Select tool to select areas of similar brightness. They automatically determine the range of pixels within an area and surround it with a selection outline. Both of these tools can be big time and labor savers.

Using the Magic Wand tool

The Magic Wand tool makes selections based on the brightness range or *tolerance* of pixels. When you need to select a solid background, for example the Magic Wand tool can be a real asset. Click an area, and adjacent pixels within the brightness range are selected. The range of pixels that the Magic Wand selects is controlled by increasing or decreasing the Tolerance setting in the Magic Wand tool's Options bar. Higher tolerances include more pixels of a brightness range. When selecting Grayscale images the range is determined by the brightness values on a single channel. When selecting RGB Color images, the range is determined by the red, green, and blue values of the sampled pixel or pixels.

TIP An efficient method of selecting an element that is surrounded by a similar colored background is to click on the background with the Magic Wand tool and then choose Select ➪ Inverse (Shift-⌘/Ctrl+I).

The sample size of the Eyedropper tool also influences the Magic Wand selection. If the Eyedropper is set to a point sample, the Magic Wand will calculate its selection based on the values of a single pixel. If it's set to an average, such as 3 x 3 for example, then the tolerance is determined by the average brightness of 9 pixels. Photoshop CS3 offers several new sampling averages for the Eyedropper tool including 3 by 3, 5 by 5, 11 by 11, 31 by 31, 51 by 51, and 101, by 101as in Figure 15.11. These new sampling sizes extend the capabilities of the Eyedropper tool and the other tools that rely on its settings to more accurately sample the color of pixels in higher resolution documents.

FIGURE 15.11

New additional sampling averages for the Eyedropper tool.

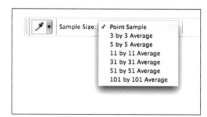

Two other features appear in the Options bar when the Magic Wand tool is chosen, which augment your ability to make selections:

- **Contiguous:** The Contiguous box is selected by default, which limits the selection to adjacent pixels. Uncheck this box to select all the pixels in the image within the same tolerance range.

- **Use All Layers:** Unselected, this check box limits the selection to pixels within the same tolerance range on a single layer. Selecting this check box includes pixels on multiple layers.

Using the Quick Selection tool

This new tool facilitates making quick selections. To use it, choose brush characteristics from the brush menu in the Options bar. Click and drag across the image. The Quick Selection tool selects areas within the tolerance range of the pixels that you touch with the brush. When the selection is made, you have the option of refining it using the new Refine Edge feature. Click the refine Edges button in the Options bar to display the Refine Selection Edge dialog box.

Modifying Selections

Several commands are accessible in the Select menu that enables you to change the selection outline after it has been made. These commands can modify the size of an existing selection or transform its shape, while leaving the content of the selection unaffected.

These are the menu items that give you greater control over the accuracy of your existing selections:

- **Show/Hide Selection Edges:** Choose View ➪ Show ➪ Selection Edges to conceal and reveal the Selection outline from view while the selection remains active. Choose View ➪ Extras or ⌘/Ctrl+H) This option also conceals and reveals the selection edges. This command is useful in seeing the results of an operation without the distracting selection border.

CAUTION With the border invisible, you may forget that an area of the image is selected. Photoshop will not perform an operation in any other location on the image until the selection border is deactivated. If you find that the program is not performing in the areas you want to affect, press ⌘/Cntrl+D to deselect.

- **Modify:** You can alter the dimensions of an existing selection by choosing one of the Select ➪ Modify commands. Each command alters the selection dimensions of the area surrounded by the selection outline. The Modify commands are:

  - **Border:** Creates a frame around the selection of specific thickness (see Figure 15.12). When you choose Select ➪ Modify ➪ Border, you can determine the thickness of the border by entering a value in pixels in the Width field.

FIGURE 15.12

You can specify a border width in the dialog box. The Border command frames the outermost portion of your selection.

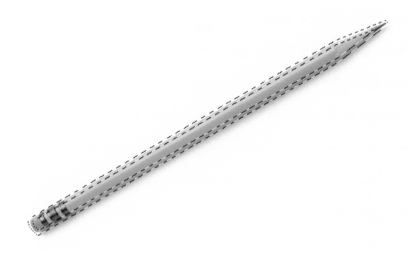

■ **Smooth:** Rounds sharp corners of a selection, eliminating protrusions and stair-stepped areas of the selection border. Choose Select ➪ Modify ➪ Smooth, and then type a Sample Radius value in the dialog box (see Figure 15.13). (The larger the value, the greater the effect.)

■ **Expand and Contract:** Both perform in the same way to enlarge or reduce the size of the selection by a specified number of pixels. This command is quite useful for trimming off stubborn, unwanted edge pixels or tightening up your selections. Choose Select ➪ Modify ➪ Expand or Contract, and in the dialog box, type a value between 1 and 100 pixels. Click OK to implement the operation. This command is redundant with the Expand/Contract slider in the new refine edges dialog box.

FIGURE 15.13

The Smooth command rounds-off jagged corners.

- **Feather:** This command feathers an existing selection by a specified pixel radius. It is redundant with the Feather slider in the Refine Edges dialog box.

- **Refine Edge:** This new feature is identical to the Refine Edge feature in the Quick Selection tool dialog box and applies the refinement to any currently active selection outline. (See the "Refine Edges" sidebar in this chapter.)

- **Grow:** When you choose Select ➪ Grow, the selection marquee expands to include adjacent pixels that are lighter or darker within the tolerance range of the value entered in the Tolerance field of the Magic Wand's Options bar.

- **Similar:** Choosing Select ➪ Similar selects all pixels within the image that are the same colors as the pixels within the area of the current selection. The additional selected pixels are determined by the Tolerance setting in the Magic Wand's Options bar.

Transforming Selections

You may want to alter the shape of a selection outline before applying an operation to its content. This differs from simply modifying the selection in that it manually changes the size orientation or the shape of the selection outline. You can scale, rotate, or move a selection border. To transform a selection, choose Select ⇨ Transform Selection to display a rectangular bounding box as shown Figure 15.14.

Choose Image ⇨ Transform to apply any of the transformation functions including size, rotate, distort perspective, skew, warp, and flip horizontal or vertical to the selection border. These operations do not affect the content, only the size, shape, and position of the selection outline.

- **Move:** To move the selection, click within the rectangular transformation box. The Move cursor appears. Press your mouse button and drag the selection into position, then release the mouse.

- **Scale:** Click one of the square handles on the corners or sides of the box. The Scale cursor appears. Press your mouse button and drag. To maintain the proportion, press your Shift key as you drag.

- **Rotate:** To rotate a selection, click outside the box and drag to rotate the selection. Holding down the Shift key enables precise rotation in 15-degree increments. Or choose a prefixed rotation, 180 degrees or 90 degrees clockwise or counterclockwise.

- **Distort:** Choose Edit ⇨ Transform ⇨ Distort or ⌘/Ctrl-click any of the corner handles and drag to distort the shape of the selection outline.

- **Skew:** Choose Edit ⇨ Transform ⇨ Skew or Opt/Alt-⌘/Ctrl-click any of the corner handles and drag to skew the selection.

- **Perspective:** Choose Edit ⇨ Transform ⇨ Perspective or Shift-Cmnd/Cntrl-Opt/Alt-click any one of the corner handles and drag to add perspective to the shape of the selection outline.

- **Warp:** Choose Edit ⇨ Transform ⇨ Warp and drag the gridlines to warp the selection outline.

- **Flip Horizontal Vertical:** Choose Edit ⇨ Transform ⇨ Flip Horizontal or Vertical to flip the section outline into a mirror of the original.

To complete the transformation, click the check mark or press Return/Enter. To cancel the transformation, click the Cancel box or press the Escape key.

FIGURE 15.14

The Transform Selection command displays a bounding box surrounding the selection. The bounding box can be altered to change the shape of the selection outline without altering its content.

Working with Selection Techniques

You can perform other operations to an active selection outline or to its contents using the following techniques. These techniques are essential to the process of modifying selection borders. They are applied to a currently active selection outline to independently reposition the marching ants or to move selection content to another location.

- **Move Selection Outline:** You must choose a Selection tool and click the New Selection Boolean icon to move a selection outline. Click inside the marquee and drag. When you reach the position you want, release the mouse.

- **Nudge Selection Outline:** Choose a Selection tool, press the right, left, up, or down arrow keys to reposition the selection outline one pixel. Press Shift plus any of the arrow keys to move the selection outline 10 pixels at a time.

- **Move a Selection's Contents:** Choose the Move tool. Click inside the marquee and drag. When you've relocated the marquee, release the mouse. You can also move the contents while in any Selection tool — Cmnd/Ctrl-click inside the marquee and drag. A scissor icon appears to let you know that you're cutting the contents of the selection outline and moving them. When you've relocated the selection, release the mouse and then the key.

NOTE The contents of a selection "floats." That is, it can be moved again providing you don't deselect it. When you deselect, the content is pasted onto the currently active layer.

- **Nudge Selection Contents:** You can nudge the contents of a selection in one-pixel increments: With the Move tool active, press the left, right, up, or down arrow keys. Press Shift and any of the arrow keys to move the selection contents 10 pixels at a time.

- **Duplicate Selection Contents:** Choose the Move tool. Press Option/Alt-Cmnd-Ctrl while you click and drag. The double Move cursor that appears indicates that you are duplicating the selection.

Summary

This chapter discussed your many options for making selections.

Some of the topics I covered are

- Modifying selections
- Transforming selections
- Working with selection techniques

Chapter 16 explores what you can do with Alpha Channels and Quick Masks to make selecting even easier.

Chapter 16

Using Alpha Channels and Quick Masks

S electing areas on a Photoshop image is by far the most labor-intensive aspect of image editing. Using alpha channels and Quick Masks can make the selection process more efficient. You create alpha channel so that you can alter a selection with the painting and editing tools or store a selection for later use. *Alpha channels* are graphic representations of selections. They are actually grayscale images that can support up to 256 shades of gray. Unlike color channels, alpha channels do not contain color information. Instead, they are composed of values of gray that represent areas of opacity or transparency of a mask.

Quick Masks are similar to alpha channels but unlike alpha channels they are temporary masks. They also enhance efficiency by enabling you to make temporary masks using the painting and editing features. Quick Masks can be converted into selection outlines or stored as alpha channels in the Channels palette for later use.

Employing both Quick Masks and alpha channels into your workflow enables you to extend the capabilities of selection making into the painting and editing tools. Rather than being limited to the cumbersome selection tools you can produce selections with more accuracy and with variable edge softness for better compositing.

After you've made a mask with the painting and editing tools on-the-fly in Quick Mask mode, and converted it to a selection outline, you can save the selection as an alpha channel and be assured that you can access it any time during the editing process. Alpha channels can be combined, duplicated, and altered in a similar fashion to Quick Masks.

You find out what you need to know to use alpha channels and Quick Masks in this chapter.

Saving and Loading Selections

Alpha channels are separate from the image and do not affect the way the image appears. When you save a selection, it is stacked underneath the color channels in the order in which it was created.

Because making an intricate selection can be difficult or time-consuming the following list describes situations when you may want to consider making an alpha channel. Use the alpha channel:

- **When making a complex selection:** Save a selection as an alpha channel during the process of making a complex selection so that if you make a mistake you can always reload the last saved version and continue from that point in the process. After the selection is complete, you can discard the interim steps.

- **After making a complex selection:** Some selections can be time-consuming. When you save a selection as an alpha channel you do not need to redraw the selection.

- **When editing a selection:** Alpha channels provide a more graphic representation of selections than the marching ants that define the selection border. They can therefore be edited with more precision.

- **When combining selections:** It is sometimes efficient to make a selection on an alpha channel and delete its black content to create a new alpha channel.

- **When using Calculations:** Before you combine the selections by using the Calculations command, save the selections as alpha channels that combine the selection with the alpha channel's content.

- **When using a selection more than once:** Save any selection as an alpha channel that you plan to use again.

- **When selecting fine detail:** When you're attempting to mask fine details such as hair, you save the selection as an alpha channel so that it can later be refined.

To save a selection, follow these steps:

1. Make a selection with one of the Selection tools (see Figure 16.1).

2. Choose Select ➪ Save Selection.

3. In the Save Selection dialog box (shown in Figure 16.2), in the Destination field, determine the following settings:

    - **Document:** You can save a selection as an alpha channel to the document where the selection was made or to any open document that is the exact same height, width, and resolution. The names of the documents that conform appear in the Document pop-up list. Choosing New creates a new document with no color channels and one alpha channel in the Channels palette.

    - **Channel:** Choosing New makes a new channel. You can name the new channel in the Name field. If you don't name it, the saved selection appears on the Channels palette titled as Alpha 1, 2, etc. Choosing an existing channel's name in the Channel pop-up list replaces it with your saved alpha channel.

FIGURE 16.1

The initial selection.

FIGURE 16.2

The Save Selection dialog box.

4. If there is an active selection on an image and you choose an existing alpha channel from the Channels pop-up menu, you can choose from four options in the Operations field:

- **Replace Channel:** Selecting this option discards the original channel and replaces it with an entirely new alpha channel made from the current selection.

- **Add To Channel:** Use this option to add the new selected area to the target alpha channel.

- **Subtract From Channel:** This option removes the currently selected area from the alpha channel.

- **Intersect With Channel:** You can replace the target alpha channel by an alpha channel that is composed of the overlapping areas of the new selection and the target channel.

5. Click OK to save the selection.

TIP You can quickly save a selection as a new alpha channel by clicking the Save Selection As Channel icon at the bottom of the Channels palette.

Alpha channels are saved with the document and can be accessed from the Channels palette at any time during the editing process. Channels can be duplicated, deleted, merged or spilt. Photoshop supports up to 56 including color channels. Each channel has the same dimensions and number of pixels as the image.

CAUTION Adding alpha Channels increases the file size of a document. The file size of each channel depends on the complexity of its pixel information. Alpha channels are saved in Photoshop, PDF, PICT, Pixar, TIFF, PSB, or raw formats. Saving in any other format discards the alpha channels.

Viewing alpha channels

A saved alpha channel can be displayed or concealed in the Channels palette. As with viewing color channels, you view or conceal alpha channels by clicking the visibility icon to the left of the channel's thumbnail. If only the alpha channel is displayed, you see a grayscale image in the Image window as in Figure 16.3. By default, black represents masked areas, white represents selected areas, and gray represents partially selected areas.

FIGURE 16.3

An alpha channel viewed in the Channels palette (a) and in the Image window as a grayscale.

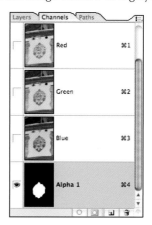

CAUTION Don't confuse channels with layers — they are really quite different even though their palettes look somewhat similar. Channels represent color information or stored selections whereas layers are regions of the image that have been separated into a stack for easy accessibility.

When both the color channels and the alpha channel are visible, you see the alpha channel as translucent color overlay superimposed over the image. By default, the overlay is 50% red as shown in Figure 16.4.

FIGURE 16.4

An alpha channel viewed as an overlay.

Changing alpha channel options

If you are looking at more than one channel at a time or if the color of the overlay closely resembles the image content, you can change the color of the transparent overlay. Double-click the thumbnail of the alpha channel to display the Channel Options dialog box (see Figure 16.5). Set display options for the channel. The radio buttons in the Color Indicates field lets you choose whether masked areas or selected areas are to be displayed as color overlays. If you are working with spot colors, you can designate a Spot Color channel (see in Chapter 10).

CROSS-REF   **To learn more about Spot Color channels see Chapter 10.**

FIGURE 16.5

The Channel Options dialog box lets you change the color and opacity of the masks.

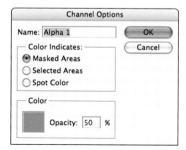

To change the color of a mask:

1. Double-click the channel thumbnail to display the Channel Options dialog box.
2. Click the swatch to bring up the Color Picker.
3. Choose a color and click OK.
4. Specify the opacity of the mask from 0% to 100%, which affects only how the mask is displayed and not its masking capabilities. Lower the opacity to see the image more clearly through the mask.

Loading selections

An alpha channel can be loaded as a selection. Loading a selection surrounds the area with a selection marquee just as if you outlined it with a Selection tool.

To load a selection:

1. Choose Select ➪ Load Selection.
2. The Load Selection dialog box (see Figure 16.6) is similar to the Save Selection dialog box. From the Document pop-up list, choose the name of the document where the channel was made. This list displays the names of open documents that are the same height, width, and resolution.

TIP If you deselect the selection, you can reselect by choosing Reselect from the Selection menu or press Shift+⌘/Ctrl+D

FIGURE 16.6

The Load Selection dialog box.

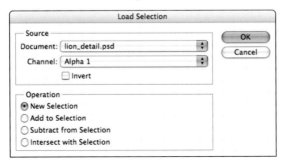

3. From the Channel pop-up list, choose the source channel to be loaded. This list displays all alpha channels and layer masks from the current document. The Invert box loads an inversed selection of the mask.

4. If you have an active selection on the image, the Operation area presents four options:

 ▪ **New Selection:** Loads a new selection on the image, replacing any currently selected area if there is one with the selection derived from the alpha channel.

 ▪ **Add To Selection:** Adds the loaded selection area to an active selection marquee.

 ▪ **Subtract From Selection:** Deletes the loaded selection area from an active selection marquee.

 ▪ **Intersect With Selection:** Loads the area where the loaded selection and an active selection marquee intersect.

5. Click OK to load the selection.

Load a selection quickly by dragging its icon to the Load Channel As Selection icon at the bottom of the Channels palette. You can also ⌘/Ctrl-click the channel's thumbnail to load a selection.

Editing Channels

You may need to change the content of your alpha channel to produce an altered selection marquee when the selection is loaded. You can edit an alpha channel with the painting and editing features, extending your selection making capabilities into an entirely new set of tools. You might edit a channel to improve the accuracy of the selection, to add a filter effect to the selection, or to produce a large variety of effects that will be applied to the image when the selection is loaded on the image and a Photoshop function is applied through it.

Fine-tuning alpha channels

Often after having saved a selection, there are inaccuracies visible on the mask that weren't visible on the selection marquee. Usually they take the form of little gray smudges that the brush may have missed or deposited. You can fine-tune these and other flaws by painting directly on the alpha channel. This process is similar to working in Quick Mask mode;, the only difference is that you are affecting the saved channel.

You can apply black to paint out protected and white to selected areas. You can also paint with gray to create semitransparent areas on the mask that will be partially affected when an affect is applied.

TIP To assure that you don't damage the alpha channel while altering it, make a duplicate first by dragging the channel to the New Channel icon at the bottom of the Channels palette and then modify the copy.

Here's how you can alter the contents of an alpha channel with the painting and editing tools:

1. Make a selection with any of the Selection tools (see Figure 16.7).

FIGURE 16.7

Make a selection.

2. Click the Save Selection As Alpha Channel icon in the Channels palette. The channel is named Alpha 1 (see Figure 16.8).

FIGURE 16.8

The saved selection appears in the Channels palette as Alpha 1.

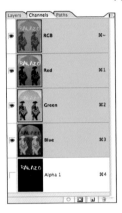

3. View the alpha channel in the Image window by pressing Opt/Alt and clicking its name or thumbnail. The black-and-white channel appears in the Image window (see Figure 16.9).

4. Press ⌘/Ctrl+D to deselect.

5. Display the composite channel by clicking on its visibility icon but be sure that the Alpha 1 channel is highlighted and visible. You'll see a red color where the channel masks the image.

6. Press the D key to make white the foreground color in the Tools palette.

TIP   The D key restores the white foreground and black background color when working on a channel or a Quick Mask. You can also press the X key to toggle back and forth between foregrouind and background color to facilitate painting.

NOTE   By default painting with black produces areas that are completely masked. Painting with white produces areas that are exposed when the selection is made. Painting with a shade of gray creates a partially masked area the degree of masking depends on how light or dark the gray is. The darker the shade of gray, the more an area will be masked.

FIGURE 16.9

The alpha channel in the Image window as a black-and-white mask.

7. Press the B key to choose the Brush tool. Choose a brush size and softness from the Options bar pop-up menu. Paint on the image where you want to alter the selection as in Figure 16.10. The resulting painting will, by default, alter the marquee to select the newly painted areas when the selection is loaded.

FIGURE 16.10

View the alpha channel in the Image window as a red mask and edit it with the Brush tool.

8. To see the result, click off the visibility icon on the alpha channel and highlight the composite channel, then load the selection as in Figure 16.11.

TIP   As you paint, you can toggle back and forth between white and black by pressing the X key.

Duplicating alpha channels

When you duplicate a targeted alpha channel, you get an exact copy of it in the Channels palette. You should duplicate the channel if you want to experiment with modifying it by painting, applying a filter effect, or any other editing function. Duplicate the channel if you want to inverse and save it for alterations. Click the arrow in the upper-right corner of the channels to displays the Channels Option Palette menu and choose Duplicate Channel.

You can also drag and alpha channel to the New Channel icon in the Channels palette to create a duplicate.

FIGURE 16.11

The result of painting on the alpha channel is that you have added to the selection.

Deleting alpha channels

You can delete a targeted alpha channel from the document by choosing the Delete channel from the Palette pull-down menu. A fast way to delete a channel is to drag it to the Delete Channel icon (the trash icon) at the bottom of the Channels palette.

Working with Alpha Channels

In early versions of Photoshop, before layers were introduced, alpha channels were used to make drop shadows, glowing effects, bevels, embossing, and other image effects. These techniques required the careful manipulation and application of filters and were quite labor intensive. Fortunately, many of these early techniques have been replaced with Layer Styles. Although they have lost much of their former importance in the Photoshop workflow, these techniques are still quite useful. Here are a few tricks that you can perform with the help of alpha channels.

Creating borders with alpha channels

Photographic edges can add an interesting dimension to your images giving them a hand-printed archival look. You can use alpha channels to create unique borders for your photographs. If you save the channel you can load it and apply the selection to another document of similar size and resolution.

1. Choose File ⇨ New Document or press ⌘/Ctrl+N. Use the specifications in Figure 16.12.

FIGURE 16.12

Make a new document.

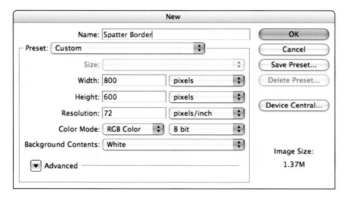

2. Click the Channels tab in the Layers, Channels, Paths palette cluster.

3. Click the New Channel icon in at the bottom of the palette to create a new channel. Name it Spatter Border.

4. Select the Rectangular Marquee tool. Choose Fixed Size in the Style menu in the Options bar and enter 700px for the width and 500px for the height. Click in the center of the channel to create a 50 pixel edge border (see Figure16.13).

5. Choose Select ⇨ Inverse (or press Shift+⌘+I) to select the bordered edge.

6. Select white as a foreground color and press Opt/Alt-Delete/Backspace to fill the area with white (see Figure 16.14). Deselect.

7. Click the Spatter Border channel. Choose Filter ⇨ Filter Gallery ⇨ Brush Strokes ⇨ Spatter. Drag the Spray radius slider to 20 and the Smoothness slider to 5. Click OK (see Figure 16.15).

FIGURE 16.13

The rectangular selection.

FIGURE 16.14

The Inversed selection filled with white.

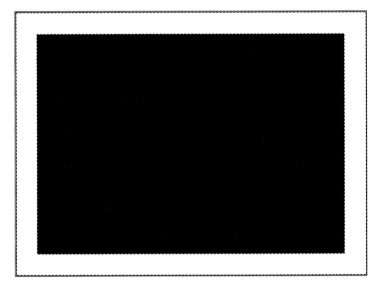

FIGURE 16.15

The Brush Strokes filter in the Filter Gallery applies a rough edge to the border.

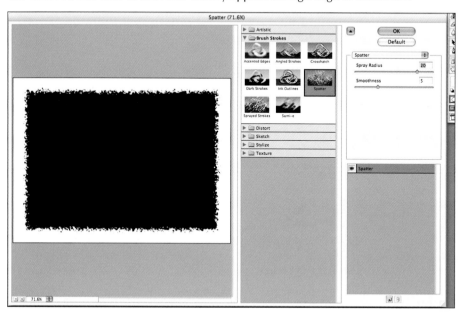

8. Click the image with the alpha channel. Target the alpha channel and Press ⌘/Ctrl+A to select all, then Press ⌘/Ctrl+C to copy the contents of the channel.

TIP Selecting All and then Copying temporarily places the image on the computer's clipboard. The Clipboard is a memory cache that holds the image so that you can paste it down at some later time. If the image is large, you may want to clear the cache after you've pasted it into the destination image. Choose Ed ⇨ Purge ⇨ Clipboard to clear the image from cache.

9. Open a photograph that is the same size and resolution as the border document. In this case it's 800px by 600px by 72 ppi.

10. In the Layers palette, click the new Layer icon to make a new layer. Press ⌘-V to paste the contents of the alpha channel into the new layer.

11. In the Layers palette, assign a Lightness Blending mode to the layer. The results should look like Figure 16.16.

TIP You can try other Brush Strokes Filter techniques and settings and settings in the filter gallery to produce different results.

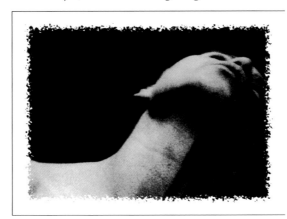
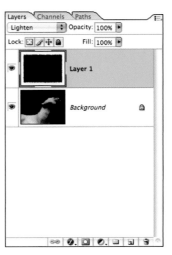

FIGURE 16.16

The Layers palette showing the border layer with the Lightness Blending mode above the content layer, and the resulting image.

Applying effects through gradient masks

You can save a channel as a gradient mask and apply a filter or color adjustment to the image to gradually distribute an effect. Gradient masks can be also used to distribute other filters and effects over a specific area.

The purpose of applying an effect through a gradient mask is to produce seamless a transition of color, a filter effect as demonstrated here, a color adjustment or image content from one area to another. Gradient mask techniques produce images with credibility because where it the technique begins and ends cannot be detected.

CROSS-REF Refer to Chapter 7 to find an example of how to make a 3D image.

1. Open the image that you want to alter.
2. Make a selection. In this image the sky was selected and then inversed.
3. Choose Window ➪ Channels to display the Channels palette.
4. Click the Save Selection as Alpha Channel icon in the Channels palette to save the selection as an alpha channel (see Figure 16.17).

A selection is saved as an alpha channel.

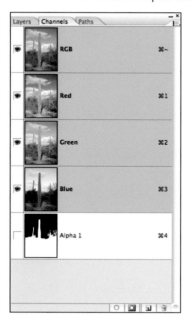

5. In the Channels palette, drag the new alpha channel to the Load Selection icon.

6. Click off the visibility icon in the Color Channels palette to display the alpha channel in the Image window.

7. Press the D key to set the foreground and background colors to black and white.

8. Press the G key to choose the Gradient tool. Click and drag the gradient tool across the selected area to apply a gradient to the alpha channel (see Figure 16.18).

NOTE   The gradient tool deposits the foreground color (black) at the point where you first clicked. The gradient becomes lighter until it becomes white where you release the mouse. Deselect.

9. Drag the new gradient alpha channel to the Load Selection icon. Click the RGB channel to target it. Click the eye next to the alpha channel to conceal it.

FIGURE 16.18

The gradient applied to a selection on the alpha channel.

10. Choose Filter ➪ Filter Gallery. Choose Artistic or any other filter (I choose the Stamp filter). Set the specifications for the filter in the Control Panel while you observe the affect in the Preview window (see Figure 16.19).

11. When satisfied, click OK. The areas of the mask that were white or light gray are most affected by the filter. On areas where the mask is dark gray areas are less affected and black areas are not affected at all.

CROSS-REF This technique can also be applied with a gradient layer mask to gradually conceal or reveal portions of an image. Gradient layer masks are discussed in Chapter 18.

FIGURE 16.19

An Artistic filter applied to the image through the alpha channel.

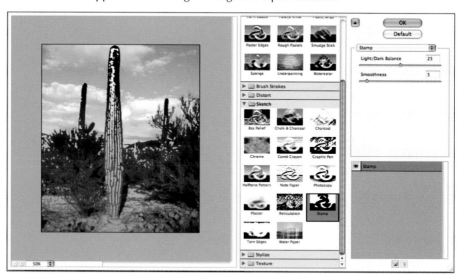

Combining selections

Alpha channels can be combined to produce a new channel. You can do this with the Calculations command (see Chapter 22) or you can combine channels with simple manipulations in the Channels palette.

Combining channels is relatively simple and involves a few very basic techniques that load a selection generated from a alpha channel onto another alpha channel and then fills the selection with white. This technique combines the contents of both channels so that a new Alpha channel with the combined selection content can be loaded onto the image.

1. Make a selection on an image with any of the Selection tools, as shown in Figure 16.20.

2. Click the Save Selection As Alpha Channel icon in the Channels palette. Photoshop names the new channel Alpha 1, as in Figure 16.21.

3. Drag the channel to the New Channel icon to duplicate it. The channel is automatically named Alpha 2, as in Figure 16.22.

FIGURE 16.20

The first selection.

FIGURE 16.21

The selection saved as an alpha channel.

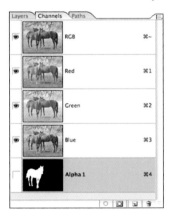

FIGURE 16.22

The Duplicate channel in the Channels palette.

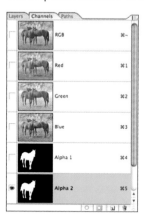

4. View the duplicate alpha channel in the Image window by pressing Opt/Alt and clicking its name or thumbnail. The black-and-white channel appears in the Image window.

5. Click on the RGB composite channel to view the image. Make another selection with any of the Selection tools, as in Figure 16.23.

FIGURE 16.23

The second selection.

TIP You can make the selection with both the RGB composite channel and Alpha 1 visible at the same time. Alpha 1 will appear as a red, translucent overlay. This will enable youyou can see where the two selections overlap.

6. Choose White as a foreground color. In the Channels palette, click Alpha 2 to target it. Press Opt/Alt-Delete/Backspace to fill the selected area on Alpha 2 with white as in Figure 16.24.

FIGURE 16.24

The selection on the Duplicate alpha channel filled with white.

CAUTION This technique requires that you select specific channels to alter. Always be aware of which channel is currently active. It is easy to make a mistake and fill the wrong alpha or composite channel with white.

7. Drag the Alpha 2 to the Load Selection icon. The Alpha 2 selection combining Alpha 1 and Alpha 2 is represented by marching ants on the image as in Figure 16.25.

The image with the new combined selection.

Entering Quick Mask Mode

Similar to alpha channels, Quick Mask mode can accelerate and enhance the precision of making selections. Quick Mask mode is an efficient method of making temporary masks using the painting and editing features.

Normally before you enter Quick Mask mode, you make a selection. Then toggle directly into Quick Mask mode in the Tools palette by clicking the Quick Mask icon or by pressing the letter Q. A temporary thumbnail labeled Quick Mask, in italics, appears in the Channels palette. The thumbnail changes appearance as you apply color to the Quick Mask. The Image window displays a red translucent mask that overlays the unselected parts of the image.

Painting and Editing Quick Masks

Quick Mask mode is ideal for cleaning up selections that you've made with one of the Selection tools. Quick Mask mode extends your selection making capabilities into painting and editing tools. You can paint a few pixels at a time with a small brush or with the Pencil tool, greatly enhancing the accuracy of the selection.

Painting on a Quick Mask is similar to painting on an alpha channel with the composite channel visible. By default, as you paint, if the foreground color is black, the paint tool will deposit a transparent red color. If the foreground color is white, the paint tool will erase the mask color. You can also paint with a tint percentage of black by adjusting the opacity of the Brush tool in the Options bar. When you paint with a tint percentage of black or choose any gray color from the Color Picker as the foreground color the mask will partially select those areas when it's converted into a selection.

To edit a Quick Mask, follow these steps:

1. Open a document and make a selection with any of the Selection tools (see Figure 16.26).

A selection on an image.

2. Click the Quick Mask icon in the Tools palette or press the Q key. The masked areas are represented by a translucent red color and the unmasked areas clearly display the image. The foreground and background swatch colors in the Tools palette are white and black. (see Figure 16.27).

FIGURE 16.27

In Quick Mask mode, the masked areas are represented by translucent red.

3. Click the Brush tool icon on the Tools palette or press the B key. Choose a brush from the Brush menu in the Options bar. Choose white as a foreground color. Click and drag the Brush tool on a masked region of the red translucent mask to erase the mask as shown in Figure 16.28. Similarly, paint with black on the transparent areas to totally restore the mask or paint with gray to partially restore the mask.

NOTE Quick masks are very similar to alpha channels. The only real difference is that they are temporary. They are can be edited with the painting and editing tools, the filters, and some of the tonal adjustment features.

TIP As you paint, you can toggle between the foreground and background color by pressing the X key.

4. In the Channels palette, click off the visibility icon next to the composite channel. Carefully examine the Quick Mask for missed areas and pinholes. Mistakes are common because it can be difficult to see omissions and errors on the translucent red mask overlay. The best way to examine the Quick Mask is to view it as a grayscale image. Click the visibility icon on all the other channels in the Channels palette except for the one to the immediate left of the Quick Mask. If necessary, edit the mask with black or white to clean up to deficient areas as in Figure 16.29.

FIGURE 16.28

Painting with white erases the mask. Painting with black restores it.

FIGURE 16.29

View the mask in grayscale and clean it up with the Brush tool.

> **TIP** You can make selections of a larger area on a Quick Mask and fill it with either black, white, or gray to save the labor of painting.

5. When you have completed painting, click the Edit In Standard Mode icon on the Tools palette or press the Q key. By default, the areas that were painted are now outlined by marching ants, as shown in Figure 16.30.

6. Save the selection as an alpha channel. Click the Save Selection As Alpha Channel icon at the bottom of the Channels palette.

> **TIP** To quickly change brushes while painting; while in the brush tool, Control/right-click the image to display the brushes palette. Release the control key and scroll down and click to select new brush.

> **TIP** You can change the color of the Quick Mask if it too closely resembles the image. Double click on the Quick Mask icon in the tools palette to display the Quick Mask Options dialog box. Click the color swatch to display the Color Picker. Choose a color and click OK twice.

FIGURE 16.30

Exit Quick Mask mode to make the selection.

Changing Quick Mask Options

You may want to change the color of the quick mask overlay if the color of the overlay closely resembles the image content. To do so, follow these steps:

1. Double-click the thumbnail of the Quick Mask icon in the Channels palette or the Quick Mask icon in the Tools palette to display the Quick Mask Options dialog box (see Figure 16.31).

2. Set display options for the channel. The radio buttons in the Color Indicates field let you choose whether masked areas or selected areas are displayed as color overlays.

3. Click the color swatch to display the Color Picker and choose a color for the mask. Specify the opacity of the mask from 0% to 100%. The opacity affects how the Quick Mask is displayed and not its masking capabilities. Lower the opacity to see the image more clearly through the mask.

FIGURE 16.31

The Quick Mask dialog box.

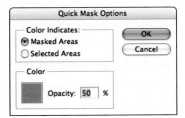

Applying Filters to Quick Masks

As with alpha channels, you can apply filters and some of the adjustment features to a Quick Mask and affect its masking capabilities. The advantage of applying a filter to a quick mask is that you can more easily gauge what the effect of the operation that you apply to the image might be.

In the example in the following step list, I apply a filter to a Quick Mask to soften its edges. This is essentially the same as feathering the selection but offers the advantage of being able to see the extent of the effect as you perform the operation:

1. Open a document and make a selection with any of the Selection tools (see Figure 16.32).

2. Click the Quick Mask icon in the Tools palette to enter Quick Mask mode. The masked areas are represented by the translucent red color (see Figure 16.33).

FIGURE 16.32

The initial selection.

FIGURE 16.33

The Quick Mask.

3. Choose Filter ➪ Blur ➪ Gaussian Blur. Make sure that the Preview check box is selected. Observe the Image window as you drag the Radius slider. Blur the edges of the mask the desired amount, as in Figure 16.34, and click OK.

TIP Enter and exit Quick Mask mode by pressing the Q key.

FIGURE 16.34

The Gaussian Blur filter applied to the Quick Mask to soften its edges.

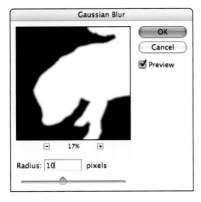

4. Exit Quick Mask mode. Apply an effect through the soft-edged selection.

Summary

In this chapter, I discussed less labor-intensive selection methods; you found out how to use alpha channels and Quick Masks.

This chapter covers the following topics:

- Editing channels
- Working with alpha channels
- Entering Quick Mask mode
- Painting and editing Quick Masks

In Chapter 17, you find out how to preserve edge detail when making selections.

Part VI

Masking Layer Content

Chapter 17

Masking Ambiguous Edges

Preserving edge detail when compositing an image is of critical importance. Poorly made selections can compromise the credibility of your image. You may encounter images that are tough to select because they have ambiguous surroundings or complex content. Perhaps fine hair or fur need to be selected, or the leaves on a tree. What do you do with these problem images? Photoshop offers a number of techniques that perform these miracle selections. The techniques vary from using the core channel information to make a selection, to implementing industrial-strength selection commands, to performing full-blown extractions with a special filter.

The purpose of creating a quality mask is to preserve as much edge detail as possible while preserving the subtle transitional tones. Ultimately, a mask is a silhouette whose edge precisely follows the contour of the area that it selects. When the edges of an image are ambiguous the mask needs to express this ambiguity in the form of variable levels of transparency.

The tools and techniques that create these types of masks are presented in this chapter. They don't necessarily make selecting ambiguous edges easy but they get the job done with precision.

IN THIS CHAPTER

Making selections with color channels

Working with color range

Selecting fine detail with adjustment layers and color range

Extracting images

Making Selections with Color Channels

You can use an image's core color information found in the Channels palette to make selections of hair and fine details. When you examine the color content of an image channel by channel, you have more choices from which to use Photoshop's features to generate an alpha channel. The differences in the contrast levels of the Red, Green, and Blue channels in an RGB image or the isolated Lightness channel in a Lab image can often provide a method of isolating regions of the image that would otherwise seem impossible to select. You can use this technique and a combination of Photoshop's painting tools and filters to select from images, such as in the image shown in Figure 17.1.

CROSS-REF There are a couple of similar techniques that help alter a copied color channel and apply industrial-strength blending modes to layers. These techniques can help select those really stubborn images where background and foreground are complex and almost indistinct.

1. Open an image that has ambiguous edges such as the seriously ambiguous edges in Figure 17.1.

FIGURE 17.1

An image with details such as hair can be difficult to select.

2. Choose Window ⇨ Channels, or press F7 on the keyboard if you still have it clustered with the Layers palette.

3. Click the Red, Green, and Blue channel thumbnails to display each channel as a grayscale in the Image window. (If the channels appear in color, choose Photoshop/Edit ⇨ Preferences ⇨ Display and Cursors and deselect the Color Channels in Color checkbox.) Determine which channel has the most contrast between the ambiguous areas. In this case, it's the Red channel (see Figure 17.2).

FIGURE 17.2

The Red channel has the most contrast.

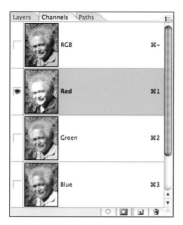

4. Click the Red channel and duplicate it by choosing Duplicate Channel from the Channels palette pull-down menu, or by dragging it to the New Channel icon at the bottom of the palette. The channel is named Red Copy.

> **TIP** The techniques used to make the selection work well on this image. But don't forget to experiment with other methods of increasing contrast, like Curves, Brightness and Contrast or even some of the Auto contrast features if you have a particularly stubborn image. Remember manipulating images is more of an art than science, so try different techniques until you get the results you want.

5. Choose Image ⇨ Adjustments ⇨ Levels. Drag the black and white Input sliders toward the center to amplify the contrast of the Red Copy channel. Adjust the sliders until the ambiguous areas are at their maximum contrast as shown in Figure 17.3. Click OK.

FIGURE 17.3

A Levels adjustment applied to a copied Red channel increases contrast.

6. Choose Filter ➪ Other ➪ High Pass. Drag the slider so that the image flattens and there is a distinct separation between the areas that you want to isolate as in Figure 17.4.

7. With the Lasso tool, select the outermost extremities of the edge surrounding everything that you want to separate in the selection.

8. Choose Select ➪ Inverse or press Opt/Alt I. Choose Black as a foreground color. Press Opt/Alt ➪ Delete/Backspace to fill the area with black. Then press ⌘/Ctrl+D to deselect (see Figure 17.5).

9. Click the RGB channel visibility icon to display the channel as a red mask. Be sure that the Red Copy is highlighted. Choose the Brush tool. Zoom into the edge. Paint out any areas around the extremities that you don't want included in the selection as in Figure 17.6. Paint with white to paint in areas that you want included.

TIP With a one- or two-pixel brush and white as a foreground color, paint in fine hairs.

FIGURE 17.4

The High Pass filter separates the tonal regions.

FIGURE 17.5

The selection filled it with black.

FIGURE 17.6

The Composite channel is visible and the details on the mask are painted with white. Areas that are masked are painted out with black.

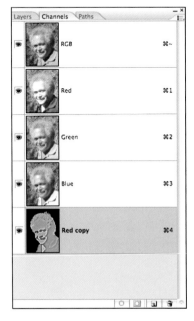

10. Click off the visibility icon next to the Composite channel to display the alpha channel in the Image window. With the Lasso tool, make a selection close to the outside edge of the image.

11. Press the X key to make white the foreground color. Press Opt/Alt ⇨ Delete/Backspace to fill the area with white as in Figure 17.7.

FIGURE 17.7

The completed mask.

12. Click the RGB channel to highlight it. Load the Red Copy by dragging it to the Load Selection icon.

13. Choose the Move tool. Click and drag the selected region image to another open image to composite it (see Figure 17.8).

FIGURE 17.8

The composited image shows the details of the original.

NOTE   After you've composited the image you might have to adjust the color on the edges with the Dodge, Burn, or Sponge tool to get it to blend with the new background.

CROSS-REF   Chapters 7, 8, and 12 tell you how to use color channel information to perform other powerful image-editing tasks.

Working with Color Range

Color Range is like having an industrial strength Magic Wand tool. It produces an accurate selection outline around a specified area within a range of color. This feature simplifies what could be a tedious task. If, for example, you have a lot of small areas of similar color situated throughout an image, you can specify a range of color to be included in the selection and all areas within the range will be selected.

When you choose Select ➪ Color Range, the dialog box displays what looks like an alpha channel. The Select pull-down menu lets you choose a specific color range to sample and it automatically selects all the pixels within the range. You can choose to select Reds, Yellows, Blues, Magentas, Greens, Cyans, Highlights, Midtones, Shadows, or Out-of-Gamut colors.

For greater control, choose the default, Sampled Colors. Before you open the dialog box, click the Eyedropper tool in the Tools palette and change the setting in the Options bar from Point Sample to 3 By 3 average for low-resolution images or 5 By 5 for images of 300 ppi. Open the dialog box and click the image with the Eyedropper to sample an initial color. Then choose the Plus Eyedropper in the dialog box and drag over other areas to enlarge the range of colors selected. If you sample colors that you don't want, drag over them with the Minus Eyedropper to reduce the range. You can click either on the image or on the preview to include or exclude pixels form the range. Drag the Fuzziness slider to extend the range of selection into adjacent pixels.

As you perform these operations the preview changes as colors are added or subtracted, as shown in Figure 17.9. The default display is a grayscale mask but the Selection Preview pop-up menu lets you choose from Grayscale, White Matte, Black Matte, Quick Mask, or None modes in which to view the mask in the Image window. These preview modes help you better determine what areas of the image will be selected and what areas will be masked. Choose the one most appropriate to the tonal or color content of your image. For example, you can choose White Matte if the image is particularly dark, because the mask will be more visible.

FIGURE 17.9

The preview changes as you add or subtract colors.

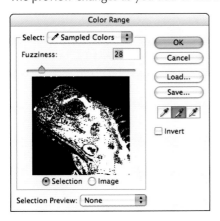

Click OK and the areas that are white (or gray) on the mask will be surrounded by a selection outline as in Figure 17.10. The selection may not include everything or include too much in which case you'll need to select or deselect those areas with the Lasso or other Selection tool.

FIGURE 17.10

The Color Range dialog box produces a selection outline so that you can edit its contents.

Selecting Fine Detail with Adjustment Layers and Color Range

Masks are black, white, or gray representations of selections. When you make a mask on an image with ambiguous edges it is helpful to think of the image as a high-contrast grayscale. You can apply a contrast adjustment such as Levels or Curves on an adjustment layer to edit the image into a high-contrast representation; then you can select the lightest portion of the image with the Color Range feature and save the selection as an alpha channel. The example image (see Figure 17.11) is particularly problematic because of its large range of contrast and the similarity of the tone of the hair to the tone of the background. But you can make a good alpha channel from the image by applying the following technique.

FIGURE 17.11

Selecting the model's hair is problematic.

NOTE During the process you may think you're ruining the image but don't worry. Because the adjustments are on adjustment layers, you can easily restore the image back to the original.

1. Click on the Eyedropper tool in the Tools palette. In the Options bar, set the Sample Size to 5 By 5 average.

2. Choose Layer ⇨ New Adjustment Layer ⇨ Curves. In the Curves dialog box click the Eyedropper and then click the lightest part of the image to color it to pure white.

3. Bend the curve into an S curve as shown in Figure 17.12 to further increase the contrast.

FIGURE 17.12

The curve is adjusted to increase contrast.

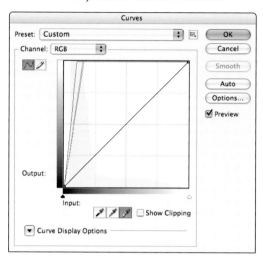

4. Choose Select ➪ Color Range to display the Color Range dialog box.

5. Click the lightest area of the image. Then choose the Plus Eyedropper. Click and drag over the lightest areas again. You can include slightly darker areas but be careful not to include any of the background in the selection. Click OK to select the lightest parts of the image, as shown in Figure 17.13.

The lightest parts of the image are selected with Color Range.

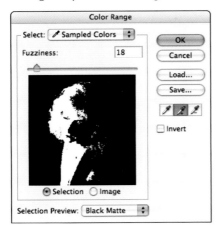

6. Go to the Channels palette and click the Save Selection as Channel icon to make an alpha channel (Alpha 1). Then Press ⌘/Ctrl+D to deselect.

7. In the Layers palette, click on the Visibility icon on the adjustment layer to conceal it. Choose Layer ➪ New Adjustment Layer ➪ Curves. In the Curves dialog box from the Presets pop-up menu choose Negative. Bend the curve until there is maximum contrast in the ambiguous area.

8. Choose Select ➪ Color Range to display the Color Range dialog box.

9. Again, click the lightest area of the image. Then choose the Plus Eyedropper. Click and drag over the lightest areas again. You can include slightly darker areas but again be careful not to include any of the background in the selection. Click OK to select the light parts of the image.

10. Go to the Channels palette and click the Save Selection as Channel icon to make an alpha channel (Alpha 2).

11. Click Alpha 1 in the Channels palette. Press the D key to make white the foreground color. Press Opt/Alt-Delete/Backspace to fill the selection with white.

12. Choose the Lasso tool and encircle inside the white portion of the channel as close to the edge as possible. Press Opt/Alt-Delete/Backspace to fill the selection with white, as shown in Figure 17.14.

FIGURE 17.14

The areas inside the selection are filled with white.

13. You might have to paint out areas with white or black to further refine the selection.

14. Discard the adjustment layers by dragging them to the Trash icon in the Layers palette. Load the alpha channel and perform the desired operation.

The Color Range command can isolate unprintable colors. If you are planning to convert an RGB document to CMYK to print color separations for offset lithographic printing, the color range feature is indispensable in selecting those colors that are outside the CMYK gamut. You need to adjust the out-of-gamut colors into the CMYK gamut prior to converting the image, so that the image you see on-screen is consistent with the printer's capabilities. You can use Color Range to select out-of-gamut colors. This example uses Adobe RGB 1998 for an RGB color space that will be converted to U.S. Sheetfed Coated V2.

1. Choose Edit ➪ Color Settings. In the Color Settings dialog box for Working RGB choose Adobe RGB 1998. For CMYK choose U.S. Sheetfed Coated V2. In the Color Management Policies field click the Ask When Opening boxes for Profile Mismatches and Missing Profiles check box, as shown in Figure 17.15.

FIGURE 17.15

Choose RGB and CMYK profiles from the color settings dialog box.

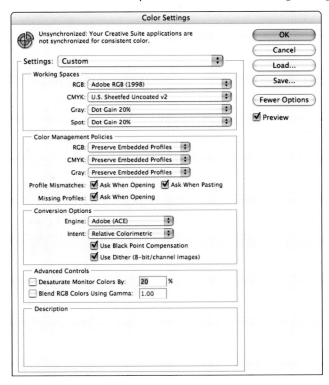

2. Open the file that you want to convert. If a Mismatched or Missing Profile dialog box is displayed choose Convert to Working Space (see Figure 17.16).

FIGURE 17.16

The Missing Profile dialog box.

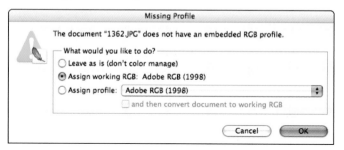

3. Make a duplicate of the document (Image ➪ Duplicate).

4. Place both images on the screen side by side.

5. Click the original image. Choose View ➪ Proof Setup ➪ Working CMYK.

6. Choose View ➪ Proof Colors. Notice that the colors in the CMYK proof are less saturated than in the RGB image, as shown in Figure 17.17.

FIGURE 17.17

Both images are placed side by side for comparison.

7. Choose View Gamut ➪ Warning to view the out-of-gamut colors, as shown in Figure 17.18. They appear as gray shapes. Press Shift-⌘/Ctrl+Y to turn off the Gamut warning.

FIGURE 17.18

The gamut warning displays a gray mask over the out-of-gamut colors.

8. Choose Select ⇨ Color Range ⇨ Choose Out Of Gamut from the bottom of the Select pull-down menu. The dialog box displays a mask of the out-of-gamut colors as shown in Figure 17.19

9. Click OK. The selection outline on the image displays a selection outline.

FIGURE 17.19

The Color Range command lets you select all colors outside the color gamut of the current CMYK profile.

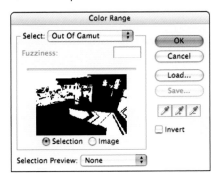

10. Press ⌘/Ctrl+H to hide the edges of the selection.

11. Choose Layer ⇨ New Adjustment Layer ⇨ Hue/Saturation. In the Hue/Saturation dialog box drag the sliders to more closely match the RGB image.

12. Choose Image ⇨ Mode ⇨ CMYK to convert the image for printing separations.

> **TIP** You can also experiment with other adjustments such as Levels and Curves to more closely match the RGB colors.

> **TIP** You can toggle in and out of Proof Colors by pressing ⌘/Ctrl+Y to compare the CMYK preview to the RGB display. Or choose Window ⇨ Documents ⇨ New Window to see another view of the image for comparing the soft-proof CMYK to the original RGB document. Or you can duplicate the document.

Extracting Images

Duplicating the best of the RGB channels to isolate images with fuzzy, complex, or indefinable edges is a good solid technique that gives you the advantage of controlling your selection. The main disadvantage is that it can be quite labor intensive. A more automated approach is to isolate a region with the extract filter. The results might not be as precise as using the channels method, but you can, by trial and error, isolate problem edges with much less effort. The Extract command is a subinterface that can gauge the subtle differences of an image edge by its color and brightness. With the extract command, you make a mask by painting and filling. The region that is masked is then physically extracted from the area around it.

You start the extraction process by painting the edge of the extraction with the Edge Highlighter. You then fill its interior and preview it. You can refine the mask and preview as many times as you need to until you have selected the image and none of the background. You then extract it, which deletes undefined areas and places the image on a transparent layer.

> **CAUTION** Because of the radical transformation that Extract produces, you should first duplicate the image or make a snapshot of it.

Specify the following tool options in the dialog panel:

- **Brush Size:** Enter a value or drag the slider to specify the width of the Edge Highlighter tool, which defines the boundary of the image.

- **Highlight:** Choose a color to display the edge boundary that you draw with the Edge tool.

- **Fill:** Choose a color to display the interior fill inside the boundary.

- **Smart Highlighting:** This option helps you keep the highlight on the edge, especially when the edge between the foreground and background is sharp with similar color or texture. To toggle Smart Highlighting on or off while you drag, press the ⌘/Ctrl key.

Follow these steps to make an extraction:

1. Open an image and choose Filter ➪ Extract to display the dialog box as shown in Figure 17.20.

FIGURE 17.20

Open the Extract filter.

2. Set the Highlight color and the Fill color to red, green, or blue.

3. Click the Edge Highlighter tool. Choose a Brush Size from the Control Panel. Select the Edge Highlighter tool and drag along the edge area you want to extract. Draw the highlight so that it slightly overlaps both the foreground and background regions around the edge about equally.

4. Use a smaller brush to precisely highlight edges that are more defined.

5. If you make a mistake, you can erase the highlight. Select the Eraser tool from the dialog box's toll palette, and drag over the highlight. This tool is available only after you've highlighted an edge. You can completely erase the highlight by pressing Option /Alt-Delete/Backspace.

TIP To toggle between the Highlighter and the Eraser while drawing an edge, press the Option/Alt key.

6. To fill the area, select the Fill tool. Click inside the outline to fill the interior (see Figure 17.21).

The extraction edge outlined with the highlighter and filled with the Paint Bucket tool.

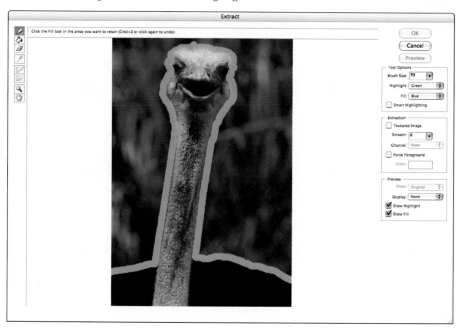

If the image is especially intricate or lacks a clear interior, make sure that the highlight covers the entire edge. To highlight an area of a single color, press ⌘/Ctrl-Delete/Backspace and then click the Force Foreground checkbox.

Previewing the extraction

To view the extracted image, click the Preview button. The edges of the extracted image appear soft, and the area outside the extraction is transparent, such as the one shown in Figure 17.22. You can better see the result of the extraction if you view it using the following techniques:

The Extraction field offers the following options:

- **Textured image:** Check this box if the foreground or background is highly textured.
- **Smooth:** This slider smoothes the edges of the highlighted edge. To help remove stray artifacts in the extraction, click the right arrow next to the Smooth field in the Extract

dialog box. Enter a value in the field or drag the Smooth Slider. The higher the number is, the greater the radius of pixels that will be affected. After you are finished editing, click Preview again to view the edited extraction. You can edit and preview the extraction as many times as you like until you achieve the results you want.

- **Channel:** The menu lets you load an alpha channel that will serve as the fill. The alpha channel can be modified with the tools.

- **Force Foreground:** Check this box if the area is intricate or lacks a specific interior.

The Preview field controls how the extraction is displayed:

- The Show menu switches between previews of the original and extracted images.

- Display menu to preview the extracted image as a grayscale mask or against a white matte or a black matte. To choose a colored background, choose Other and a color from the Color Picker. To display a transparent background, choose None.

- Show Highlight /Fill option to display the object's extraction boundaries or interior.

FIGURE 17.22

The extraction is previewed against the Transparency checkerboard.

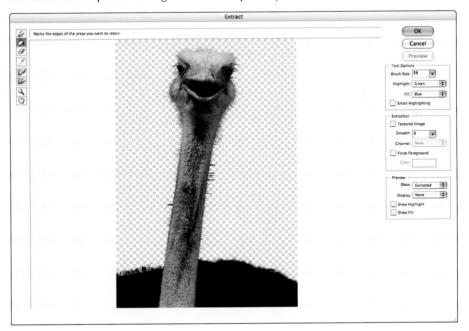

Refining the extraction

These tools let you refine the edges and interior of the extraction, enabling you to add to the extraction or eliminate unwanted pixels.

■ **The Cleanup tool:** You can edit and refine the extraction with the Cleanup tool, which is only available when you preview the extracted image. The Cleanup tool subtracts opacity. Making multiple passes has a cumulative effect. Drag over an area to erase it to transparency. Press the Option/Alt key while painting with the Cleanup tool to restore opacity.

■ **The Eraser and Fill tools:** You can use this tool to edit the previewed image. The Eraser restores the edge to transparency. Clicking a filled area with the Fill paint bucket removes the fill.

■ **The Edge Touchup tool:** Use the Edge Touchup tool to edit the extraction boundaries. The tool, which is available when you show the extracted image, sharpens the edges of the extracted image. It has a cumulative effect as you make multiple passes over the edge. If the image has no clear edge, the Edge Touchup tool adds opacity to the image or makes the background more transparent.

Extracting the image

To apply the final extraction, click OK. All pixels on the layer outside the extracted image are eliminated. If necessary, use the History brush or the Background Eraser to touch up stray edge pixels. When you perform the extraction, the original image is extracted from its surroundings; therefore, duplicating the image prior to applying this filter is a good idea.

Summary

The techniques I discussed in this chapter can help you make selections of items with ambiguous edges.

Specifically, I discuss the following topics:

■ Making selections with the Color Range dialog box

■ Selecting fine detail

■ Extracting images

Chapter 18 is packed with information on how to use Layer Masks, Clipping Masks, and Smart Objects.

Chapter 18

Working with Layer Masks, Clipping Masks, and Smart Objects

S elections, alpha channels, and Quick Masks all work to the same ends: to protect a region from the application of a tool or operation while exposing other areas to their effects. But Photoshop's masking capabilities can also combine visual elements in unique and rather surprising ways. Layer masks reveal or conceal areas of a layer from view. They offer the capability of manipulating the opacity or transparency of pixels on isolated areas of a content layer.

Photoshop also offers the ability to use the transparent portions of layers to mask content by creating clipping masks; a very useful method of superimposing one image over another. And to pile even more onto the heap, in Photoshop CS3, Smart Object layers offer the ability to mask filter effects. This chapter shows you how to use these extremely useful features to your best advantage.

Working with Layer Masks

The Opacity slider on the Layers palette is a global adjustment — it controls the transparency of all the pixels on a layer. Reducing the opacity gives you the ability to see through the layer content to the layers below. With a layer mask you can control the transparency of the specific region of a layer. Layer masks look similar to alpha channels but they reside in the Layers palette next to the thumbnail of the layer. They use the same visual iconography as alpha channels. On an alpha channel, black areas fully mask an area, white fully exposes an area to the effects of a tool operation, and gray partially exposes an area. On a layer mask, black completely conceals layer contents from view, white fully reveals contents, and gray partially reveals an area.

Layer masks can be made several different ways.

- **Reveal All:** Choose Layer ➪ Layer Mask ➪ Reveal All to display an empty white thumbnail in the Layers palette. The content of the layer in its entirety is visible in the Image window. If you click on the layer mask to target it, a double border indicates that it is ready for editing. You can then paint with 100% black, to conceal areas on the targeted layer and reveal the content of the layer beneath it. Paint with gray to partially conceal areas or with white to erase any black or gray that you may have painted.

- **Hide All:** Choose Choose Layer ➪ Layer Mask ➪ Hide All and a black thumbnail is displayed that layer conceals layer contents. As you paint with white, you reveal portions of the layer.

- **Reveal Selection:** If a selection is active when you create a layer mask and you choose Layer ➪ Layer Mask ➪ Reveal Selection, the contents of the selection outline on the layer mask fills with white and areas outside the selection outline fills with black. The contents of the selection are visible in the Image window. All pixels that are not selected are not visible.

- **Hide Selection:** Choose Layer ➪ Add Layer Mask ➪ Hide Selection, the contents of the selection outline on the layer mask fills with black and areas outside the selection outline fills with white. The contents of the selection are not visible in the Image window. All pixels that are not selected are visible.

> **NOTE** Not having the correct layer or layer mask targeted is perhaps the most common mistake made by users.

Controlling layer masks

Layer masks can be controlled by key commands or menu commands:

- **Disable/Enable a Layer Masks:** Shift/click the layer mask to turn it on or off, or choose Layer ➪ Enable or Disable Layer Mask.

- **View a Layer Mask:** Option/Alt-click the mask thumbnail to view the layer mask in the Image window.

- **Make a Selection from a Layer Mask:** Press ⌘/Ctrl click the layer mask to generate a selection outline.

- **Move a Layer's Mask and Content:** Click between the two thumbnails to reveal or conceal the link icon. When the two thumbnails are linked and you drag on the image with the Move tool, both the image on the layer and layer mask move as a unit. When the link is concealed, only the content of the targeted thumbnail will move.

- **Removing a Layer Mask:** Choose Layer ➪ Remove Layer Mask ➪ Discard or Apply. Discard removes the layer mask and does not apply the effect. Apply removes the layer mask and applies the effect directly to the pixels of the layer. You can also drag the Layer Mask icon (not the Layer icon) to the trash can on the Layers palette. You will see a dialog box that asks if you want to apply the layer mask to the image before discarding it.

Making layer masks

1. Open a file that is composed of at least two layers. The example has three — two content layers and a background (see Figure 18.1).

FIGURE 18.1

This image has three layers. The topmost layer will contain the layer mask.

2. Choose Layer ➪ Layer Mask ➪ Reveal All. A Layer Mask icon appears in the Layers palette that is, by default, targeted for editing (see Figure 18.2).

FIGURE 18.2

The new empty layer mask.

3. Choose black as the foreground color and white as a background color. Choose the Brush tool and a Soft brush from the Brushes palette. In the Options bar, set the opacity to 100%. Pass over areas that you wish to totally conceal (see Figure 18.3).

4. In the Options bar, lower the opacity of the brush tool and paint areas that you want to partially conceal. The lower the opacity, the less that is concealed.

5. Apply multiple passes of the lower opacity of the brush to mold and model the image.

6. Choose a blending mode from the Layers palette to intensify the effect. In this example I chose Hard Light (see Figure 18.3).

FIGURE 18.3

Painting on the layer mask with a lower opacity of black partially conceals the topmost layer. The Hard Light Blending mode enhances the effect.

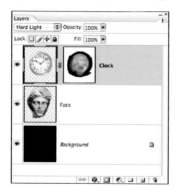

TIP You can restore areas of the topmost image by painting on the layer mask with white.

Seamless Blending with Gradient Masks

One of the advantages of a layer mask is that pixels can be superimposed and blended from one layer to another. You can visually control color relationships by applying a gradient to a layer mask and subtly blend the content of two layers for a seamless composite. Here are a couple of techniques that will deliver the goods:

This method blends two layers together over the entire surface of the image. It's a good technique for superimposing a sky over a landscape, for example, and seamlessly blending them together. The sky should be the same size or slightly larger than the landscape.

1. Open a landscape image (see Figure 18.4).

FIGURE 18.4

The landscape image.

2. Open the sky image with the content that you want to composite.

3. Click and drag the sky image and place it on the landscape image and release the mouse (see Figure 18.5).

4. Choose Layer ⇨ Layer Mask ⇨ Reveal All.

5. Reduce the opacity of the sky layer to 50% so that you can determine where to blend the images together.

6. Click on the layer mask to target it.

7. Press the D key to set the foreground and background colors to black and white.

8. Choose the Gradient tool. Click a point that you want to blend and drag away from it. It deposits black (the foreground color) that will fade to white (the background color) on the layer mask gradually blending the layer's contents with the layer below it. The length of gradient drag line will determine the distance of the transition.

9. Set the topmost layer's opacity to 100% to reveal its full intensity. Figure 18.6 shows the Layers palette with the gradient mask and the resulting image.

FIGURE 18.5

The layer is superimposed above the background in the stack.

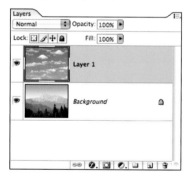

FIGURE 18.6

The Layers palette and gradient mask.

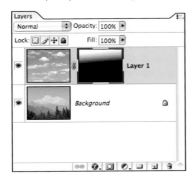

Here's another method that blends layers with a layer mask. This method blends a region of an image using a layer mask that has an active selection.

1. Open the image (see Figure 18.7).
2. Make a selection around the content that you want to composite (see Figure 18.8).

The top of the cactus needs repair.

Make a selection of the area you want to composite.

3. Choose Layer ➪ New ➪ Layer Via Copy.

4. Drag the contents of the new layer into place. If necessary transform it so that it fits (see Figure 18.9).

FIGURE 18.9

Drag the selected area and position it into place.

5. Choose Layer ➪ Layer Mask ➪ Reveal All.

6. Drag a rectangular marquee around the place where the layer and the background overlap (see Figure 18.10).

FIGURE 18.10

Make a rectangular selection around the overlapping areas.

7. Click the layer mask to be sure it is selected. Choose the Gradient tool. Click the edge of the selection that you want to blend and drag away from it. It deposits black (the foreground color) that will fade to white (the background color) on the layer mask gradually blending the layer's contents with the layer below it. The length of Gradient tool's drag line determines the distance of the transition (see Figure 18.11).

FIGURE 18.11

Blend the overlapping areas with a gradient layer mask.

8. The portion of the cactus is seamlessly blended with the bottom, as shown in Figure 18.12. It may be necessary to make color or tonal adjustments to best match the two parts.

FIGURE 18.12

The cactus tip is seamlessly repaired with the gradient layer mask.

Masking Color Adjustments

Masking adjustment layers is an effective way to isolate an area of the image and to apply color manipulations to it without affecting the rest of the composition. It works well when you want to alter the color depth/contrast of the subject of an image without affecting the background.

Selective adjustments

You can use adjustment layers to selectively apply a color adjustment to an image. When you make an adjustment layer, you contain the color information on a layer that affects the layer (or layers) immediately below it in the stack. A layer mask is automatically created that can conceal portions of the effect so you can selectively apply an adjustment over specific areas while concealing it from other areas.

Here is how to selectively apply a color adjustment.

1. Open an image whose color you want to adjust (see Figure 18.13).

FIGURE 18.13

The original image.

2. Choose Layer ➪ New Adjustment Layer ➪ and one of the adjustments from the list. In this case I chose Hue/Saturation. The New Layer dialog box appears. Click OK.

3. In the Hue/Saturation dialog box that is displayed, adjust the color of the image by dragging the sliders. Click OK when satisfied (see Figure 18.14).

FIGURE 18.14

Adjust the Hue/Saturation sliders to change the color of the image.

4. Click the layer mask. Choose the Brush tool and a brush shape from the Brush Presets menu. Press the D key to set black as the foreground color and white as the background color. Paint out the areas on the layer mask that you don't want to affect.

5. You can gain even more control by painting on the layer with mask various opacities of black to partially affect the image as shown in Figure 18.15.

FIGURE 18.15

Paint the image with the layer mask icon selected to mask the color adjustment.

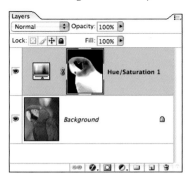

6. At any time you can click the Hue/Saturation icon in the Layers palette to display the Hue/Saturation controls and readjust the color. And you can repaint the layer mask.

> **TIP** If you select an area prior to creating the adjustment layer, the layer mask will automatically mask the areas outside the selection outline.

> **TIP** Most filters work with the adjustment layer masks. If, for example, you want to separate color adjustments between subject and background, but don't want an abrupt change, you can apply Filter ➪ Blur ➪ Gaussian Blur to soften the edges of the layer mask.

Controlling contrast

The contrast of an old photograph may fade over time because of the instability of the emulsion. This emulsion may react chemically with non-archival photo paper or it may have been exposed to sunlight; both of these may cause discoloring or fading. A photo may have developed a gradual fade from one side to the other. You can use a layer mask to apply precision contrast adjustments to restore the image to its former glory.

Apply this technique to an image that has a gradual fade:

1. Open the file. It's a nice sepia print that has faded diagonally with age (see Figure 18.16).

FIGURE 18.16

The image has a diagonal fade that goes from top left to bottom right.

2. Choose Image ⇨ Mode ⇨ Grayscale to convert the image to black and white.

3. Choose Layer ⇨ New Adjustment Layer ⇨ Levels. In the New Layer dialog box that appears, leave the defaults and click OK. When the Levels dialog box is displayed, click OK again.

4. Target the adjustment layer's layer mask by clicking on its thumbnail.

5. Press the D key to choose black as a foreground color and white as a background color.

6. Choose the Gradient tool. In the Options bar, choose the Linear Gradient icon. Click on the Gradient menu in the Options bar. Click the third gradient swatch (black to white).

7. Click and drag the gradient in the direction of the fade. In this case diagonally from the top left to the lower right. The gradient appears on the adjustment layer mask as in Figure 18.17.

FIGURE 18.17

With the layer mask selected, click and drag a gradient slider in the direction of the fade.

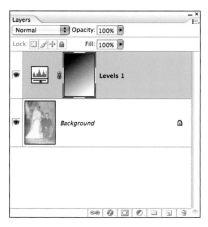

8. Double-click the Levels 1 adjustment layer thumbnail. The Levels dialog box appears.

9. Be sure the preview box is checked. Drag the Black Shadow slider to the right and the Gray Input slider to the right until the lightest areas of the fade darkens and has good contrast. Click OK (see Figure 18.18).

FIGURE 18.18

Adjust the sliders in the Levels dialog box to even out the fade.

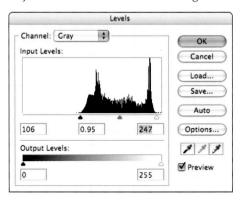

10. Choose Image Mode RGB color to convert the image back to RGB.

11. Choose Image ⇨ Adjustments ⇨ Hue Saturation. Click the Colorize button. Drag the Hue and Saturation sliders until the sepia color is fully restored (see Figure 18.19).

FIGURE 18.19

Adjust the sliders in the Hue/Saturation dialog box to restore the image back to sepia.

Masking Solids, Gradients, and Patterns

You can fill a region by using the Fill command, but a more powerful method involves creating a Fill layer. Fill layers are more dynamic than the other methods of filling because they combine the potential of the Fill command with the flexibility of layers. You can create Fill layers with solid colors, gradients, or patterns. These fills support all the properties of layers including transparency, blending modes, and adjustment layers and when you create a Fill layer it automatically creates a layer mask.

Creating a solid Fill layer

Follow these steps to create a Solid Color Fill layer:

1. Open an image that you want to fill (see Figure 18.20).

FIGURE 18.20

Open the image that you want to fill.

2. Choose Layer ➪ New Fill Layer ➪ Solid Color.
3. The New Layer dialog box is displayed, with the layer named Color Fill 1 by default. Enter a name or keep the defaults and click OK.
4. The Color Picker is displayed. Choose a color and click OK.

5. The new layer that appears in the Layers palette is a solid color and has a layer mask linked to it, as in Figure 18.20. The layer mask enables you to conceal portions of the image by painting on it as in Figure 18.21.

FIGURE 18.21

Choose a blending mode so that the image content is mixed with the solid color fill. Then paint on the layer mask with solid black to conceal all color and a percentage of black to create tints.

 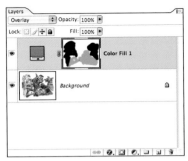

6. Choose a blending mode in the Layers palette (I chose Overlay) and paint on the layer mask with a solid black for pure color and a percentage of black to create tints.

7. To change the color of the layer click on the color swatch in the Layers palette and pick a new color from the Color Picker.

Creating a Gradient Fill layer

Gradient layers offer the advantage of being able to precisely control the gradient from a single interface and mask regions of the image with a layer mask.

1. Open an image that you want to apply a gradient to Figure 18.22.

2. Choose Layer ➪ New Fill Layer ➪ Gradient.

3. The New Layer dialog box appears. The name of the new layer defaults to Gradient Fill 1. Click OK. The Gradient Fill dialog box shown in Figure 18.23 appears.

FIGURE 18.22

Open the image.

FIGURE 18.23

In the Gradient Fill dialog box, you adjust the characteristics of a gradient. The Gradient Editor lets you edit a gradient or create a new one.

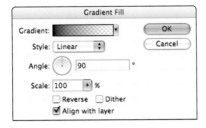

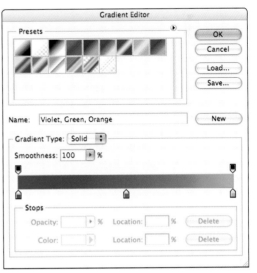

4. The colors of the gradient default to the last gradient chosen. If you want a gradient other than the one presented, click the down arrow to the right of the gradient swatch to choose a saved gradient, or click the swatch itself to display the Gradient Editor, as shown in Figure 18.23. Create a new one. In the Gradient Fill dialog box, set the following specifications:

   ▪ **Style:** Choose a gradient type from the Style pop-up list.

   ▪ **Angle:** Enter a number, or click the diagram, to choose an angle to control the direction of the gradient.

   ▪ **Scale:** Choose a scale by clicking on the arrow and moving the slider or by entering a value, to control the gradient's relative distribution over an area.

   ▪ **Reverse:** Select Reverse to flip the gradient's direction over the entire layer.

   ▪ **Dither:** Select Dither to soften the blending of the gradient. Dithering may help prevent banding that sometimes occurs when the gradient is printed.

   ▪ **Align With Layer:** If the gradient is contained within a selection, check Align With Layer to distribute the gradient within the selection; not checking this box distributes it over the entire layer but reveals only the selected portion.

5. Click OK to fill the layer. The image displays the solid color gradient. The Layers palette displays a color swatch of the gradient and a layer mask.

6. You can choose a blending mode and mask areas of the gradient by painting on the layer mask as shown in Figure 18.24.

FIGURE 18.24

The image with the blending mode and layer mask applied.

Creating a Pattern Fill layer

A pattern chosen from the Pattern presets can be applied to a layer in the same way a Solid Fill or a Gradient Fill can:

1. Choose Layer ➪ New Fill Layer ➪ Pattern.
2. The New Layer dialog box appears with the layer named Pattern Fill 1 by default. Enter a name for the layer to better identify it and click OK; the Pattern Fill dialog box appears (see Figure 18.25).

FIGURE 18.25

The Pattern fill dialog box.

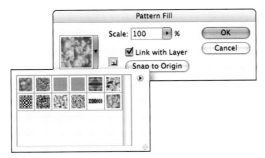

3. Click the down arrow to choose a pattern, and set the following options:
    - **Scale:** Choose a percentage to determine the size of the pattern.
    - **Snap To Origin:** You can move the pattern by placing your cursor on it in the Image window, or you can snap it back to its origin by clicking the Snap To Origin button.
    - **Link With Layer:** Checking this box aligns the pattern's layer mask to the layer.

As with Solid and Gradient Fill layers you can paint on the layer mask to adjust the visibility of the pattern.

Color Fill, Gradient Fill, and Pattern Fill layers can be edited by double-clicking their thumbnails in the Layers palette to reveal the Color Picker, the Gradient Fill dialog box, or the Pattern Fill dialog box.

Clipping Images

Grouping layers together can create a unique graphic effect called a *clipping mask*. You can superimpose one image on top of another and create a virtual "tattoo". If you combine this effect with an opacity adjustment, a layer mask, or a blending mode, you can mold and model the superimposed layer into superbly realistic surfaces.

Defining areas to be clipped

To create a clipping mask, the image on the bottom layer must be surrounded by transparency. The clipped layer is positioned immediately above it in the stack. When a layer is clipped, it fills the shape of the pixels. The transparency of the bottom layer masks the pixels outside the shape area.

Creating a "virtual tattoo"

To see how clipping groups work, clip two layers together to create a virtual tattoo:

1. Open the file. The image should be separated into at least two layers. The topmost layer is the image and the bottom layer will be used as a clipping mask. The example has two layers and a solid black background.

2. Option/Alt and click between the two layers. The top layer is clipped to the bottom layer and conforms to the shape of the pixel content (see Figure 18.26).

FIGURE 18.26

When you clip two layers together the content of the topmost layer is masked by the shape of the layer beneath it.

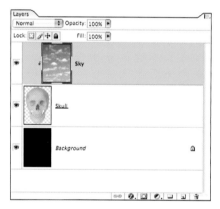

3. Experiment with blending modes to enhance the effect. Target the top layer and choose Hard Light from the pop-up menu at the top of the Layers palette. The lightning becomes more saturated. Try Pin Light and Linear Light, too. Adjust the Opacity slider to modify the effect shown in Figure 18.27.

FIGURE 18.27

A blending mode applied to the image to bring out the detail.

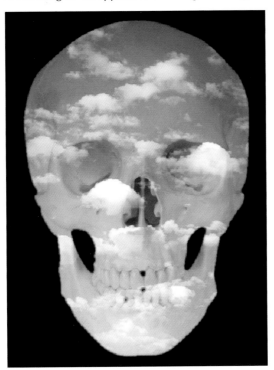

Combining clipping masks and layer masks

You can add a layer mask to model the content of the topmost layer. The layer mask can produce a 3-dimentional modeled look attainable by painting with an opacity percentage of black.

1. Click the topmost layer to target it. Choose Layer ➪ Layer Mask ➪ Reveal All. A new layer mask appears in the Layers palette.

2. Choose black as a foreground color. Choose the Paintbrush and set its opacity in the Options bar to 20%. Choose a Soft brush from the Brush panel. Paint on the image in various places to increase dimensionality. As you do, the layer mask displays the changes and the topmost layer is partially masked revealing more of the bottommost layer.

3. Paint on the layer mask with multiple passes with opacities of black until you are satisfied with the image (see Figure 18.28).

FIGURE 18.28

Paint on the layer mask to mold and model the image.

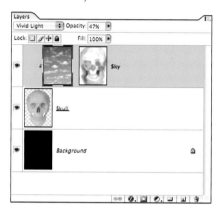
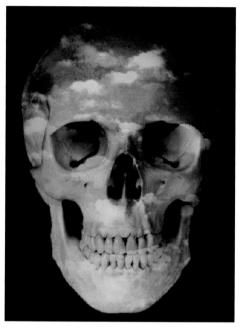

TIP Type in a two-digit numerical value while the Brush tool is selected to change the opacity setting in the Options bar.

Working with Smart Objects

Compositing a vector based image like a piece of clip art, a logo or an illustration that was created in Adobe Illustrator might present problems. Transforming the image or increasing its scale after it has been placed in Photoshop can diminish its quality.

When you open or place a vector image, Photoshop rasterizes it, which simply means that the vector data is converted into pixels. When you attempt to resize it, the quality can become inconsistent with the rest of the image.

Is the loss of image quality inevitable? Do you have to except inconsistent rendering elements on your images? Absolutely not! You can place a vector image onto a *Smart Object* layer and then size, transform, warp and even filter it without loss.

There are several ways to work non-destructively in Photoshop. Take Adjustment Layers for example. You apply settings to an independent layer that can be changed, concealed, or discarded at any time. The actual pixels are unaffected. *Smart Objects,* too are nondestructive. The information does not affect the layer per se, but instead is processed using information from the source document.

Smart Objects combine raster and vector images into a kind of hybrid layer. The vector data is placed on a special layer that links to the original file. Nondestructive transformations can then be preformed to layer content. You can create a Smart Object to embed vector files from Adobe Illustrator or Adobe Acrobat or raster images from a Photoshop file and apply transformations, layer styles, opacity, filters, and blending modes. When you create a Smart Object layer, a small icon in the lower-right corner identifies it as such.

You can work with Smart Object layers several ways:

- **Effects:** You can apply layer styles, opacity, blending modes and filters to Smart Objects.
- **Transformations:** You can perform nondestructive transformations like scale, rotate, or warp to layer content without compromising quality. The transformations don't diminish the quality of vector images.
- **Filters:** You can perform nondestructive filtering to Smart Objects with *Smart Filters.*
- **Shadow/Highlight:** You can apply the Shadow/Highlight command to Smart Objects as a Smart Filter.
- **Updates:** You can update a Smart Object and automatically update all its linked instances.
- **Conversions:** Convert one or more selected layers of a regular Photoshop document into one smart object layer.
- **Placement:** Place an existing file inside an existing Smart Object.
- **Pasting:** Paste existing vector content from Adobe Illustrator inside an existing smart object.
- **Duplicate:** Duplicate an existing smart object to create two versions that refer to the same source contents. Editing the source content of one version updates them both.
- **Drag and Drop:** Drag-and-drop selected PDF or Adobe Illustrator artwork into a Photoshop document.
- **Camera Raw:** Placing a Camera Raw file as a smart object enables you to reconfigure the Camera Raw settings at any time, even after you've made edits to the file in Photoshop.

CAUTION You can't directly paint, dodge, burn, clone, or perform any other pixel altering operation to a Smart Object. You must first click on the smart object layer to display the source document and edit with the tools of the source program. Or you can convert or duplicate the smart object to a regular layer.

Creating and Editing Smart Objects

Vector-based Smart Objects maintain resolution even if they are enlarged because the Smart Object layer is directly linked to the original image. When the layer is modified the Smart Object uses the vector data of the original file as its source, which is resolution independent.

Creating Smart Objects

There are several methods for converting layers containing pixels or vector files into Smart Objects. The method you choose will depend on the layer content and your image editing goals.

Here three methods for creating Smart Objects

■ Select one or more layers. Choose Layer ➪ Smart Objects ➪ Group Into New Smart Object (the same option is available in the Layer Options menu). The Smart Object icon appears on the layer's thumbnail in the Layers palette shown in Figure 18.29.

FIGURE 18.29

The Smart Object icon appears on the layer's thumbnail in the Layers palette.

■ Drag layers or selected vector objects from PDF or Adobe Illustrator files into a Photoshop document to automatically create a Smart Object layer.

■ Copy and paste selected vector objects from Illustrator into a Photoshop document. When the Paste dialog box is displayed, click the Smart Object checkbox (see Figure 18.30).

NOTE Enable the PDF and AICB (No Transparency Support) File Handling & Clipboard preferences in Illustrator for optimum flexibility in pasting images between programs.

FIGURE 18.30

When the Paste dialog box is displayed, click the Smart Object checkbox.

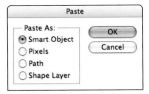

Editing Smart Objects

If you create a Smart Object layer and the source content is raster like a Photoshop or a Camera Raw image, click the layer. Click OK on the dialog box that opens, and the layer contents open as a separate document that you can edit in the source program. Choose File ➪ Save and the Smart Object layer (or layers) updates.

If the content is vector based, click on it to open it in Adobe Illustrator. Edit the image in Illustrator and save the changes (Figure 18.31). The edits are updated in all linked instances of the smart object in the Photoshop document.

FIGURE 18.31

You can reedit the Smart Object in Illustrator.

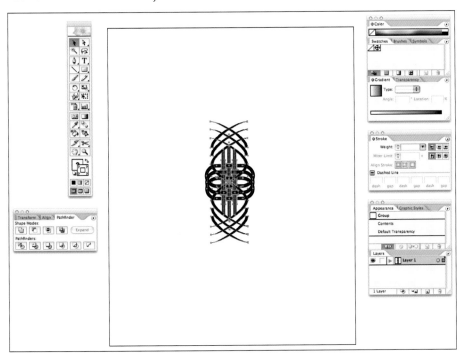

You can also select the Smart Object in the Layers palette and choose Layer ⇨ Smart Objects ⇨ Edit Contents. Click OK on the dialog box that opens. Make edits to the source content file, and then save the image.

Duplicate a Smart Object

Smart Objects can be duplicated. The duplicate and the original Smart Object can be linked to the same source document. You can link the duplicate Smart Objects so that when you edit one version, the second is also updated. Or you can specify that the Smart Objects are unlinked so that your edits to one Smart Object do not affect the other.

In the Layers palette, select a Smart Object layer. To create a duplicate Smart Object that is linked to the original, choose Layer ⇨ New ⇨ Layer Via Copy, or drag the Smart Object layer to the Create A New Layer icon at the bottom of the Layers palette. Edits you make to the original Smart Object affect the copy and vice versa.

To create a duplicate Smart Object that is not linked to the original, choose Layer ⇨ Smart Objects ⇨ New Smart Object Via Copy. This type of copy is unaffected by edits you make to the original Smart Object.

Creating and Editing Smart Filters

If you're working in Photoshop CS3, you can apply a filter to a Smart Object called, not coincidentally a *Smart Filter*. Smart Filters appear in the Layers palette below the Smart Object layer to which they are applied. They are nondestructive. In other words, because the filter data is on a separate layer you can you can adjust, reorder, conceal, or delete it without affecting the image pixels.

All filters except for Extract, Liquify, Pattern Maker, and Vanishing Point, can be applied as a Smart Filter plus you can also apply third party filters and the Shadow/Highlight adjustment as a Smart Filter.

Applying Smart Filters

To work with Smart Filters, you click on a Smart Object layer. Choose a filter from the Filter menu and then set filter options (Figure 18.32).

A Smart Filter that has settings can be edited at any time. Double-click the Smart Filter in the Layers palette to display the settings. Readjust the filter settings and click OK to apply them to the Smart Object.

CAUTION While you're editing a filter, any filter stacked above it doesn't preview.

FIGURE 18.32

An artistic Smart Filter applied to a Smart Object.

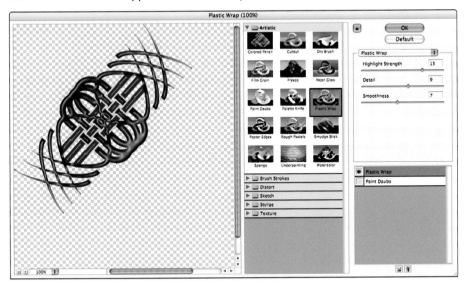

Applying blending modes

Another trick that can be applied to Smart Objects is the ability to edit blending options If you Ctrl-click (Mac OS) or right-click (Windows) the Smart Filter in the Layers palette you can choose Edit Blending Options. The dialog box that is displayed shows a nice preview as you adjust the mode and the opacity (see Figure 18.33). Click OK to commit the blending options.

FIGURE 18.33

You can apply blending modes to enhance the color of a Smart Object.

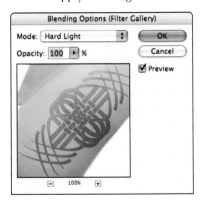

Masking Filter Effects

Use filter masks to selectively mask Smart Filters. When you mask Smart Filters, the masking applies to all Smart Filters attached to a specific Smart Object. Individual Smart Filters cannot be masked separately. If you want to apply a Smart Filter to another area, you have to create a new Smart Object.

When a Smart Filter is created, Photoshop displays an empty mask thumbnail in the Layers palette below the Smart Object. Selecting an area before applying the Smart Filter produces a masked selection instead of an empty mask.

Smart Filter masks are like layer masks in your ability to edit them. They can be painted with black, white, or gray (see Figure 18.34). Like layer masks, filter masks are stored as alpha channels in the Channels palette that can be loaded to produce a selection outline.

FIGURE 18.34

Paint on the Smart Filter mask to reveal or conceal the effects of a filter.

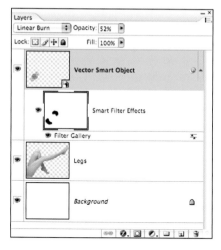

Summary

In this chapter, you found out about ways to manipulate the opacity or transparency of pixels on isolated areas of a content layer.

Specifically, this chapter covered the following topics:

- Working with layer masks
- Masking solids, gradients, and patterns
- Clipping images
- Creating and editing Smart Objects

You are now ready to go to Part VII. You'll learn how to use type masks and vector masks.

Part VII

Working with Type Masks and Vector Masks

Chapter 19

Working with Type Masks

Type is an important part of the overall appeal of any layout that contains words and images. A word's appearance can communicate just as much to a viewer as does its meaning. Photoshop's has several features that control typographical characteristics.

There are tools that determine whether type is vertical, horizontal, or follows the curve of a pre-established path. The Character and Paragraph palettes specify all the basic type attributes. Type can be generated in layers, on paths, in boxes, and in type masks. In combination with Layer Styles and Filter effects, Photoshop's type features can offer unlimited possibilities for creating interesting type effects. This chapter shows you ways of working with type and how to use type masks to create cool effects that add character and interest to your images.

Examining Type Features

Photoshop generates fully editable type. If you need a single line of text, you can create type on a straight path called *point text*. You can also generate text on a predefined or curved path that can wrap around an area. If you want to confine your text to a specific area you can create type in a bounding box (called *paragraph text*) and then apply paragraph specifications such as indents and Space Before or After for even more control. You can also bend and distort text for with the warp feature, and you can generate type shaped selection outlines that you can paste images into or apply filters to.

Using the Type Controls

You can find several of the type controls on the Options bar when one of the Type tools is selected (see Figure 19.1). More extensive controls are accessed from the Character and Paragraph palettes (see Figure 19.2). You can set type attributes before you enter text, or edit selected characters after you type them.

The Options bar controls basic type characteristics.

The Character and the Paragraph palettes control type characteristics.

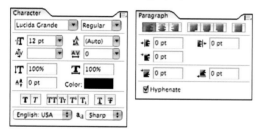

The following list describes how Photoshop controls the basic type characteristics:

- **Font:** The style or appearance of a complete set of characters is the font. Your choice of font can greatly influence the appearance of a publication. When a type tool is selected you can choose a font for your selected text from the Options bar or from the Character palette.

- **Size:** In traditional typography, the *type size* of a character is determined by the distance from the top of a capital letter to the bottom of a descender. Size is measured in *points*. There are 72 points in an inch. When a type tool is selected, size is specified in the Options bar or in the Character palette.

- **Style:** By controlling the *style* of a character, you place a visual emphasis on its meaning. In Photoshop, style is chiefly a function of font *weight* (thickness or heaviness) and *obliqueness* (whether it leans). You can specify either of these two type characteristics in the Options bar by choosing a bold or italic typeface from a type family on your system or by applying faux styles from the Character Palette Options menu.

- **Alignment:** Aligning text is an important step in maintaining readability. The *alignment* choices in the Options bar are flush left, flush right, and centered. In the Paragraphs palette, you can choose from four types of justification, last line left, last line right, last line centered, and last line justified.

- **Leading:** *Leading* is the typographic term that describes vertical spacing between lines; the word originates from the time when typesetters hand-set wooden or metal type. The space between lines was filled with lead slugs of specific sizes that controlled the vertical spacing. This term has been adopted throughout the industry as a way to describe the distance, in points from baseline to baseline, of rows of type characters. Software with a typography component (such as Photoshop) usually, by default, applies autoleading for body copy at 120% of the type's size.

- **Tracking and Kerning:** These terms refer to the space between characters. *Tracking* is the global space between selected groups of characters, and *kerning* is the space between two individual characters. You apply kerning and tracking by selecting or typing percentages of an EM space in their respective boxes in the Character palette.

NOTE An Em space is a unit of measurement based on the width of a capital M of a particular font.

- **Horizontal and Vertical Scale:** The horizontal scale of type stretches or squeezes it from side to side. When you vertically scale a letterform you stretch it from top to bottom. You can perform these operations in the Character palette.

- **Baseline Shift:** Shifting the *baseline* of a character moves it horizontally or vertically from its baseline. Unlike leading, which affects all the characters in a paragraph, baseline shift can target a selected individual character or a group of characters and moves it up or down. The Baseline shifty is implemented from the Character palette.

- **Indent/Space Before/Space After:** These operations are performed in the Paragraph palette.

Using the Type tools

To generate text, choose one of the four Type tools (see Figure 19.3). Click the point in the image where you want the text to appear and enter the text from the keyboard. You can preprogram the Type tool prior to entering the text by entering values in the Options bar or in the Character or Paragraph palettes, or you can highlight the text after it has been entered and modify its specifications.

Use these functions to modify text:

- To highlight text so that it can be edited, click the path or drag over it.
- To select a word, double-click it.
- To select a line of text, triple-click it.
- To select all characters in a bounding box, quadruple-click anywhere in the box, or press ⌘/Ctrl+A (Select All).

The Type tool generates either horizontal or vertical type on a type layer. You can edit the layered type, mask it with a layer mask, or you can apply Layer Styles to your text, but you cannot apply filters or color adjustments.

The Type tool flyout menu lists the Horizontal and Vertical Type Mask tools, which produce a selection marquee in the shape of the specified character on a currently targeted layer. When you enter text with either of the Type Mask tools it appears as a red mask until you click the check mark icon on the Options bar or press the Return/Enter key to commit the type.

The Type tool Options bar contains the following options:

- **Orientation:** The icon to the right of the Type tool Preset picker toggles between a horizontal and a vertical orientation of type.

- **Font:** Choose a font and style from the menus.

- **Size:** Choose a size in points from the list, or enter a numeric value.

- **Anti-Alias:** This setting determines how the type blends into its background in varying degrees. None produces a jagged character, Strong makes a heavier character, Crisp a sharper character, and Smooth a softer character.

- **Alignment:** From the Options bar you can align either flush left, centered, or flush right. The type aligns to the insertion point. When the type is vertically oriented, the top, center, or bottom of the text aligns to the insertion point. To justify type, use the Paragraph palette discussed later in the chapter.

- **Color:** Click the swatch and select a fill color for the type from the Color Picker.

- **Warp Text:** You can place your text on a path, twist it, or bend it using this function (see "Warping Text" later in this chapter).

- **Character/Paragraph:** This icon opens the Character and Paragraph palettes where you can enter global specifications for your text.

- **Commit/Cancel:** After you input your type specs, click one of these buttons to commit the edit or to cancel it.

FIGURE 19.3

The Type tools.

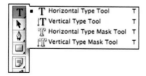

Creating Type

There are three ways of entering type in Photoshop: You can simply click anywhere on the image to enter type from a single point; you can click on a predefined vector path made with the Pen tool or one of the Shape tools and type the text which will follow the curve of the path; you can click and drag the Type tool to create a bounding box of a specific size and then type the text inside the box.

Creating point text

You generate type on a point when you want to create a single line of text or don't need to apply paragraph specifications to multiple lines. Choose the Type tool. Set the specifications in the Options bar or the Character palette. Click the image to display a blinking insertion point (see Figure 19.4) and then enter the text. If you want a second line of text, press the Return/Enter at the end of the first line and then continue to type. Each, though separated by leading, is part of the same path. If you want to edit the path, click under any character with the Type tool to activate the path, and then highlight the text by dragging over it. Type the new characters, and they replace the type content of the highlighted characters.

FIGURE 19.4

Point text is generated on a straight line. You cannot assign paragraph attributes to it.

Creating paragraph text

As you enter text in the bounding box, a return is automatically inserted at the end of each line as the text flows to the bounding box edge19. The text automatically hyphenates as shown in Figure 19.5. After the bounding box has been drawn and the type entered, you can size the box to reflow the text by dragging its corner handles.

To create type in a bounding box, follow these steps:

1. Choose the Type tool.

2. Click in your image and drag the box to size. Release the mouse and the bounding box appears. There will be a blinking insertion point positioned in the text box. By default, the insertion point appears in the upper-left corner of the box.

3. Set your type specifications in the toolbar and type the text. The text automatically returns when it reaches the right border of the box.

4. If you want to start a new paragraph, press the Return/Enter key at the end of the line.

5. Commit the test by clicking the check mark in the Options bar.

6. Readjust the size of the bounding box by dragging any of the corner or side handles.

FIGURE 19.5

Box text automatically returns the text to a new line when it reaches the box's borders. You can assign paragraph attributes to box text.

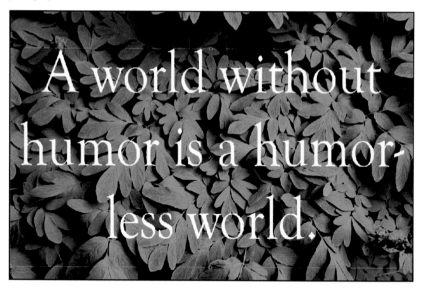

 **TIP**   You can convert point text to paragraph text and vice versa. Target the Type layer and choose Layer ➪ Type ➪ Convert To Point Text or Convert To Paragraph Text.

Type on a path

This feature places type on a pre-existing vector path, as shown in Figure 19.6. The cross at the beginning of the text is the entry point, or the leftmost extremity of the text. The circle at the end of the text is the rightmost extremity. These elements can be moved to alter the position of the text on the path. These two elements also determine the alignment of the text when a specific alignment option is applied.

1. Draw either a shape layer or a path using the Pen tool or any of the shape tools.

2. Choose any variation of the Type tool and set options on the Options bar.

3. Click the path or on the outside of the shape; you'll see a blinking insertion point, and type the text.

4. To move the text along the path or to the inside of the shape, choose the Path Selection tool, click on the cross at the beginning of the text or the circle at the end of the text depending on the alignment, and drag it into the desired position.

FIGURE 19.6

Type can flow around a path made by the Shape tools or the Pen tool.

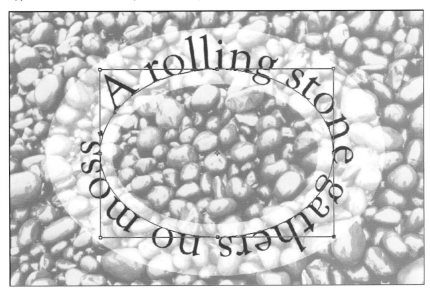

Warping text

If you want to produce awesome shapes from your text you can warp the text using the warp feature. You can bend type to conform to almost any of 15 warp styles plus you can control the amount of bend and horizontal and vertical distortion. The Warp Text option is accessible from the Type tool Options bar or from the Layer ➪ Type menu. When you click the icon, the Warp Text dialog window appears. Choose a style and adjust the controls as shown in Figure 19.7. For even more control, you can manually adjust the warp of the text by choosing Edit ➪ Transform ➪ Warp and dragging the gridlines or handles.

FIGURE 19.7

Text can be warped using one of the predefined warp features in the Warp Text dialog box or manually with the Warp option in the Transform menu.

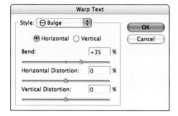

Rasterizing type

Photoshop uses vector-based fonts that preserve the ability to edit the text on a type layer at any time. Features such as filters and color adjustments don't work on vector-based type. If you want to apply those effects, you'll have to *rasterize* the type, or convert it into pixels.

Pixel-based type has its advantages and disadvantages. The main disadvantage is that after you render your type, it appears at the same resolution as the document. This is particularly problematic for small type on low-resolution documents, because there may not be enough pixels to do a decent job of smoothing the type's edges.

The advantage of pixel-based type is that it enables you to apply filter effects, color adjustments, and other effects. To rasterize your type into pixels, click the Type layer and choose Layer ➪ Rasterize ➪ Type. The text on the type layer is now no longer editable.

Generating and Editing Type Masks

There are two different type tools. With the Type tool, text can be generated as layer-based text which resides as an independent layer in the layers palette and maintains its editability until it is rasterized. The layer is merged with another layer, or the image is flattened. Like any layer, a type layer can be positioned anywhere in the stack and Layer styles can be applied to it. The second type tool generates a type mask. A type mask is applied to an existing empty layer, or a layer with content.

A type mask can be generated with the Type Mask tool which can be accessed in the Type tool fly-out or by pressing Shift -T. When you create a type mask, the image turns a light red color with a blinking insertion point. Type the letters and click the check mark in the Options bar to commit the type. The type transforms to a selection outline. If you want to change the type specifications, highlight the text by dragging over it and then change the specifications in the Options bar or the

Character palette. If you want to change the size or position of the type, press the ⌘/Ctrl key and drag the bounding box to move the text, or a corner handle to resize it.

You can produce some very cool image effects by pasting type into a type mask. Here is a technique that produces image text:

1. Open an image. In this case, I opened a picture of some clouds (see Figure 19.8).

FIGURE 19.8

The original cloud image.

2. Choose the Type Path tool. Set the specifications in the Options bar.
3. Click the image and enter the text (see Figure 19.9).

FIGURE 19.9

The Type Mask tool produces a red type mask over the image.

4. Press the Return/Enter key to convert the type mask into a selection outline (see Figure 19.10).

FIGURE 19.10

The text is converted into a selection.

5. Choose Layer ⇨ New ⇨ Layer Via Copy. The image pastes into the selection and there will be no visible change on the image. A new layer will appear in the Layers palette in the shape of the characters (see Figure 19.11). Name the layer.

6. Click the Layer Style icon at the bottom of the Layers palette. Choose the Drop Shadow Layer Style from the list (see Figure 19.12).

7. Set the specifications for the drop shadow and click OK (see Figure 19.12).

FIGURE 19.11

Make a new layer from the selected area.

FIGURE 19.12

The Drop Shadow Layer Style applied to the layer.

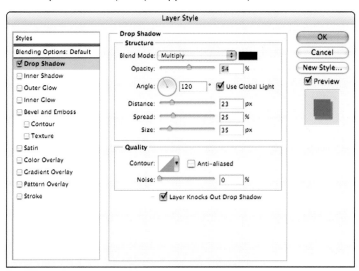

Summary

This chapter details how to make cool type effects in Photoshop.

Specifically, I cover the following topics:

- Examining type features
- Creating type
- Generating and editing type masks

Chapter 20 covers paths and shapes.

Chapter 20

Masking Paths and Shapes

P aths and shapes are vector objects. They are mathematically defined curves. Vector objects are composed of anchor points and line segments, known as Bézier curves. The advantage of using vectors is that they are resolution independent and when printed from Photoshop they retain their vector data, even though they are part of an image that contains pixels or raster information. This chapter explains the nature of vector-based objects in Photoshop, and how to make and mask them. There are two fundamentally different methods used to create still images. Vector graphics are objects composed of mathematically defined points, curves, and shapes called objects. Raster images use a grid of colored squares, called pixels, to render variations of color.

Understanding Vector Objects

The shape of a vector object is composed of line segments and anchor points called paths. In Photoshop the Vector tools are used to draw and edit these objects that vectors are used for the following purposes:

- To make and store accurate selections.
- To create shapes.
- To create smooth lines.
- To stroke and fill areas.
- To mask layer content.
- To mask areas imported to other programs.

Working with vector objects is rather different than working with pixels, and the different techniques are quite independent of each other. You can't create, select, or edit a path with a Selection tool, nor can you create, select, or edit a selection with a Vector tool. Vector objects are created by depositing points and line segments with the Pen tool or by dragging a shape onto the Image window with one of the Shape tools. These paths or *Bézier curves* can be created in any combination of straight or curved paths. They can be open-ended or closed.

CROSS-REF **To further understand the difference between vector and raster images, see Chapter 1.**

Drawing Paths

The Path tools enable you to create editable straight lines and curves with greater precision than you can with the Selection tools. If you create an open-ended path, for example, you can stroke it with a color to form a curved line. The stroke is composed of pixels, but the path is independent of the stroke. If its two end points have joined, the path encloses a *shape*. You can then fill the shape with color, stroke it with an outline, or store it in the Paths palette or in the Shape library for later use. It can also be converted into a selection outline.

The primary Path tool is the Pen tool. To choose the Pen tool, click its icon in the Tools palette or type **P** (Shift-P cycles through all the tools in the flyout).

Path-drawing and editing tools

The Path tools deposit or change line segments or anchor points. This set of tools includes the following:

- **Pen tool:** Draws paths by clicking and dragging.
- **Freeform Pen tool:** Draws a freeform line that converts itself into a path when the mouse is released.
- **Freeform Pen tool:** With the Magnetic Option: Sometimes simply called the Magnetic Pen, this tool intuitively defines edges based on contrasting colors.
- **The Add Anchor Point tool:** Adds anchor points to existing paths.
- **The Delete Anchor Point tool:** Removes anchor points from existing paths.
- **The Convert Point tool:** Changes a corner point to a curve, or a curve to a corner point.
- **Path Selection tool:** Selects and moves the path as a unit.
- **The Direct Selection tool:** Selects and moves individual anchor points and segments.

Learning to draw accurately with the Vector tools can be challenging at first. But with a little practice you can become proficient.

Using the Pen tool

For first-time users the pen tool can be a bit tricky. Drawing with the basic pen tool is unlike drawing with a pencil. The techniques deposit anchor points, segments or curves to make basic lines or shapes that can later be tweaked to a great level of precision. The best way to become facile with the Pen tool is to practice drawing different types of paths.

The Freeform Pen tool and its Magnetic option behaves more like the lasso tool is less precise than the basic Pen tool an d usually deposits two many anchor point and consequently needs more editing.

The Pen tool generates anchor points and line segments. A path can quickly be drawn or modified with one of the Pen tools to define a general area and then be edited and refined. The Pen tool Options bar displays options that enable you to modify its behavior (see Figure 20.1). The Boolean icons enable you to make a new Shape layer or a new work path. Choosing one of the icons affects how the shape can later be edited. If you choose the Shape Layer icon, Photoshop generates an independent Shape layer. If you choose the Work Path icon, Photoshop draws an independent path and creates a work path in the Paths palette. Check the Auto Add/Delete feature to automatically add anchor points when one of the Pen tools is placed on a segment or to delete a point when a Pen tool is placed over an anchor point.

FIGURE 20.1

The Pen tool flyout (left) and the Options bar. (right)

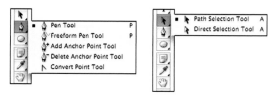

You can constrain the direction of the path to horizontal, vertical or 45 degrees by pressing the shift key w when you click to deposit the anchor point.

Straight paths

Two anchor points joined by a straight line segment create a single segment. You can add additional segments to the straight path by moving the cursor and clicking the mouse:

1. Click the Pen tool. Click the Path Boolean icon in the Options bar. Click the image where you want to begin the path. An anchor point appears; release the mouse button.

2. Move the cursor and click your mouse at the next point. A line segment with another anchor point appears between the two points.

3. Continue to move and click your mouse to produce a series of straight-line segments connected to each other by corner anchor points, as shown in Figure 20.2.

FIGURE 20.2

Connecting straight paths on an image.

Curved paths

A curved path consists of two anchor points connected by a curved segment. *Direction handles* radiate from the anchor point and determine the position and shape of the line segment. The length and direction of the handles can be adjusted when drawing the curve or later with the path editing tools. To make a perfectly smooth curve, the anchor points will be positioned on the sides of the curve rather than at the apex. The direction handles are ideally approximately one-third the size of the curve.

To draw a curved path, follow these steps:

1. Select the Pen tool. Click the paths Boolean icon in the Options bar.

2. Click the image where you want the path to begin. An anchor point with a direction handle appears. Without releasing the mouse button, drag the handle in the general direction you want the curve to travel.

3. Release the mouse and move the cursor to the next point on the image.

4. Click your mouse and drag again, this time in the opposite direction. A curved segment with another anchor point and direction handle appears. With the mouse button still depressed, adjust the direction handle until the curved line segment is in the desired position, and then release the mouse as in Figure 20.3.

FIGURE 20.3

FIGURE 20.3

A curved path showing the direction handles.

Changing the direction of a curved path

Scalloped paths abruptly change direction. This technique requires you to press the Option/Alt key while clicking and dragging. This technique can be a little tricky but if you think of the Option/Alt keys as a turn signal it might help facilitate the drawing of scalloped paths. These paths define areas that don't undulate like the standard S curve but have corner points at their junctions. Follow these steps:

1. Click the Pen tool. Choose the Paths Boolean icon in the Options bar.

2. Click the image where you want to begin the path and drag. An anchor point with a direction handle appears. Without releasing the mouse button, drag to adjust the direction handle, then release the mouse.

3. Click where you want the segment to end. Click your mouse and drag down. A curved segment with another anchor point and direction line appears. Release the mouse. Adjust the direction handle to end.

4. Opt/Alt-click the last anchor point and drag a direction handle away from it.

5. Move your cursor to the next location, click your mouse, and drag in the opposite direction of the last direction handle you created. Adjust the segment so that the curve is the desired length and position (see Figure 20.4).

FIGURE 20.4

A scalloped curve is drawn by re-establishing a new direction for the curve with the Opt/Alt keys.

Combining straight and curved paths

Usually the paths you draw are combinations of straight and curved paths. There are two types of points in a Bezier curve. A smooth point where the next path flows fluidly from the former path, and a corner point, in which the path suddenly changes direction. Often the continuous paths you draw are combinations of straight and curved paths. A straight path is really just a curved path with the direction handles placed all the way into the anchor point. You can combine straight and curved paths using the Option/Alt key (the turn signal) to extract the handles or to inhibit the curve. These techniques simply change the end anchor point form a curve point top a smooth point or visa versa bine the two into one continuous path.

To try this technique, follow these steps.

1. Select the Pen tool and click the image where you want to path to begin. An anchor point appears. Release the mouse button.

2. Click the next point on the image. A straight segment with another anchor point appears.

3. To add a curved segment, Opt/Alt-click the last anchor point and drag.

4. Release your mouse button and move your cursor to the next location.

5. Click your mouse and drag down to finish the curve. Release the mouse when the position and size of the curve is achieved, as shown in Figure 20.5.

FIGURE 20.5

A straight path can be added to a curve or a curve can be added to a straight path.

You can also add a straight path to a curve:

1. Select the Pen tool, click the image where you want to begin the path, and drag the direction handle in the direction of the curve.
2. Release the mouse and move the cursor to the next point.
3. Click your mouse and drag to create the curve.
4. Opt/Alt-click your mouse on the last anchor point.
5. Move your cursor to the next location and click your mouse to complete the segment.

Closing a path

A closed path is a shape. To close a series of straight paths, draw at least two paths. Place the cursor over the first anchor point. A little circle appears beside the cursor to indicate that the path is ready to be closed. Click the mouse. To close one or more curved paths, draw at least *one* path and click the first anchor point.

Tips for Drawing Curved Paths

Keep these suggestions in mind when you are drawing curved paths:

- Drag the first point in the direction of the peak of the curve and drag the second point in the opposite direction. If you drag the first and second point in the same direction you form an S curve which is difficult to control.
- For a smoother curve, draw as few anchor points as possible.
- Anchor points work best on the sides of the curve, not on the peaks or valleys.
- You can add anchor points to the middle of a segment, but you can only add segments to the end points of an open path.
- An anchor point can only connect two segments.
- If you stop drawing and want to add a new segment to a path, resume drawing by first clicking one of the end points with a Pen tool.
- If you are drawing an open path and want to begin a second path that is not connected to the first. Click the Direct Selection tool. Then click off the path and release the keys. Choose the Pen tool and resume drawing the new path.
- If you want to edit the path as you draw press the Opt/Alt key to toggle into the Direct Selection tool. Edit the path, release the key, and resume drawing.
- If possible, avoid drawing S-curves with one path. Instead, connect two individual curves to form an s-shaped path, the path will be smoother.

Making Freeform paths

The Freeform Pen tool is a quick way to draw a curve, but it doesn't offer the same level of control and precision as the Pen tool. You can't control the number or placement of anchor points. And often paths created by the Freeform Pen require editing or removal of excess anchor points.

Using the Freeform Pen tool is similar to drawing with the Lasso tool. Click and drag your mouse across the image to a draw line and release the mouse and the line changes to a path. Type a value between 0.5 and 10.0 pixels in the *Curve Fit* box in the Geometry Options menu in the Options bar (see Figure 20.6 to determine the sensitivity of the tool to the movement of your mouse). A lower tolerance produces a finer curve with more anchor points. A higher tolerance produces a simpler path with fewer anchor points and thus smoother curve.

FIGURE 20.6

The Geometry Options menu for the Rectangle tool.

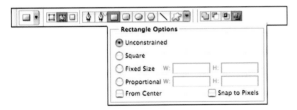

The Magnetic Pen option

The Freeform Pen tool with Magnetic option checked is similar to the Magnetic Lasso. It intuitively snaps to areas of high-color contrast within an image. As you drag, the Magnetic Pen converts to a path. To access the Magnetic Pen, select the Freeform Pen tool (click and hold the cursor on the Pen tool in the Tools palette, and choose the Freeform Pen from the flyout; or type Shift+P once or twice to select the tool) and check the Magnetic box in the Options bar. Then use the Geometry Options menu to display the Magnetic options:

- **Width:** Type a distance in pixels from the edge that the tool will be active. Higher values mean the tool is "attracted" to the edge from a greater distance.

- **Contrast:** Type a value between 1% and 100% to determine the tool's sensitivity in detecting contrasting borders. Higher values detect edges of greater contrast, while lower values increase the tool's sensitivity to low-contrast edges.

- **Detection:** You can increase the detection width in one-pixel increments *while drawing* by pressing the] key. You can decrease the width by pressing the [key.

- **Frequency:** Type a value between 1 and 100 to establish the rate at which the Magnetic Pen deposits anchor points. Higher values place more anchor points over a shorter distance.

- **Pen Pressure:** If you are working with a graphics tablet, check Pen Pressure. As you drag, the pressure of the stylus will correspond to the Width setting. An increase of pressure on the stylus will thicken the pen width.

Editing Paths

All or part of a path can be moved or reshaped. Anchor points can be added or omitted, and corners can be converted into curves or curves into corners. The path-editing tools include the Path Selection tool, the Direct Selection tool, the Add Anchor Point tool, the Delete Anchor Point tool, and the Convert Point tool.

The Path Selection tool

The black arrow, the Path Selection tool, selects all the anchor points and segments of a path. Drag the path to reposition it.

> **TIP** Another method of selecting a path is to use the Path Selection tool to click and drag a marquee that touches any part of the path. All the anchor points will appear solid, indicating that the entire path is selected.

> **TIP** Duplicate a path by Opt/Alt-clicking and dragging and then dropping it with the Path Selection tool.

The Direct Selection tool

The Direct Selection tool selects or modifies a segment, or the position of an anchor point, on a path. Use this tool to revise and reshape the path after it has already been drawn.

To select, move, or edit a segment or anchor point, choose the Direct Selection tool. Click on a segment or anchor point. Click and drag an anchor point to reposition it or a segment to reshape it. To deselect a path, click anywhere on the image.

> **TIP** Toggle into the Direct Selection tool while in Pen tool by pressing Opt/Alt.

Adding and deleting anchor points

You usually need to refine it by adding or deleting anchor points. To add an anchor point, choose the Add Anchor Point tool and click the path. A new anchor point appears where you've clicked. To delete an anchor point, choose the Delete Anchor Point tool and click an anchor point. The two segments connected by the point join into one.

> **CAUTION** It might be tempting to add dozens of anchor points to facilitate the drawing of a path. That's not always a good idea; too many extra points increase the path's complexity and compromise the smoothness of the shape.

> **TIP** You can click the Auto Add/Delete checkbox in the Pen tool Options bar to automatically convert the Pen tool into the Add Anchor Point tool when you touch a segment or the Delete Anchor Point tool when you touch an Anchor point.

Converting anchor points

Smooth anchor points connect curved or straight lines that flow into each other. *Corner points* connect lines that change direction abruptly. An anchor point can be converted from one type of point to another by clicking the point with the Convert Point tool. Click a smooth point and it converts to a corner point. To convert a corner point, click and drag out the direction handles until the desired curve is achieved and then release the mouse.

Transforming paths

You can modify paths with the Transform tools. Select the path with the Path Selection tools. Then choose either Edit ➪ Free Transform Points or Edit ➪ Transform Points and any of the transformation operations including Scale, Rotate, Skew, Distort, Perspective, or Flip, to edit the entire path. If you select one or more points or segments with the Direct Selection tool, you can apply any of the transformation operations to the selected part of the path.

Combining paths

If you've drawn two or more paths that intersect, you can combine them into one path. Select a path by using the Path Selection tool. Click and drag the marquee that touches both of the paths, or you can Shift-click them in sequence. On the Options bar, click the Combine button. The elements of both paths combine into a group of paths (see Figure 20.7). If you click on any member of the group with the Path Selection tool, then all will be selected.

FIGURE 20.7

Paths can be combined.

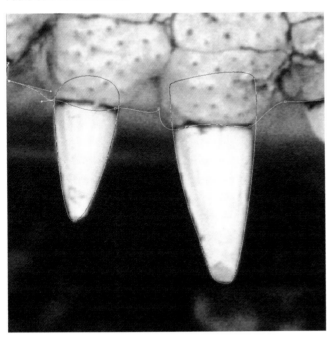

Working with the Paths Palette

The Paths palette displays a list of paths with thumbnails that display the path contents. Paths can be saved and stored in the palette so they can later be edited or converted into a selection. Access the Paths palette (see Figure 20.8) by choosing Window ➪ Paths. (If you still have the Paths palette in the default cluster — grouped with the Layers palette — pressing the F7 function key will also bring it up.)

FIGURE 20.8

The Paths palette.

Using work paths

When you begin to draw a path with the Pen tool, it appears as a thumbnail in the Paths palette, named Work Path. The work path is a temporary element that records changes as you draw new sections of the path. If you complete a path on an image, click the Pen tool and draw another path, it will appear on the same Work Path thumbnail as the first path. To create separate additional paths, you must save the work path to the Paths palette.

TIP You can increase or decrease the size of the Paths palette thumbnails by choosing Palette Options from the Palette pull-down menu and clicking the radio button next to the desired thumbnail size.

Saving paths

After a path has been drawn and appears as a Work Path thumbnail, you can save it by choosing Save Path from the Palette menu as shown in Figure 20.9. A dialog box appears where you can name the path; if no name is entered, the path name defaults to Path 1. You can also save a path by dragging the Work Path to the New Path icon at the bottom of the palette.

The Paths palette lists saved paths from top to bottom in the order in which they were created. The paths can be reorganized within the list by clicking the path's name or thumbnail and dragging it to the desired location.

FIGURE 20.9

The Save Path dialog box is accessed from the Paths Palette Options menu.

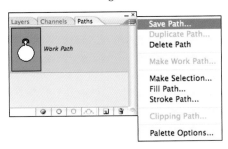

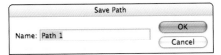

Displaying paths

To display a path, click the path's name or thumbnail image in the Paths palette. You can only display one path at a time. When displayed, the path is visible on the image. To conceal all paths from view in the Image window, click the empty portion of the Paths palette.

Deleting paths from the Image window

To delete a path from the image, do one of the following:

- Select an entire path with the Path Selection tool. Press the Delete or Backspace key. If it's a work path, the path and its icon are deleted. If it's a saved path, the path is deleted from the Image window, but its empty thumbnail remains in the Paths palette.

- To discard part of a path, click on the part of the path that you want to delete with the Direct Selection tool. Press the Delete or Backspace key once to delete the selected part of the path or twice to delete the entire path.

Deleting paths from the palette

If you no longer need a path you can delete it. To do so, click the path's name in the palette and perform one of the following operations:

- Drag the path thumbnail to the trash icon at the bottom of the palette.
- Choose Delete Path from the Paths Palette pull-down menu.
- Click the trash icon in the Paths palette. In the dialog box that appears, click Yes.
- Click on the path in the Paths palette. Press the Delete or Backspace key.

Filling a path

There are many ways to fill areas in Photoshop. You can fill a selection outline or you can crate aF Layer which uses a vector mask. But if you want to fill the contents of a simple path, you should first highlight a content layer. The color that you fill the path with will consist of pixels and will not be editable with the vector tools.

To fill the area within a path, draw an open or closed path or display an existing path from the Paths palette by clicking its thumbnail. Choose a foreground color and then choose Fill Path from the Paths Palette pull-down menu.

The Fill Path dialog box appears (see Figure 20.10). Type the specifications for the fill and click OK. You can also fill a path with the current Fill Path dialog box settings by clicking the Fill Path icon at the bottom of the Paths palette.

FIGURE 20.10

The Fill Path dialog box enables you to fill the pixels contained within the path's boundaries with color.

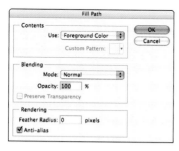
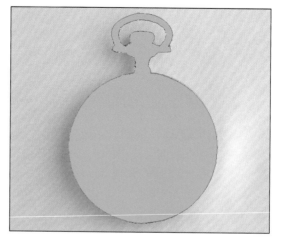

Stroking a path

Stroking a path is the only way to precisely create smooth curved lines. Try drawing a curved line with the Paintbrush or Pencil; you'll see that it's quite difficult to achieve satisfactory results. Drawing an open path, editing it to your exact specifications, and then stroking it with a color produces perfect results.

To stroke a path, draw a path, or load one from the Paths palette, choose a foreground color; then, from the Paths Palette pull-down menu, choose Stroke Path. The Stroke Path dialog box appears (see Figure 20.11). Pick a tool from the pop-up list. When you click OK, the stroke is painted with the current characteristics of the chosen tool as defined in the Options bar.

All of the characteristics of the current brush will appear on the stroke. For example, if the brush that you apply the stroke with has low hardness specified in the brushes palette then the stroke will look quite fuzzy.

 A path can be quickly stroked with the current tool characteristics set in the Stroke Path dialog box by clicking the Stroke Path icon at the bottom of the Paths palette.

 You can stroke a selection outline using the Edit ⇨ Stroke command. You can also apply a stroke around layer content using the Stroke option in the Layer Styles dialog box.

The Stroke Path dialog box enables you to color pixels with the characteristics of a painting or editing tool.

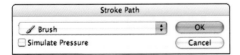

 You can quickly stroke a path with the current tool characteristics set in the Stroke Path dialog box by clicking the Stroke Path icon at the bottom of the Paths palette.

Converting paths

Paths offer ease and flexibility, so you can precisely define regions of an image. Paths are easy to edit and require less real estate on your hard drive than selections saved as alpha channels. Eventually, though, you may need to convert your path into a selection before you can apply a Photoshop operation The purpose of converting a path into a selection is so that you can affect the pixels contained within its boundries.

Converting a path to a selection does not eliminate the path, it simply generates a selection from an existing path and the path remains in the Paths palette. Converting a selection into a path however eliminates the selection and converts oit into a new work path.

The Make Selection dialog box enables you to specify the characteristics of a selection and its relationship to active selections on the image. Click the path in the Paths palette and choose Make Selection from the Paths Palette pull-down menu. The Make Selection dialog box is displayed (see Figure 20.12). Choose from the following specifications:

- **Feather Radius:** Creates a soft-edged selection.
- **Anti-Aliased:** Determines whether the selection will possess an anti-aliased edge.
- **New Selection:** Makes a selection from the path.
- **Add To Selection:** Adds the area defined by the path to an existing selection.
- **Subtract From Selection:** Omits the area defined by the path from the existing selection.
- **Intersect With Selection:** Makes a selection from the overlap of the path and the existing selection.

Click OK to convert the path into a selection.

FIGURE 20.12

The Make Selection from Path dialog box.

TIP You can convert a path into a new selection by clicking the Load Path As Selection icon at the bottom of the Paths palette.

Converting a selection into a path

To convert a selection into a path, draw a selection with one of the selection tools. Choose Make Work Path from the Paths Palette menu. A dialog box appears that enables you to set the tolerance of the path in pixels. Tolerances with low values produce more complex paths with greater numbers of anchor points, while tolerances with higher values produce simpler paths. Click OK to convert the selection into a path.

You can also convert a selection into a path by clicking the Make Work Path from Selection icon at the bottom of the Paths palette.

Masking Vector Images

Sometimes it's necessary to "knock out" portions of an image so that elements in layers below can show through. You can create vector masks to knock out areas within a Photoshop document or clipping paths to mask areas you intend do export to desktop publishing or illustration programs.

Creating vector masks

Vector masks reveal the interior portion of a path. The areas outside the path are concealed. Vector masks are similar to layer masks except they are edited with path tools. Vector masks produce a clean, crisp edge, which is not always easy to achieve with regular selection methods.

To create a vector mask:

1. Draw a path around an area on the image that you want to isolate (see Figure 20.13).
2. From the Paths Palette pull-down menu, choose Save Path and give it a name.
3. With the path selected in the Paths palette, choose Layer ⇨ Add Vector Mask ⇨ Current Path.
4. The path outline conceals anything outside the path, and letting any layer beneath show through. The vector mask is represented in the Layers palette, to the right of your layer's thumbnail.

FIGURE 20.13

A vector mask starts with a path on a layer.

The vector mask also resides in the Paths palette. If you deselect the vector mask path in the Paths palette the path outline will no longer be visible. You will still be able to edit it at any time by selecting it again. You can also add a Layer Style to the layer as in Figure 20.14.

Using clipping paths

The Clipping Path option has essentially the same effect as a vector mask except that clipping paths are exported with your image into a vector illustration program (such as Adobe Illustrator) instead of embedded within a Photoshop layer. You create a clipping path to knock out areas from an image that you want to export to a desktop publishing program or a vector-based illustration program.

FIGURE 20.14

The vector mask knocks out the area on a layer outside of the path.

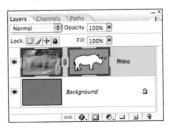

To create a clipping path:

1. Create your path around an area of your image as before using the Path tools.

2. From the Paths Palette pull-down menu, choose Save Path, and give it a name.

3. Choose Clipping Path from the palette menu to display the dialog box (see Figure 20.15).

4. Select the name of the path you want to convert to a clipping path from the pull-down submenu. Click OK.

FIGURE 20.15

To create a clipping path, first save the path. Then choose Clipping Path from the Path Options menu to display the Clipping Mask dialog box.

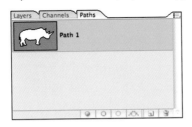
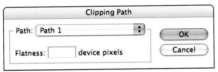

NOTE For most paths, leave the Flatness setting blank. When you print the image, the printer's default flatness setting will be used to define the shape. However, if you experience printing problems, try saving the path with new settings.

Saving clipping paths

If you want to export an image containing clipping paths to a desktop publishing or illustration program, you must save it as an Encapsulated Postscript image (Photoshop EPS). The knock out will appear only in programs that support this format. Duplicate the image first so that the original image retains Photoshop's attributes.

To save an image with a clipping path as an EPS:

1. Choose File ⇨ Save As. Select the As a Copy option.

2. From the Format list, choose Photoshop EPS to display the EPS Options dialog box (see Figure 20.16).

FIGURE 20.16

The EPS Options dialog box.

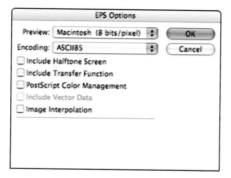

3. Choose a Preview option, depending on the type of computer and the platform you are using: Macintosh or Windows, 1 bit or 8 bit.

4. For the Encoding type, choose Binary.

5. Click OK.

6. Open a document in a desktop-publishing program or vector-drawing program, and place the EPS image. The clipping path masks out everything outside the path, similar to what a vector mask does within Photoshop (see Figure 20.17).

NOTE The preview in Illustrator can look pixilated as the example shown here, when printed, the quality will be much better.

The clipping mask placed in Adobe Illustrator knocks out areas outside the boundaries of the path.

Masking Shapes

As with type, lines and shapes are vector objects that are drawn and defined by paths. You draw a predefined shape using one of the Shape tools or a custom shape using the Pen tool. Shapes can then be edited by adjusting their anchor points with the path-editing tools.

Creating shape layers

When you create a shape on a shape layer, either with the Pen tool or the Shape tool it appears on an independent layer as a color swatch thumbnail with a vector mask thumbnail next to it. You can edit the color by double-clicking the color swatch to reveal the Color Picker. You can edit the vector mask with the Pen tools, the Shape tools, or with the Path Selection tools.

To create a shape layer:

1. Choose a Pen tool or a Shape tool.
2. Click the Shape Layer Boolean icon in the Options bar.
3. Draw the path or shape on the image. A shape layer is automatically formed in the Layers palette with a vector mask to the right of the thumbnail, as in Figure 20.18. The shape also appears as a separate path in the Paths palette.

FIGURE 20.18

A shape layer automatically creates a vector mask next to its thumbnail.

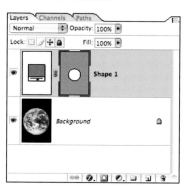

NOTE To apply a filter to a shape, it must first be *rasterized* or turned into pixels. If you flatten the image, shapes are automatically converted to pixels.

Working with Shape tools

The Shape tools can instantly create precise shapes, such as rectangles, rounded rectangles, ellipses, polygons, lines, and custom shapes that are editable using the path-editing tools. When you click the Shape tool icon in the Tools palette, it expands to reveal all the available tools. After you've chosen a shape from this flyout, click in the image and drag to size the shape.

Using the Shape Tool Options bar

When you choose a different shape from the Tools palette or from the Shape list in the Options bar, as shown in Figure 20.19, the Options bar changes to accommodate specific characteristics of the shape. These are the items in the Options bar:

- **Create New Shape Layer:** The far left icon makes a shape on a new layer.
- **Create New Work Path:** The middle Boolean icon makes the path outline of the shape on an existing layer or background.
- **Create Fill Pixels:** The third Boolean icon fills an area with the foreground color in the form of the shape.
- **Shape List:** You can choose a shape from the list. The Shape List Options menu displays categories for even more shapes that you can add to the list.
- **Geometry Options:** You can type specifications for the size and proportion of the shape.
- **Style:** You can attach a Layer Style to the Shape layer (available with New Shape layer).
- **Shape Characteristics:** Assign a value for the characteristics of a particular shape, or choose a custom shape.
- **Mode:** This feature lets you select a blending mode for the shape (available only with Create Fill Pixels).
- **Opacity:** This feature controls the shapes' opacity (available only with Create Fill Pixels).
- **Anti-Alias:** Click the checkbox to add an anti-alias to the shape (available only with Fill Pixels).

FIGURE 20.19

The Shape Tool Options bar sets specifications when a Shape tool is selected.

Drawing shapes

To draw a shape, choose a foreground color. Click the Shape tool in the Tools palette and choose a tool from the expanded palette or from the Options bar. Click in the image and drag to form the shape. Because shapes are vector objects, you can use the Path Selection tool, the Direct Selection tool, or the path-editing tools to move or edit a shape or to add and delete anchor points.

Each shape performs slightly differently. The Options bar of each shape lets you adjust its individual characteristics. For example, you can enter a value for the radius of the corners on the Rounded Rectangle tool or for the number of sides on the Polygon tool.

Creating rectangles and ellipses

As with the selection Marquee tools, icons on the Shape tool Options bars let you add, subtract, intersect, or exclude areas from a shape as you draw. Clicking the arrow to the right of the Shape tool icons on the Options bar offers additional controls on a pop-up menu (see Figure 20.20). When you choose the Rectangle, Rounded Rectangle, or Ellipse tool, the down-arrow button on the Options bar offers you these choices:

- **Unconstrained:** Sizes and proportions the shape as you draw it.

- **Square (or Circle):** Constrains the shape.

- **Fixed Size:** Lets you type values for the shape's width and height.

- **Proportional:** Lets you type proportional values for the Width and Height.

- **From Center:** Radiates the shape from a center point.

- **Snap To Pixels:** Aligns the shape to the on-screen pixels (Rectangle and Round-Cornered Rectangle only).

TIP To constrain the Rectangle or Round-Cornered Rectangle to a square or the Ellipse to a circle, hold down the Shift key as you drag.

FIGURE 20.20

The Ellipse Tool pop-up menu.

Creating polygons

Select the Polygon tool and type a number of sides in the Size field in the Options bar. The Polygon Options panel, shown in Figure 20.21, differs from those of the other shapes. Choose from the following options:

- **Radius:** Enter a corner radius for a round-cornered polygon.

- **Smooth Corners:** Rounds the corners of the polygon.

- **Indent Sides By:** Enter a percentage value to curve the sides inward.

- **Smooth Indents:** Rounds the indents.

FIGURE 20.21

Polygon Tool pop-up menu enables you to produce a variety of polygons.

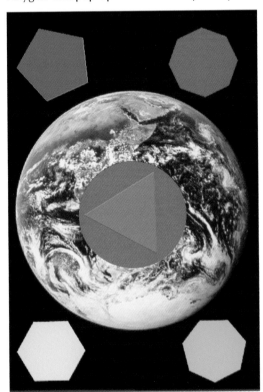
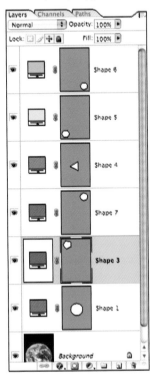

Creating lines and arrows

Select Line tool and type a value in the Options bar for the weight of the line in pixels. Choices in the Line Options panel determine what type of arrow appears at either end of the line. Check the Start or End boxes, or both, to produce an arrowhead at the beginning and/or end of the line (see Figure 20.22). Enter values in Width, Length, and Concavity for these characteristics of the arrowhead. Then click and drag on the image to create the line or arrow. Press the Shift key while dragging to move the arrows position.

FIGURE 20.22

The Line Tool pop-up menu produces a variety of arrows.

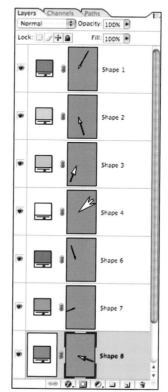

Creating custom shapes

You can generate custom shapes with the Shape tool. With the Custom Shape tool selected, the Options panel displays these options:

- **Unconstrained:** Manually determines the proportion of the shape as you draw.
- **Defined Proportions:** Drag to constrain the proportion of the shape.
- **Defined Size:** Draws the shape at the size it was created.
- **Fixed Size:** Enter values for the shape in the Height and Width fields.
- **From Center:** Radiates the shape from a center point.

You can choose from many predefined custom shapes in the Options bar shape menu (see Figure 20.23) and can create additional shapes with the Pen tool and save them to this list.

The pull-down submenu on the panel provides a list of commands that lets you Save, Load, Reset, Delete, and Replace custom shapes, plus several palette-viewing options. The options at the bottom rung of the submenu replace the default list with additional shapes. With the All option, you can view a comprehensive list of all available shapes.

You can choose from many predefined custom shapes in the Options bar Shape menu.

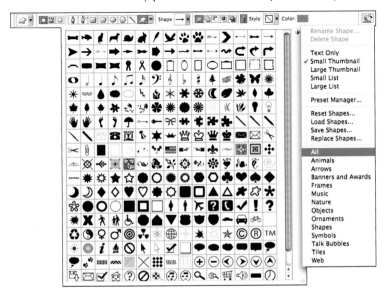

It's easy to apply a shape to your image. Open an image or create a new one, then follow these steps:

1. Choose a foreground color.

2. Make a new empty layer by clicking the New Layer icon in the Layers palette.

3. Click the Shape tool in the Tools palette. In the Options bar, click the Custom Shape icon to display the Shape Options panel. Click the Unconstrained radio button.

4. In the Options bar, click the Shape menu arrow to display the default custom shapes. Click the arrow on the panel to display the list of commands in the pull-down submenu; choose All to load all the additional shapes as in Figure 20.23.

5. Click a shape in the Shape menu. Place your cursor on the image, click, and drag until the shape is the size and proportion you want. To reposition the shape, press the spacebar while dragging. Then release the mouse to produce the shape in the specified color as in Figure 20.24.

FIGURE 20.24

The Custom Shape tool creates predefined custom vector shapes of a specified color.

Defining custom shapes

To create your own custom shape, follow these steps:

1. Use the Pen tools and draw a shape outline (see Figure 20.25).
2. Choose Edit ⇨ Define Custom Shape. The Custom Shape dialog box as shown in Figure 20.26 appears.
3. Type a name for the shape.
4. Choose the Custom Shape tool. The new shape will appear in the Custom Shape menu, as shown in Figure 20.27.

FIGURE 20.25

The shape outline is drawn as a path with the Pen tool.

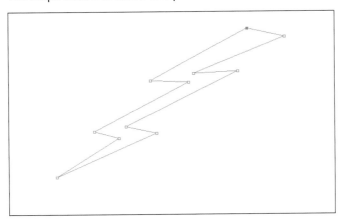

FIGURE 20.26

The Custom Shape dialog box.

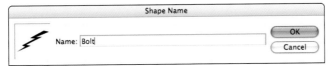

FIGURE 20.27

Your custom shape is now on the Custom Shape list, ready to be applied to the image.

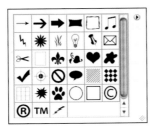

Masking shapes

A shape layer is simply a solid-colored fill masked by a vector mask. It is a kind of hybrid layer that combines a color swatch with a path. Click the Shape Layer icon in the Options bar and draw a shape with the Shape tool or the Pen tool. A vector mask is automatically created that conceals the areas outside the boundaries of the shape. The vector mask resides in the Layers palette to the right of the shape layer's swatch thumbnail. The shape can be edited with the Pen tools or the Path Selection and the Direct Selection tool. You can also edit a vector mask with the Transform features if you choose Edit ➪ Transform Point.

If you want to change the color of a shape, double-click the Color Swatch icon on the shape layer to display the Color Picker. Specify a color and click OK.

The advantage of making a shape layer is that you can apply layer features such as opacity adjustments, blending modes, and Layer Styles to the shape. You can't apply filters and adjustments unless you rasterize the layer first by choosing Layer ➪ Rasterize ➪ Shapes.

Summary

This chapter explains the nature of vector-based objects in Photoshop, and how to make and mask them.

Specifically, I cover the following topics:

- Drawing paths
- Editing paths
- Working with the Paths palette
- Masking vector images
- Masking shapes

Chapter 21 details how to blend layers to create amazing color relationships.

Part VIII

Compositing with Channels and Layers

Chapter 21

Blending Layers

Blending can extend Photoshop's capability to create amazing color relationships. By blending layer content you can heighten saturation, apply special lighting effects, darken, lighten, and improve overall image quality.

Applying a blending mode to a layer is similar to superimposing two transparencies on a light table. The colors mix with each other and the intensity and color of the light that shines through them also affects the color. Suppose that you could control the relationship of the two images by illuminating them with special gels. Blending modes work in a similar way; the two layers are the transparencies and the gel is the blending mode.

Blending layer content is a smart way to alter the color relationships of an image. Layers can be blended together using a variety of blending modes that control the brightness, hue, and intensity of the image's colors. Painting and editing tools can also be programmed to blend color as can some of the other features that apply color or composite images. In this chapter, I explain what blending modes are and how they can help you create superb color in your image.

Compositing Color

In Photoshop color can be composited through a variety of tools and methods each having a specific purpose, but in general, all accomplishing similar results—to ultimately combine the values on the color channels. Because the application of blend modes can be layer specific, you can apply layer masks, clipping masks, and opacity to enhance control. Blend modes can also be assigned to painting and editing tools that affect the application of color to the image. Blend modes can also be assigned to a number of other features such as the Apply Image, Calculations, Fill and Stroke commands, among others. These features affect how images or colors are superimposed on each other.

 **Learn more about compositing color in Chapter 22.**

Blending Layers

When a blending mode is assigned to a layer with the mode menu in the Layer's palette, the target layer is affected by the content on the layer immediately below it in the stack. You can apply any of 25 specific blending modes to an individual layer.

All types of layers support blending modes. The modes are divided into five categories on the Layers palette (see Figure 21.1). Figures 21.2 to 21.31 show how blending modes affect the content of two consecutive layers in the stack.

The Blend options in the Layer Styles dialog box.

Combination blend modes

The two modes at the top of the palette are influenced by the opacity slider. The two modes are

- **Normal:** The default mode applies the color at 100% opacity. Any portion of the top layer that is not transparent simply blocks out the pixels in the layers below (see Figure 21.2). If the Opacity is reduced, the content of both layers is visible as in Figure 21.3.

- **Dissolve:** A stipple effect is produced by breaking the image up into tiny dots, as shown in Figure 21.4.

FIGURE 21.2

Normal

FIGURE 21.3

The result of adjusting the Opacity slider of the top layer in Normal mode to 50%.

FIGURE 21.4

Dissolve

Darken blend modes

The four Darken blending modes lower the value of pixels on the bottommost layer. They darken by applying color values that are darker than 50% gray.

- **Darken:** Lighter pixels are replaced with darker pixels. It has no effect on pixels with values darker than the blended layer. Darken is not usable on Lab images (see Figure 21.5).

FIGURE 21.5

Darken.

- **Multiply:** Darkens all pixel values by multiplying the values of the original color by those of the applied color, producing a darker color (see Figure 21.6).

FIGURE 21.6

Multiply.

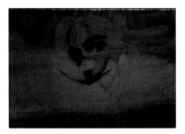

- **Color Burn:** Darkens the original color increasing contrast values. Blending with white does not change the image. Color Burn is not usable on Lab images (see Figure 21.7).

FIGURE 21.7

Color Burn.

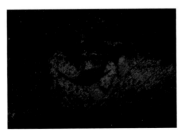

- **Linear Burn:** The most extreme darkening mode. It pushes the darkest colors in the image to black and darkens the base color by decreasing the brightness. Blending with white produces no change (see Figure 21.8).

FIGURE 21.8

Linear Burn.

Lighten blend modes

The four Lighten blending modes raise the value of pixels on the bottom layer. They lighten by applying colors values that are lighter than 50% gray.

- **Lighten:** Darker pixels are replaced with lighter pixels. It has no effect on pixels with values lighter than the blended layer. It's not usable on Lab images (see Figure 21.9).

Lighten.

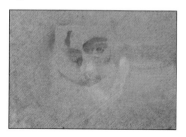

■ **Screen:** All pixels are lightened and contrast is reduced. Blending with black has no effect. Blending with white produces white (see Figure 21.10).

FIGURE 21.10

Screen.

■ **Color Dodge:** Light-colored pixels are made even lighter and contrast is decreased. Blending with black does not change the image. Color Dodge is not usable on Lab images (see Figure 21.11).

FIGURE 21.11

Color Dodge.

■ **Linear Dodge:** This blend mode is the most extreme lightening mode. It brightens the target color by increasing the brightness. It pushes the lightest colors in the image to white. Blending with black produces no change (see Figure 21.12).

Linear Dodge.

Contrast blend modes

The seven Contrast blend modes darken the darkest range of pixels and lighten the lightest pixels thereby increasing the contrast. The midtone range of colors is remapped to conform to the dark and light color extremes.

■ **Overlay:** Multiplies the dark pixels and screens the light pixels to produce higher contrast (see Figure 21.13).

Overlay.

■ **Soft Light:** This mode bathes the area in defused light. Depending on the color applied, this mode either softly lightens or darkens the area. Applying a color that is less than 50% gray lightens the area, as with the Color Dodge mode (see Figure 21.14).

FIGURE 21.14

Soft Light.

■ **Hard Light:** An effect similar to casting a glaring light on the area is produced. Depending on the color applied, this mode either lightens or darkens the area. Applying a color that is less than 50% gray lightens the affected area, as with the Screen mode. Applying a color that is more than 50% gray darkens the area, as with the Multiply mode (see Figure 21.15).

FIGURE 21.15

Hard Light.

■ **Vivid Light:** Harsher than Hard Light, this blending mode can create highly saturated effects or obliterate detail with high contrast. Burns or dodges the colors by increasing or decreasing the contrast, depending on the blend color. If the blend color is lighter than 50% gray, the image is lightened by decreasing the contrast. If the blend color is darker than 50% gray, the image is darkened by increasing the contrast (see Figure 21.16).

FIGURE 21.16

Vivid Light.

■ **Linear Light:** This mode hyper-saturates the layer. It burns or dodges the colors by decreasing or increasing the brightness, depending on the blend color. If the blend color is lighter than 50% gray, the image is lightened by increasing the brightness. If the blend color is darker than 50% gray, the image is darkened by decreasing the brightness (see Figure 21.17).

FIGURE 21.17

Linear Light.

■ **Pin Light:** Softer than Soft Light, this mode often has a graying effect that can offer subtle shading. It replaces colors, depending on the applied color. If the applied color is lighter than 50% gray, pixels darker than the blend color are replaced, and pixels lighter than the blend color do not change. If the blend color is darker than 50% gray, pixels lighter than the blend color are replaced, and pixels darker than the blend color do not change (see Figure 21.18).

Pin Light.

■ **Hard Mix:** The image is posterized into eight colors: red, yellow, green, cyan, magenta, blue, black, or white based on the mix of the base and blend colors (see Figure 21.19).

Hard Mix.

Comparative blend modes

The two Comparative blend modes create a negative of the images by inversing colors. The modes compare the pixels on the applied and affected layer Comparative blend modes.

■ **Difference:** The color on the topmost layer is blended with the bottom color by subtracting the color values of the least brightest color from the brighter color. White inverts the base color values. Black produces no change. Not usable on Lab images (see Figure 21.20).

FIGURE 21.20

Difference.

- **Exclusion:** This mode is similar to Difference mode, but with less contrast. White inverts the base color values. Black produces no change. Not usable on Lab images (see Figure 21.21).

FIGURE 21.21

Exclusion.

Component blend modes

The six Component blend modes target and change specific components of color characteristics of layer content:

- **Hue:** The colors are blended by assessing the luminance and saturation values of the target area and the applied color's hue value (see Figure 21.22).

FIGURE 21.22

Hue.

■ **Saturation:** The colors are blended by applying the hue and luminance values of the target areas and the saturation value of the applied color (see Figure 21.23).

FIGURE 21.23

Saturation.

■ **Color:** The applied color's hue is blended with the target color's luminance and saturation values to maintain the original brightness values (see Figure 21.24).

FIGURE 21.24

Color.

■ **Luminosity:** The colors are blended by using the target color's hue and saturation values and the applied color's luminance value (see Figure 21.25).

FIGURE 21.25

Luminosity.

■ **Lighter Color:** The mode excludes colors on the blended layer that are darker than 50% gray (see Figure 21.26).

FIGURE 21.26

Lighter Color

■ **Darker Color:** The mode excludes colors on the blended layer that are lighter than 50% gray (see Figure 21.27).

FIGURE 21.27

Darker Color.

Additional blending modes

There are additional blend modes that are used with the painting tools and some of the other features that are not found in the Layers palette.

- **Add:** Available in the Apply Image and Calculations dialog boxes, Add mode lightens the image by increasing the value of pixels. Add totals the brightness value of each pixel in the source image to the aligned pixels in the target image, and then it divides the difference by the scale and then adds the offset value. The formula is: [(Target + Source) ÷ Scale] + Offset = Brightness value (see Figure 21.28).

FIGURE 21.28

Add.

- **Subtract:** Available in the Apply Image and Calculations dialog boxes, it subtracts brightness from the value of each pixel in the source image from the aligned pixel in the target image, divides the difference by the scale, and then adds the offset value. The Subtract mode darkens the image. The formula is: [(Target − Source) ÷ Scale] + Offset = Brightness value (see Figure 21.29).
- **Behind:** Used with the painting tools. It limits the action of the current tool to only the transparent portions of the layer provided that the transparency lock is not checked.
- **Clear:** Used by the painting tools. It fills an area with transparent pixels.
- **Subtract Threshold:** This is the default mode for Bitmap or Indexed Color images which don't support layers. The appearance is similar to Normal.

FIGURE 21.29

Subtract.

Blending layers with similar content

Blending layers with the same content can have the effect of producing much richer colors. To demonstrate how this effect works, follow these steps:

1. Open an image (see Figure 21.30).

The original image is pretty dull.

2. Duplicate the background layer by dragging it to the new layer icon at the bottom of the Layers palette. Repeat the process one more time.

3. Target the new layer and choose Linear Light from the Mode pull-down menu. It looks more saturated but has a little too much contrast.

4. Click on the second duplicate. Assign a Hard Light blending mode. The image is further enhanced (see Figure 21.31).

The Linear Light is assigned to the first duplicate layer and Hard Light is applied to the second duplicate layer.

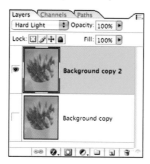

5. Drag the Opacity Fill sliders of each layer to better balance the color and contrast. Figure 21.32 shows the results.

FIGURE 21.32

Assign the blending modes to the new layer and adjust opacity.

The image now appears much richer. The colors in the targeted areas are more saturated and have better contrast. Experiment with different blend modes and with creating additional layers and applying at varying degrees of opacity to vary the effect.

Blending with Tools and Commands

If you assign a blending mode to a brush or image-editing tool or command, the color you are applying with the tool blends with color in the target area, as in Figure 21.34. Table 21.1 shows the tools that apply blending and the blending modes they support.

TABLE 21.1

Tools and Commands Blending Modes

Brush	Normal, Dissolve, Darken Multiply Color Burn, Linear Burn Lighten, Color Dodge, Linear Dodge, Overlay, Soft Light, Hard Light, Vivid Light, Linear Light, Linear Light, Pin Light, Hard Mix, Difference, Exclusion, Hue, Saturation, Color, Luminosity, Darker Color, Lighter Color
Pencil	Normal, Dissolve, Darken Multiply Color Burn, Linear Burn Lighten, Color Dodge, Linear Dodge, Overlay, Soft Light, Hard Light, Vivid Light, Linear Light, Linear Light, Pin Light, Hard Mix, Difference, Exclusion, Hue, Saturation, Color, Luminosity, Darker Color, Lighter Color
Color Replacement	Hue, Saturation, Color, Luminosity
Spot Healing Brush	Normal, Replace, Multiply, Screen, Darken, Lighten, Color, Luminosity
Healing Brush	Normal, Replace, Multiply Screen Darken Lighten, Color, Luminosity
Clone Stamp	Normal, Dissolve, Darken Multiply Color Burn, Linear Burn Lighten, Color Dodge, Linear Dodge, Overlay, Soft Light, Hard Light, Vivid Light, Linear Light, Linear Light, Pin Light, Hard Mix, Difference, Exclusion, Hue, Saturation, Color, Luminosity, Darker Color, Lighter Color, Darker Color, Lighter Color
Pattern Stamp	Normal, Dissolve, Darken Multiply Color Burn, Linear Burn Lighten, Color Dodge, Linear Dodge, Overlay, Soft Light, Hard Light, Vivid Light, Linear Light, Linear Light, Pin Light, Hard Mix, Difference, Exclusion, Hue, Saturation, Color, Luminosity, Darker Color, Lighter Color
History Brush	Normal, Dissolve, Darken Multiply Color Burn, Linear Burn Lighten, Color Dodge, Linear Dodge, Overlay, Soft Light, Hard Light, Vivid Light, Linear Light, Linear Light, Pin Light, Hard Mix, Difference, Exclusion, Hue, Saturation, Color, Luminosity, Darker Color, Lighter Color
Art History Brush	Normal, Darken, Lighten, Hue, Saturation, Color, Luminosity
Gradient	Normal, Dissolve, Darken Multiply Color Burn, Linear Burn Lighten, Color Dodge, Linear Dodge, Overlay, Soft Light, Hard Light, Vivid Light, Linear Light, Linear Light, Pin Light, Hard Mix, Difference, Exclusion, Hue, Saturation, Color, Luminosity, Darker Color, Lighter Color

continued

TABLE 21.1	*(continued)*
Paint Bucket	Normal, Dissolve, Darken Multiply Color Burn, Linear Burn Lighten, Color Dodge, Linear Dodge, Overlay, Soft Light, Hard Light, Vivid Light, Linear Light, Linear Light, Pin Light, Hard Mix, Difference, Exclusion, Hue, Saturation, Color, Luminosity, Darker Color, Lighter Color
Blur	Normal, Lighten, Hue, Saturation, Color, Luminosity
Sharpen	Normal, Lighten, Hue, Saturation, Color, Luminosity
Smudge	Normal, Lighten, Hue, Saturation, Color, Luminosity
Fill Command	Normal, Dissolve, Darken Multiply Color Burn, Linear Burn Lighten, Color, Dodge, Linear Dodge, Overlay, Soft Light, Hard Light, Vivid Light, Linear Light, Pin Light, Hard Mix, Difference, Exclusion, Hue, Saturation, Color, Luminosity, Darker Color, Lighter Color
Stroke Command	Normal, Dissolve, Darken Multiply Color Burn, Linear Burn Lighten, Color Dodge, Linear Dodge, Overlay, Soft Light, Hard Light, Vivid Light, Linear Light, Linear Light, Pin Light, Hard Mix, Difference, Exclusion, Hue, Saturation, Color, Luminosity, Darker Color, Lighter Color

Using Advanced Blending

The Blending Options in the Layer Styles dialog box allow you to control certain aspects of blending layer content or color channels (see Figure 21.33). The following list explains what the blending options enable you to do:

- **General Blending:** In this field you can choose two items that affect the color of the image. These are actually the same controls you see on the Layers palette.

    - **Blending Mode:** Affects the color of pixels as they align with the pixels on the layer beneath.

    - **Opacity:** Controls whether the pixels are opaque, transparent, or semi-transparent.

- **Advanced Blending:** Shows controls for superimposing layers and blending layer content and styles. Included in the field are:

    - **Channels:** Lets you include or exclude the color information of a channel when blending layers by selecting or deselecting their boxes.

    - **Fill Opacity:** Affects layer content without affecting the opacity Layer Styles.

    - **Blend Interior Effects As Group:** Applies the blending mode of the layer to modify opaque pixels in Layer Styles such as Inner Glow, Satin, Color Overlay, and Gradient Overlay.

    - **Blend Clipped Layers As Group:** Applies the blending mode of a layer to all layers included in the clipping mask. Deselecting this option, which is always selected by default, maintains the original blending mode and appearance of each layer in the group.

    - **Layer/Vector Mask Hides Effects:** Select or deselect these check boxes to choose whether a Layer Style hides the effects of a Layer Style.

■ **Blend If:** These controls can be tricky. The field includes:

  ▪ **Pop-Up Menu:** Gray specifies a blending range for all channels. The individual color channels for example, Red, Green, or Blue in an RGB image specifies blending for the color of a specific color channel.

If you use exclusion sliders to omit pixels of a specific brightness range from the layer, you force colors to disappear. This can produce harsh color transitions and jagged edges. You can diminish the effect by adjusting the Fuzziness setting, which softens the transition. Here's how: Press Option/Alt and click Reset. This time, press the Option/Alt key as you drag the left half of the white slider to the left.

FIGURE 21.33

The Advanced Blending Options in the Layer Style dialog box.

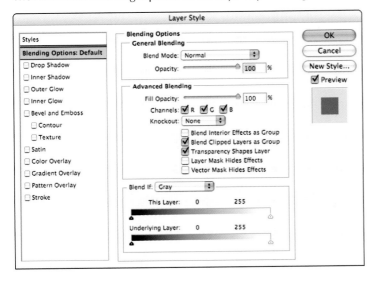

CROSS-REF To see an example of how the Blend If sliders can affect two consecutive layers, see Chapter 7

Replacing Backgrounds

When compositing images from multiple sources, a situation that frequently arises is that a background image needs to be replaced, or you may want to drag and drop a selection from one document to another. This can present problems, because the selection may produce unwanted edge pixels when you select the region on the layer or eliminate the background of the layer content and replace it with another background below it in the stack. The superfluous edge pixels can't be seen until they reach their destination or until the background is replaced — when you see them as a rough fringe around the edge of the layer content.

Matting is the key to clean composites. Most edge pixels can be eliminated using Photoshop's matting commands. The matting functions blend your layer into the layer beneath it. There are three ways to matte an image and, if your edge pixels are particularly stubborn, there is also a workaround that does the job every time. It's usually a row of one or two pixels that are significantly darker or lighter than the color behind them, as in Figure 21.34.

FIGURE 21.34

Edge pixels are produced by the anti-alias when a selection is cut from an image.

To matte an image, it must be on an independent layer surrounded by transparency.

Defringe

Choose Layer ➪ Matting ➪ Defringe and enter a value in the dialog box that is shown in Figure 21.35. Defringe is a very effective method of eliminating the off-color edge pixels selected by the anti-alias because it replaces the color of the edge pixels with the colors of the nearby pixels on the layer (see Figure 21.36).

FIGURE 21.35

FIGURE 21.35

The Defringe dialog box.

FIGURE 21.36

The result of defringing the image.

Removing White or Black Matte

Choose Layer ➪ Matting ➪ Remove White Matte or Remove Black Matte to darken the white edge pixels or lighten the black pixels. This is helpful if you are moving a selection from a white or black background to another background.

If none of these operations works to your satisfaction — and sometimes you just can't eliminate enough of that edge — here's a workaround:

1. Select the area on the layer that you want to replace and delete it.

2. Choose Select ➪ Modify ➪ Expand. Enter the amount (in pixels) to contract the selection. View the edge close-up to see how far into the image the marquee has contracted.

3. Press Delete/Backspace to delete the edge.

NOTE You can also choose Layer ➪ Add Layer Mask ➪ Reveal All to convert the selection into a layer mask that will conceal the edge pixels.

Summary

Mix colors and expand your creativity. In this chapter, I covered how to use blending modes.

Specifically, I discussed:

- Blending layers
- Replacing backgrounds

Chapter 22 details how to combine images

Chapter 22

Compositing with Channels

Much of Photoshop's power lies in its ability to combine images. Multiple images can be collaged together as layers, and their transparency can be precisely controlled with opacity adjustments, blending modes, and with layer masks. The shape of layer content can be altered with clipping groups. Selections and alpha channels can also be combined as can other types of masks.

The two Photoshop channel operations that this chapter covers, Apply Image and Calculations, were essential in earlier versions of Photoshop to produce many of the effects that Layer Styles and Blend modes now can do with considerably more ease. Still, these commands can still be extremely useful for accurate compositing and making accurate selections. Because they use formulas that compare the brightness values of channels they are sometimes called *Chops* short for *channel operations*. Chops affect the core color or selection information that constitute Photoshop documents. Compositing information from multiple channels can produce amazing results.

Applying Images

Many of the Apply images features are similar to the blending modes in the Layers palette. But there are two big differences. Apply image combines the contents of two separate documents into a single document. Within the dialog box you have the ability to target individual layers and channels that give it additional functionality.

The Apply Image command can apply the contents of a layer, the composite channel, a color channel, or an alpha channel to an image. The Apply Image feature works with RGB, CMYK, Lab, and Grayscale images. The target

IN THIS CHAPTER

Applying images

Using calculations

image (the image that is affected) is the image that is currently active. The source image must be the same size and resolution as the target image and be open on the desktop. To access the dialog box choose Image ⇨ Apply Image. When you open the Apply Image dialog box, you are presented with the following options:

- **Source:** This field represents characteristics of the image that is applied, or overlaid. Choose the desired image from the pop-up list.

  - **Layer:** The pop-up lists all the layers and the background in the source image. You can overlay all the layers if you choose Merged.

  - **Channel:** Select a channel to apply to the image from this list. If you choose the composite channel (RGB, CMYK, etc.), the entire channel will be mixed.

  - **Invert:** Select this check box to invert the contents of the selected channel. Pixels that are black will be applied as if they are white and vice versa.

- **Target:** The target image is the current active image on the desktop. The target lists the channel(s) and layers that the image will be applied to.

- **Blending:** Choose a blending mode from the pop-up list to affect how the color is applied.

  - **Opacity:** Enter a percentage value for the opacity or the applied image.

  - **Preserve Transparency:** This check box leaves transparent areas on a layer unaffected.

  - **Mask:** Selecting this option masks off a part of the source image. When you choose Mask, the Apply Image dialog box expands. From the menus, choose an image and a layer. Choose a color channel, an alpha channel, or an active selection on the source image to isolate the application of the affect.

- **Add and Subtract:** If you choose either the Add or Subtract modes, you can enter values for scale and offset. These values are used in the calculation to determine the brightness values of the superimposed pixels.

  - Add lightens the image by applying this formula: [(Target + Source) ÷ Scale] + Offset = Brightness value

  - Subtract darkens the image by applying this formula: [(Target − Source) ÷ Scale] + Offset = Brightness value

CROSS-REF See Chapter 7 for other uses of the Apply Image command.

Using Apply Image to make a difficult selection

The image shown in Figure 22.1 has a lot of fine detail. It would be quite difficult to select the edges of the radio tower, but Apply Image can do the job quickly.

FIGURE 22.1

This image has a lot of detail that would be difficult to select.

1. Open the image that you want to select.
2. Display the Channels palette and examine each color channel to determine which one has the most tonal difference between the areas you want to select. In this case it's the Blue channel.

TIP Press ⌘/Ctrl+1,2, or 3 to toggle through the channels.

3. Duplicate the blue channel by dragging it to the New Channel icon at the bottom of the Channels palette (see Figure 22.2).
4. With the Blue copy channel active choose Image ➪ Apply Image.
5. Choose Hard Light from the Blending Pop-Up menu to further increase the contrast, or experiment with the blend modes to produce maximum contrast as in Figure 22.3.

FIGURE 22.2

Duplicate the channel with the most tonal variation.

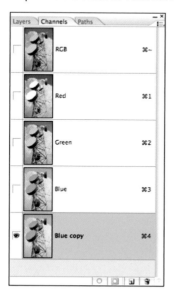

FIGURE 22.3

The Apply Image command with the Hard Light blend mode increases contrast in the image.

6. Choose Image ⇨ Adjustments ⇨ Invert to change the white areas to black and the black areas to white (see Figure 22.4).

7. Choose Image ⇨ Adjustments ⇨ Curves to further enhance contrast (see Figure 22.5).

FIGURE 22.4

Inverting the alpha channel produces a negative.

FIGURE 22.5

Apply a Curves adjustment to increase contrast.

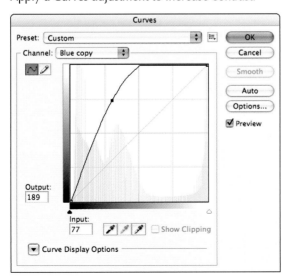

8. With the Magic Wand tool select the lightest areas of the image. With the Lasso tool exclude any of the areas that are outside of the areas that you want to ultimately select (see Figure 22.6).

FIGURE 22.6

Select the lightest areas of the image that you want in the ultimate selection.

9. Press the D key and then the X key. To make white the foreground color, press Opt/Alt-Delete/Backspace to fill the areas with white.

10. Inverse the selection (Shift+⌘/Ctrl+I), press the X key, and then hit Opt/Alt-Delete/Backspace to fill the areas with black (see Figure 22.7).

11. Choose Select ➪ Load Selection ➪ Blue copy to load the new selection (see Figure 22.8).

CROSS-REF See Chapter 5 for more about Adjustment layers and the new Photoshop CS3 Curves dialog box.

FIGURE 22.7

Fill the selection with white, inverse the selection, and fill the inversed selection with black to produce a perfect alpha channel.

FIGURE 22.8

Load the blue copy alpha channel on the image.

Enhancing images

The Apply Image feature can be used to enhance color and produce solarization effects by applying channel information through a blending mode. To do so, follow these steps:

1. Open an image. Look at the color channels to see which one has the tonal variation. In this case it's the Blue channel.

2. Click on the thumbnail of the composite channel. With the channel active, choose Image ⇨ Apply Image. The Apply Image dialog box appears (see Figure 22.9). Set the channel to Blue and the Blending to Exclusion. Be sure the preview box is checked.

FIGURE 22.9

The Apply Image dialog box with Blue channel information applied through the Difference blend mode.

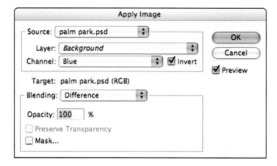

3. Try other Channel and Blending modes combinations. Also try checking the Invert box. You'll find that you can produce some pretty wild results as shown in Figure 22.10.

4. Click OK.

FIGURE 22.10

Two other examples of blend mode combinations:. (left) Exclusion, (right) Vivid Light, Inverted.

Combining multiple images

The Apply Image command can produce some beautiful artistic effects. A broadly painted version of the image mixed with a photograph can produce some very interesting results. The effect can be further altered by adjusting the blending modes and the opacity.

1. Open a grayscale image (see Figure 22.11).

2. Choose Image Mode, RGB, and convert the color mode.

3. Choose Image ➪ Duplicate to make a copy of the image. Name the new image **Paint**.

FIGURE 22.11

The grayscale image.

4. With the painting tools, color the image with broad strokes as in Figure 22.12.

FIGURE 22.12

Paint the duplicate image broadly with the paint tools.

5. Choose Filter ➪ Blur ➪ Gaussian Blur. Drag the Radius slider to blur the image slightly as in Figure 22.13. The amount you specify depends on the resolution of the image.

FIGURE 22.13

Blur the image to soften the edges.

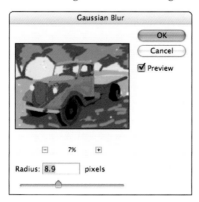

6. Click the original image to make it active. It will become the target image.

7. Choose Image ➪ Apply Image. Enter the following; then click OK:

   ▪ **Source:** Old Truck copy

   ▪ **Layer:** Background

   ▪ **Channel:** RGB

   ▪ **Blending:** Soft Light

   ▪ **Opacity:** 100%

8. Figure 22.14 shows the specified settings in the Apply Image dialog box and the result. Try different combinations of modes, channels, and opacities to produce different results.

FIGURE 22.14

The application of the image with a Soft Light blending mode (top) and the result (bottom).

Using Calculations

Despite the complex appearance of its dialog box, the Calculations command actually performs a simple operation — it creates only one channel from two sources. The Calculations command works to combine two source channels into a new channel, selection, or document. Unlike Apply Image, Calculations do not produce color documents. Calculations command can be used to create a new grayscale image, or to combine two masks into either a single alpha channel or an active selection.

Calculations requires that the images combined be identical in height, width, and resolution. When you go to Image ➪ Calculations, it has two source fields and a destination field. The two source areas let you choose two channels to combine.

Calculating one image

Calculations can be used to combine channels to make optimal grayscale images:

1. Open an image and examine its color channels for contrast. In this example, the Red and Green channels are both usable (see Figure 22.15).

Open an image and observe the channels.

2. Choose Image ⇨ Calculations. Enter the following:
   - **Source 1**: Red
   - **Source 2**: Blue
   - **Result**: New Document
   - **Blending**: Hard Light

3. Because each image is unique, Calculations requires experimentation with all the settings to produce the best possible results (see Figure 22.16). Keep an eye on the preview to see the results of your experiments.

FIGURE 22.16

With the Calculations command, combine the two channels with a blending mode to produce a fine grayscale with a good tonal range.

Calculating two images

You can also use the Calculations command to blend channels from two source documents and create a new alpha channel that can be used to alter the colored image. The images must be the same size in height, width, and resolution.

1. Open the two documents that you want to combine. In this case I have a document called Austin Building that has an alpha channel and an image called texture (see Figure 22.17).

2. If you need to resize the images so that they are identical in height, width, and resolution, click the least important image to make it active.

3. Choose Image ⇨ Image Size. Then choose Window and click the name of the image whose size you want to match. The specifications appear in the Image Size dialog box. Click OK.

> **NOTE** You can use this technique with the File ⇨ New; Image ⇨ Canvas Size; and Image ⇨ Image Size commands.

FIGURE 22.17

The two original documents that can be combined into a new document or alpha channel.

4. Choose Image ➪ Calculations. Enter the following specifications to produce a new grayscale document, as in Figure 22.18:

   1. **Source 1**: Austin Building
   2. **Channel**: Red
   3. **Layer**: Background
   4. **Source 2**: Texture
   5. **Channel**: Gray
   6. **Blending**: Pin Light
   7. **Layer**: Background
   8. **Result**: New Document

CAUTION The Calculations feature is complex and, as always, there are several workarounds that perform the same operations. Mastering it, however, gives you the skills you need to quickly combine channels, and that can extend your selection-making capabilities.

FIGURE 22.18

FIGURE 22.18

The resulting image

Summary

In this chapter, I showed you that compositing information from multiple channels can produce remarkable results.

Specifically, I covered the following topics:

- Applying images
- Using Calculations

Index

C

501

L

L channel, Lab Color mode, 233–234
Lab Color mode
    a channel, 233–234
    Apply Image command support, 477
    Apply Image techniques, 240–244
    b channel, 233–234
    black-and-white techniques, 251–256
    Blending Options, 240–244
    Color Picker, 84
    Curves techniques, 244–245
    device independent, 77, 233
    high radius sharpening, 235–236
    hiraloam sharpening, 235–236
    image sharpening techniques, 234–239
    International Commission on Illumination, 76
    L channel, 233–234
    luminance mask, 237–239
    monochrome image creation, 195–197
    noise addition/reduction, 246–251
    RGB Color mode conversion, 80
    two pass sharpening, 237–239
laser printers, color separations, 11–12
Lasso tool, selections, 304, 311
Layer characteristic, Apply Image command, 478
layer comps, multiple version saves, 29
layer content
    layer type changing, 29
    printing, 107
Layer Group Properties dialog box, color channels, 30–31
layer groups, layer organization, 29
layer masks
    alpha channel similarities, 162, 377
    clipping mask combination, 399–400
    concealing/revealing contiguous layers, 29
    content moving, 378
    creating, 378–380
    enabling/disabling, 378
    gradient mask blends, 381–387
    moving, 378
    removing, 378
    selections, 378
    viewing, 378
    when to use, 41, 296–297
Layer Palette Options dialog box, thumbnail size, 25

Layer Properties dialog box, layer naming, 24
Layer Styles dialog box
    advanced bending controls, 472–473
    color exclusions, 176–178
    combination blend modes, 456–457
    drop shadows, 277–280
    glare reduction techniques, 175
    layer styles, 39
layer styles, drop shadows, 277–280
layer variable, blending color channels, 171
layers
    adjustment, 29, 142, 364–372
    background, 23–24
    blending modes, 29, 37–38
    clipping masks, 29, 297, 397–400
    combination blend modes, 456–457, 465–467
    comparative blend modes, 464–465
    comps, 29
    consolidating, 40
    content, 29
    content transferring, 35–36
    content viewing, 25
    contrast blend modes, 461–464
    copying, 33
    copying individual, 33, 35
    copying multiple, 35
    creating, 31, 33–34
    cutting to a new layer, 34
    darken blend modes, 458–459
    discarding, 37
    dragging/dropping between documents, 36
    duplicating, 36
    fill, 29, 393–397
    Gradient Fill, 394–396
    gradient mask blends, 381–387
    grouping, 29–31
    highlighting, 25
    image flattening, 40
    lighten blend modes, 459–461
    linking, 28–29
    locking, 31–32
    masking, 29
    multiple layer selections, 28
    naming conventions, 24
    noncontiguous selections, 25, 28

M

Read Less–Learn More®

There's a Visual book for every learning level...

Simplified®

The place to start if you're new to computers. Full color.

- Computers
- Mac OS
- Office
- Windows

Teach Yourself VISUALLY™

Get beginning to intermediate-level training in a variety of topics. Full color.

- Computers
- Crocheting
- Digital Photography
- Dog training
- Dreamweaver
- Excel
- Guitar
- HTML
- Knitting
- Mac OS
- Office
- Photoshop
- Photoshop Elements
- Piano
- Poker
- PowerPoint
- Scrapbooking
- Sewing
- Windows
- Wireless Networking
- Word

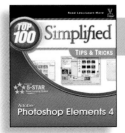

Top 100 Simplified® Tips & Tricks

Tips and techniques to take your skills beyond the basics. Full color.

- Digital Photography
- eBay
- Excel
- Google
- Mac OS
- Photoshop
- Photoshop Elements
- PowerPoint
- Windows

Build It Yourself VISUALLY™

Do it yourself the visual way and without breaking the bank. Full color.

- Game PC
- Media Center PC

...all designed for visual learners—just like you!

Master VISUALLY®

Step up to intermediate-to-advanced technical knowledge. Two-color interior.

- 3ds Max
- Creating Web Pages
- Dreamweaver and Flash
- Excel VBA Programming

- iPod and iTunes
- Mac OS
- Optimizing PC Performance
- Photoshop Elements

- QuickBooks
- Quicken
- Windows
- Windows Mobile
- Windows Server

Visual Blueprint™

Where to go for professional-level programming instruction. Two-color interior.

- Ajax
- Excel Data Analysis
- Excel Pivot Tables
- Excel Programming

- HTML
- JavaScript
- Mambo
- PHP & MySQL
- Visual Basic

Visual Encyclopedia™

Your A-to-Z reference of tools and techniques. Full color.

- Dreamweaver
- Excel

- Photoshop
- Windows

Visual Quick Tips™

Shortcuts, tricks, and techniques for getting more done in less time. Full color.

- Digital Photography
- Excel
- MySpace
- Office

- PowerPoint
- Windows
- Wireless Networking

For a complete listing of Visual books, go to wiley.com/go/visual

Visual
An Imprint of ⑨WILEY
Now you know.